IT'S A JOURNEY

The MUST-HAVE Roadmap to Successful Succession Planning

Navigate the Complicated Terrain of
Private & Family Business Transitions

Elizabeth Ledoux & Laura Chiesman

SKY TO SEA
PUBLISHING

ISBN (paperback): 978-1-7363623-0-3
ISBN (ebook): 978-1-7363623-1-0

Sky to Sea Publishing, LLC
1300 Highway AIA, Suite 103
Satellite Beach, FL 32937

www.SkytoSeaPublishing.com
www.TheSuccessionPlanningBook.com

DISCLOSURE - Investment advisory services offered through First*Wave* Financial, Inc., an SEC Registered Investment Adviser. Succession planning services offered through The Transition Strategists. Elizabeth Ledoux/The Transition Strategists and Laura Chiesman/First*Wave* Financial are not affiliated with each other. This presentation is designed for informational and educational purposes. It is not designed as a substitute for advice from professional financial advisors or succession planners. Each individual's circumstances may be different. Individuals should seek financial, legal, and tax advice or other professional or expert advice based upon their particular circumstances.

If you want to go fast,
go alone...

If you want to go far,
go together.

-African proverb

TABLE OF CONTENTS

SECTION I

Establish the Rules of the Road

You very likely picked up this book because you have given some thought to the day you will leave your business in the hands of someone else. Perhaps you have a new business or personal adventure to pursue, you are eager to see your children carry on your entrepreneurial legacy, or you have simply grown weary of the stress inherent in business ownership. Maybe the death of someone close to you has you thinking about what else you'd like to do in your life. Perhaps your business requires an injection of cash that you aren't willing to make or your younger business partner is ready to take over the reins. Maybe the activity in the mergers & acquisitions (M&A) market makes it an ideal time to sell or a dip in the economy creates a great opportunity to gift ownership to your children. Perhaps you have simply heard how few business transitions succeed.

No matter what emotion, condition or event prompts you to think ahead, we guarantee you are not alone if you cannot see a clear path from where you are now to your Next Adventure™ (your life after you leave your business). In fact, you are part of a large crowd if: 1) you are somewhat overwhelmed by the number of decisions you know you will have to make, 2) and you have more questions than answers about how you will make the transfer work, or 3) you wonder what will give your life purpose after you are no longer an owner.

We Get It.

Transferring a business of any type is a big deal. You want to get it right, and the choices you make will impact the lives not only of your successors, but also of all the people who rely on your business for their success and well-being. Any mention of "moving on" will likely elicit some strong reactions from those around you. In addition if your successors are not as adept as you were in running the company, it could bankrupt the company.

We know just how much is at stake for you. For the last 30 years, we've walked hundreds of business owners through the journey of transitioning business ownership from one owner to the next and from one generation to the next. In this book we will share with you the process we've used to achieve our 100 percent success rate. We will also identify the tools we've developed to help owners just like you create clear paths to successful ownership transition.

Yes, you read that correctly. One hundred percent of the owners who have completed the process we describe in this book (The Transition Roadmap Developer Process™) have successfully transferred their companies to their successors and are living happy and meaningful lives.

In this book we will introduce you to a unique approach to business succession: one that recognizes that a business transfer must meet your emotional and material desires. We will share the process we use to craft successful business transfers: The Transition Roadmap Developer Process. We will show you how to anticipate and avoid as many obstacles as possible, and we will explain how to design a plan that prevents one choice from resulting in consequences from which you cannot recover. We will show you how to create a unique Transition Roadmap to prevent you from wasting time on dead ends and detours, and we will move you toward your destination. Our Transition Roadmap Developer Process puts the odds in your favor that you will join our 100 percenters.

What's Ahead

In this section we describe our seven principles. Some, such as putting your relationships first, may seem to be counterintuitive, but in Section II you'll see how they come into play. At the conclusion of Section I, you can use the Business Owner Transition Confidence Survey™ to gauge your certainty about the path you will take to reach the next phase of your life.

In Section II we ask you to consider and answer six important questions that will point you toward your desired destination and show you routes you might take to get there.

Section III introduces you to four elements of a Transition Roadmap: 1) a timeline for the transfer of ownership and knowledge, 2) a statement to motivate you—and all those involved—to keep doing the work necessary to make the transfer, 3) a structure for comparing your transfer options, and 4) a project management tool that breaks major steps into component parts.

Transferring a business to another person impacts the lives of not only your successor, but also of all the people who rely on your business for their success and well-being.

To help you gauge where you are in your journey to transfer your business to a successor, we include Points of Interest at the end of nearly every chapter. We designed them to give you the opportunity to pause, assess your progress, make adjustments and chart a new path if appropriate. Most chapters also include two lists: one identifying potential consequences of failing to act and a second showing the benefits of taking action.

So how does the entire process play out? Here's an overview.

The Transition Roadmap Developer Process Overview™

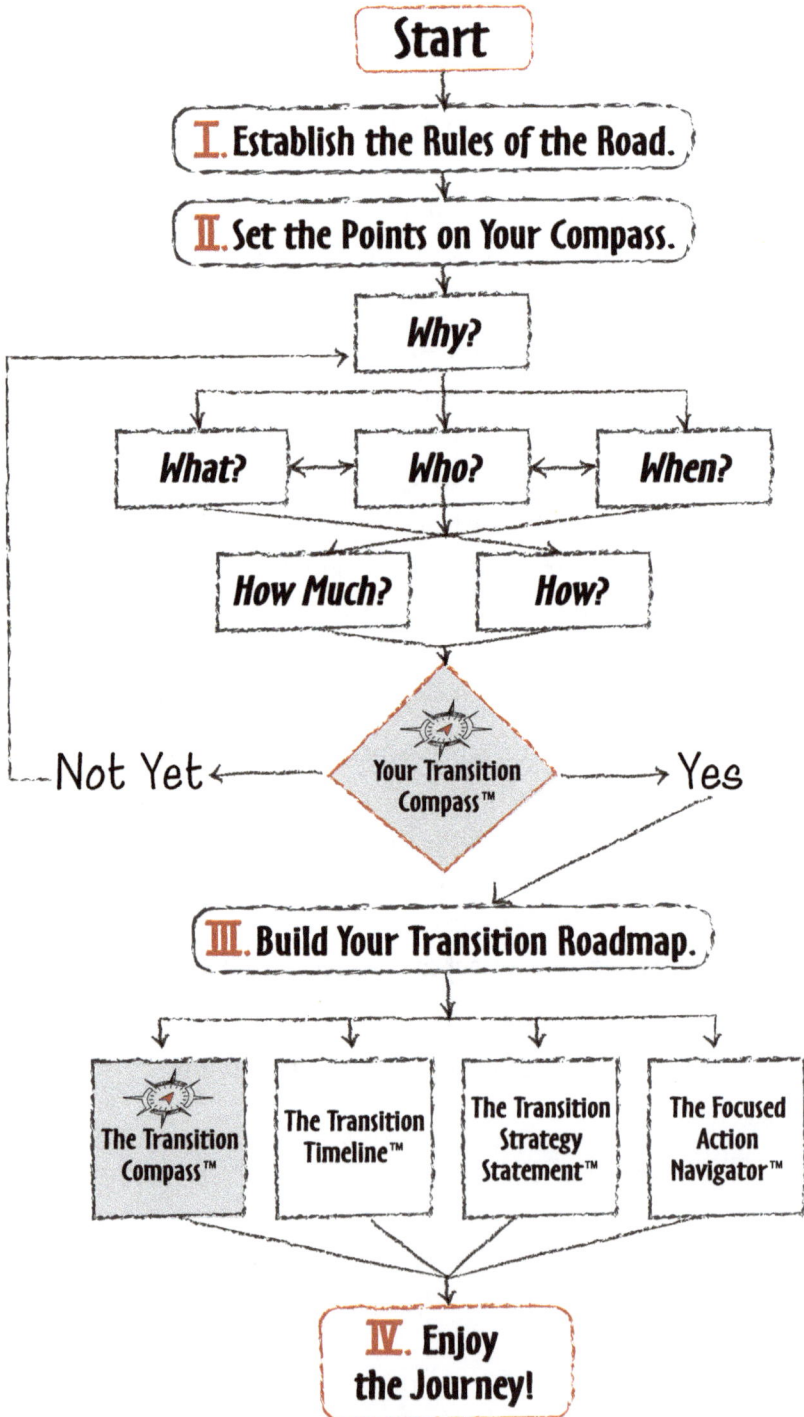

Start

I. Establish the Rules of the Road.

II. Set the Points on Your Compass.

Why?

What? ← → **Who?** ← → **When?**

How Much?   **How?**

Not Yet ← **Your Transition Compass™** → Yes

III. Build Your Transition Roadmap.

| The Transition Compass™ | The Transition Timeline™ | The Transition Strategy Statement™ | The Focused Action Navigator™ |

IV. Enjoy the Journey!

CHAPTER ONE

SUCCESSFUL BUSINESS TRANSITION IS A JOURNEY

The true metric of prosperity is time.

Matt Ridley, Author

A s you know, there are a number of books on the topic of transferring, selling and exiting companies—many of which we've read. What's different (and we think better!) about our approach to business transfers is that it:

- Meets both the emotional and material goals of owners.
- Is flexible enough to work in multiple ownership scenarios and in any industry.
- Makes it possible to create "a win" for all involved: owner, successor and business.
- Views transition as a journey rather than a one-time event.
- Follows seven guiding principles, or rules of the road.
- Has a 100 percent success rate for those who complete it.

Defining Success

A 100 percent success rate is a bold claim, so it is worth sharing how we define "success" in our consulting practice.

A business transition is successful if at its conclusion:

- Owners achieve their most important quantifiable and experiential goals. Of course, every owner has different goals. For some, success might mean achieving both a desired level of financial independence and putting the business in the hands of a son, daughter or longtime employee. To another, it might mean leaving when the business reaches a certain level of market share or revenue and fulfilling a promise to a spouse to live abroad for two years. But all owners must leave in a way that honors what they have built and maintains relationships with those who are important to them.

- Successors are ready and able to assume all of the responsibilities of ownership, leadership, financial management and operations once held by the prior owner.

- Companies are as successful under new ownership as they were under past ownership.

- Owners are as engaged in moving toward their Next Adventure as their successors are in moving the business forward.

Unless a business transition meets all four conditions, it is, in our opinion, not completely successful.

Business Succession: A Journey

To achieve these high standards, a succession plan must include a carefully orchestrated, progressive series of decisions and actions owners need to take to prepare themselves, their successors and their companies for a change of ownership. Even if a transfer of business equity is a one-time event (as is often the case in a sale to a third party), a series of actions leads up to that event. For that reason, we view business succession as a journey.

For good reason, many observers compare handing over business ownership with the passing of a baton in a relay race. Just as runners do, owners and successors must coordinate their movements to complete a handoff successfully. The problem with this analogy is that runners are able to practice the baton handoff in advance and each handoff is similar. Transferring business ownership, however, involves multiple events, varies in each situation, and owners and successors cannot practice the "handoff."

Instead of considering a relay race analogy, think, for a moment, of your business as a car moving at 70 miles per hour. You are the driver, and your successor is in the passenger seat. Your goal is to switch places without losing any speed or running off the road. Without a plan, could you and your passenger trade seats while maintaining a consistent speed and staying in the correct lane?

Even with a plan in place to exchange seats, there would be points at which elbows jab into ribs, one person is smashed into the seat, and the other has one eye on the road and just a toe on the gas pedal. That high-speed seat switch is a more accurate reflection of business succession than the previous example of baton passing. It's also an amusing scene to imagine, but the situation is far from funny when you are involved in the transition of your business whose value you are trying to preserve and worked for years to build.

As you prepare your successor to take your position, your business should not lose momentum and you, your successor and your business must arrive safely at your intended destination. That means you must:

- Carefully choreograph the position change and take charge of an organized process to transfer crucial knowledge, wisdom, fiscal awareness, skills, experiences and expertise to your successor.

- Resolve dilemmas in ways that are consistent with the priorities, objectives and guidelines that you will establish at the beginning of your journey.

- Be sensitive to the desires of all stakeholders and communicate well.

- See yourself charting a journey to a new beginning rather than to a career-ending event.

> *When you approach business succession as a journey that involves a number of decisions and actions, you position your business, employees and successor to succeed without you.*

When owners look at the exit from their companies as a one-time event, they usually leave without preparing their successors or their companies to continue successfully without them. This typically happens when owners are anxious to leave, tired, burned out or bored. In some unfortunate situations, owners die or become disabled and unintentionally leave their successors and companies unprepared. Some owners don't know that there is a proven process that other owners have used to successfully transfer their companies to successors. Still others jump ship too quickly because they can't wait to start the part of their lives that comes after business ownership—their Next Adventures.

When owners don't take time to create roadmaps that prepare their successors to assume control and that leave their companies prepared to thrive under new owners, they:

- Risk damaging the relationships they value. In family-owned companies, the business that acted as the glue binding family members together can become the dynamite that blows a family apart.

- Put the performance of their companies in jeopardy. When that happens and assuming owners are still alive, they may be forced to retake the reins when businesses falter without their leadership.

- Put in jeopardy the "life after ownership" that they dreamed of living and deserve.

RULES OF THE ROAD

Like any journey, business succession has rules of the road that make travel both efficient and safe. In business succession we refer to those rules as "principles," and we'll refer to them again and again as we show you how to craft your own successful business transfer.

Principle 1: Put relationships first.

> A business transfer is only successful if it protects or enhances your relationships with the people who are important to you. Seems simple. It's not.

Principle 2: You are in charge of your journey.

> It is your job and privilege as the owner of a successful company to create a vision and a transfer plan that generate successful outcomes for you, your company, successors and family.

Principle 3: No transition is perfect.

> No transition will meet every one of your desires, but if crafted properly, a transition plan should deliver what is most important to you.

Principle 4: It's your Next Adventure: Go for it!

> Owners who understand they are not just leaving a business but are beginning a new and exciting phase of their lives are highly motivated to do the work necessary to craft successful business transfers.

Principle 5: Choose your destination with intention.

It can be tempting to ignore the fact that all owners leave their businesses at some point or to pretend that the dilemmas that can arise during a transfer of ownership will magically disappear. Owners who ignore reality, however, lose an incredible opportunity to take charge of what they want the transfer of their businesses to accomplish for themselves, their families, their successors and their companies.

Principle 6: Step away from mutual dependency.

Mutual dependency between you and your company must end if you are to successfully move on to your Next Adventure and your company is to succeed after you leave it.

Principle 7: Your Transition Roadmap is indispensable.

One hundred percent of the owners who have completed The Transition Roadmap Developer Process have successfully transferred their companies to successors. Your Roadmap keeps you moving forward, shows you alternate routes when you run into roadblocks and keeps all parties accountable when circumstances change. It is your key to success.

If you can even consider transferring your business to someone else, you own a successful business. That's a testament to your hard work. It's a privilege to be able to turn over a successful business to someone else.

In the following chapters we'll show you how each of these principles increases the odds that you will successfully move on to a great new phase of your life.

The purpose of this book is to help you capitalize on your hard work and realize that it is a privilege to embark on a business transition journey. We want to add you to our very happy group of 100 percenters. We're ready if you are to create a plan to transfer your business to a successor in a way that meets your financial and emotional objectives and positions both your successor and company for future success. Let's get started!

CHAPTER TWO

THE TRANSITION ROADMAP DEVELOPER PROCESS™

A Different And More Successful Approach To Business Transition

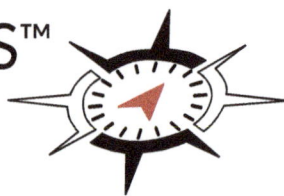

Nothing will ever be attempted if all possible objections must be first overcome.

Samuel Johnson, English writer 1700s

"What percentage of business transitions actually succeed?" That's one of the most common questions owners ask us. While estimates of failure run as high as 70 percent, we can't provide a data-based response for several reasons. First, owners of privately held businesses are not required to publicly report changes of ownership, much less report on the result of those transfers. Second, few owners voluntarily share information about their companies' equity transfers with researchers. Based on the surveys that are available, business successions that involve children are especially challenging. Our experience mirrors that finding.

Many of our clients are private businesses that may or may not have multiple generations working or owning equity in the business but do have cultures in which owners and employees think of and treat each other like family. All the owners we work with want to craft business transitions that satisfy all involved, but leaders of family businesses generally shoulder an additional burden: Their choices will impact not only their businesses, but also multiple family generations.

Rather than spend time looking for raw data about transition failure and success rates, we concentrate on why too many transitions fail and we have developed a process that results in success.

A Different Approach to Business Transfers

It is natural for most owners to think about strategies when they begin to consider their business transfer. They read or hear about an employee stock ownership plan, a sale to a private equity group or a merger, and they attempt to figure out how to apply that method of transfer to their own situation. Too often we watch these owners waste time and, in the worst cases, destroy their companies and relationships, because they didn't use our seven principles to guide them or didn't think about where they wanted to go before choosing a path to take.

When you employ the seven principles of The Transition Roadmap Developer Process, you:

1. Put relationships first.

2. Lead the process to achieve successful outcomes for all.

3. Do not expect perfection.

4. Keep your eye on your Next Adventure.

5. Take intentional action.

6. Eliminate the dependency between you and your business.

7. Use a Transition Roadmap.

In short, this Process maximizes your chances of a successful transition and minimizes (and possibly eliminates) conflicts about money, control and unmet expectations that can destroy both relationships and businesses.

The Transition Roadmap Developer Process, benefits your business by providing your successor the foundation necessary to lead and grow the business. In addition, the Process gives your successor their own Next Adventure.

A More Successful Approach to Business Transition

We know that transferring businesses to new owners is never easy and is a high-risk endeavor, yet the owners who do so successfully tell us it brings a huge sense of personal fulfillment.

Imagine how you will feel when:

- You gain the choices afforded by time and money. In other words, you can live the way you want during the next phase of your life after ownership—your Next Adventure.

- Everyone you care about moves closer to their Next Adventures.

- Your business continues to support and serve the people who depend on it.

We want to help you create your own transition plan and avoid joining those business owners whose only "transfer plan" is actually a rolling five-year retirement plan, so the day of retirement never arrives. We don't want to count you among those whose failure to take the lead in the transfer of their businesses results in the liquidation of the companies they worked years to build. We want you, your company and those you care about to succeed.

Are you a candidate for our approach to business succession?

Over the years we have found that the owners most likely to try our approach share some common characteristics:

- At a future date, they want to transition some or all of their current ownership to family members, employees or a third party. They have strong relationships with employees and care deeply about the security of their people.

- They are highly committed to their clients or customers.

- They are often charitably inclined and have made a positive impact on their communities over the years.

- They are not willing to put their families or companies at risk should something happen to them before they can transition successfully.

- They want their businesses to continue to thrive after they leave and are willing to create and implement a plan to make that vision a reality.

If you share any of these characteristics, you, your successor, your relationships and your company will benefit from engaging in The Transition Roadmap Developer Process.

If you fail to put in place a carefully designed succession plan:

- You miss the opportunity to prepare your successor to assume the responsibilities of ownership, leadership and business operations.

- You put your family's financial security and the survival of your business at risk should something happen to you.

If you design a succession plan for your business:

- You are far more likely to achieve both your financial and emotional goals.

- You lay a solid foundation for the ongoing success of your business.

POINT OF INTEREST

When you imagine your ideal business transition, whom do you see taking over for you:

- One or more family members not active in the business?
- One or more family members active in the business?
- One or more employees are active in the business?
- One or more current business partners?
- A person not working in the business today whom you will bring in, work with and mentor over a planned or unplanned period of time?
- A third party that will assume immediate control and ownership at the time of sale with little to no mentoring period?
- Someone else?

Take a moment to jot down your thoughts about your "ideal" successors as well as those you are not considering. This is an important exercise and will help you clarify your thoughts and feelings regarding various successors.

Successors Under Consideration

	Are you considering this option? Absolutely! Maybe. No possible way!	Note your thoughts, concerns, feelings, questions, etc.
One or more family members not active in the business		
One or more family members active in the business		
One or more employees active in the business		
One or more business partners		
A person not working in the business today whom you will bring in, work with and mentor over a planned or unplanned period of time		
A third party that will assume immediate control and ownership at the time of sale with little to no mentoring period		
Someone else		

CHAPTER THREE

PUT RELATIONSHIPS FIRST

PRINCIPLE 1

No road is long with good company.
Turkish proverb

The foundation for a successful business transfer is to put relationships first. Family members, employees, customers, vendors and community all contribute to your company's success, and many of them are important to you personally. When you put relationships at the top of your priority list:

- The transfer of your business is not a one-time event, but a journey that you share with your successor.

- You establish a standard you can use to evaluate whether a decision or strategy moves you closer to or further from your goals (transferring your business in a way that benefits all those you care about).

- You design the transfer so it is only successful if it benefits those you have cared for over the years: your family, employees, customers, vendors and community. And don't forget yourself!

- You receive a positive emotional return on the investment you make in helping others to be successful as they carry on the mission of your business.

- You create the opportunity to increase the value of your business and the return on your financial investment.

Establishing your relationships as a primary principle provides a litmus test for all of the options that you will consider as you make decisions during your business transition journey.

Customers **Vendors**
Employees **Community**
Family **You**

Valued Relationships

Caring For The People Who Are Important To You

When we help owners lay the foundation for their Transition Roadmaps, we ask them to first identify the people who are most important to them. We know that when they are able to preserve and protect both family and nonfamily relationships as they transition out of ownership, owners are more likely to engage in the transition process and actually enjoy positioning everyone involved for long-term success.

Whether you plan to stay in your business until you die or leave in the next few months, your Transition Roadmap tells everyone you have invested the time and resources necessary to plan what will happen to your company, its people and your family after your departure. Your Transition Roadmap also prepares your successors to run the business so it continues to provide for those who depend on it.

Owners who put people first understand that a business transfer is only successful if it protects or enhances their relationships with the people who are important to them.

A business transition that puts relationships first is necessarily a journey rather than a singular event because it takes time to plan for and execute a transfer of skills, responsibilities and wisdom from one generation of ownership to the next.

The more time you give yourself to take this journey, the more options you have. Having more options increases the odds your journey will end with the transition that you and your successors desire.

As you begin to create your Transition Roadmap, you will have the opportunity to explore many paths and eventually you will make numerous critical decisions. In many of those decisions, you will have to balance honoring yourself with maintaining your valued relationships. Answering the following questions will help you to achieve that important balance.

- Does the person you want as your successor actually want to take over the business?
  - ~ If so, will they be capable of running it or will the business run them?
  - ~ If not, who will take over after you leave?
- If one person takes over the business, how will you treat fairly those whom you do not choose?
- Will the people you care for now (children/team members active in the business, children not active in the business, employees and other family members) be taken care of when you leave?
- How likely is a potential successor to value and take care of customers and vendors as you have? Will customers and vendors trust a potential successor as they have trusted you?
- How will the business and/or the successor afford to pay you the amount you want for your ownership equity?
- How will you optimize taxes to minimize their impact on you, your successor, family and business?
- If something happens that jeopardizes your company's success, what then?
- Once you leave, will you have a fulfilling and meaningful purpose in your life?

As you consider possible responses to these questions, you will find your choices will yield some of the outcomes you want, but not typically all of them. For example, you might want to consider bringing your younger brother—an average performer at best—into ownership. If you don't offer him ownership, will you hurt his feelings and, by extension, other family relationships? If you do offer him ownership, will you have to continue to carry him, will your top performers leave, and will the business falter and put your financial security at risk? Or, on the other hand, will your brother rise to the occasion and contribute at the level you desire?

Answering questions that put relationships at risk is often difficult, and it almost always triggers deep thinking and emotions. Thoughtful answers may require some tough conversations with colleagues and family. Avoiding those conversations is certainly a pleasant hike on the path of least resistance, but that's not the journey you are on if your goal is to optimize the effects of your business exit on yourself and on everyone you care about. In Chapter Five we explore how to tactfully engage in difficult conversations to produce tremendous clarity as you create your Transition Roadmap.

No Assumptions

When you are thinking about questions whose answers will affect your important relationships, it is easy to make assumptions. You may assume your successor would be "crazy" to take a pass on the "amazing opportunity" to take over your business or that they already know how to run the business. But are your assumptions accurate?

How do you know your successor is interested in taking over the business? Is running a company what *they* desire for their lives or is that your dream? Unless you work to understand the truth, you don't know.

When you put relationships first, you focus on your needs and desires and those of the people you care for. You determine what you want to provide for them. You test assumptions and clarify perceptions—both yours and those of the key people involved in and affected by your transition out of ownership.

This relationships-first approach gives you an incredible opportunity for open, honest discussions about tough subjects. These discussions provide a way to dispel assumptions and answer questions together.

If you fail to make valuing relationships a guiding principle:

- Your life after you leave your business could be a lonely one.

- You may jeopardize both your legacy and the success of your business.

When you put relationships first as you create your Transition Roadmap:

- You establish a litmus test to evaluate every decision you will make on your journey.

- You show others that your relationships are critically important to you, and they recognize you have their best interests at heart and tend to honor your decisions.

- You gain the clarity and confidence you need to create a transition strategy that is a win/win for you and others involved.

POINT OF INTEREST

When you think about your transition, who are the individuals and groups in your family, business and community that you want to take care of? Please list them and outline your reasons on the chart "People and Groups I Would Like to Care For Through My Transition."

People and Groups I Would Like to Care For Through My Transition

Family Member and Why	Business Member and Why	Other People or Groups in the Community and Why

Are there any philanthropic organizations that you'd like to contribute to or care for as part of your transition? Please note them below.

CHAPTER FOUR

YOU ARE IN CHARGE OF YOUR JOURNEY

PRINCIPLE 2

I will not follow where the path may lead, but I will go where there is no path, and I will leave a trail.

Muriel Strode, American poet

At some point you will vacate the role of CEO/owner/investor, relinquish all the duties and privileges these positions entail, and step aside. Given time, you have the opportunity to create and execute a plan to transfer these duties to a successor in a way that sets up your successor and your business to succeed without you.

Some owners are not given the gift of time. They die, become disabled or leave their businesses too soon without the opportunity to instill in their successors the knowledge and insight they need to maintain a company's success. When that happens, not only is the financial security of the owners' families at risk, so is the ongoing viability of their companies.

Today you have the opportunity to create a plan for yourself, your business and your successor, and you are the only one who can lead a successful transition. If you do not lead the transition process, the choices of others—not your choices—will determine the outcome for you, your family and your business.

> *If you do not lead the transition out of your business, the outcome for your family and business will be the result of others' choices, not yours.*

When you design a Transition Roadmap that charts the journey to the transfer of your business to a successor:

- You leave your business in good hands and positioned to thrive.

- Your successor is prepared to seamlessly pick up where you left off.

- You preserve the relationships that are most important to you.

- You launch yourself into the next—and possibly most fulfilling—phase of your life: your Next Adventure.

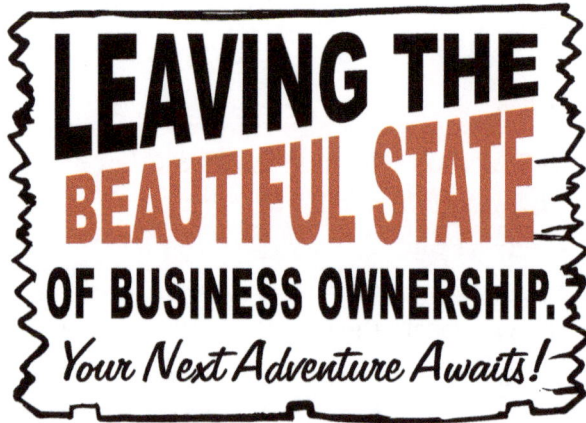

LEAVING THE BEAUTIFUL STATE OF BUSINESS OWNERSHIP. *Your Next Adventure Awaits!*

Leading The Business Transition Process

As the current owner, you set the goals for your business transition and lead the journey. Advisors can help you with various details, but only you can lead the way.

On the journey you will spend time training and mentoring your successor. When you decide they are ready, you will shift total responsibility for your company's success to them. At that point your role will change from leader of your business to proud observer, but until then you are responsible for meeting the goals you set for yourself, your family, your successor and your company.

As a mentor, you will share your past experience in navigating the ups and downs of the business cycle and do your best to transfer your entrepreneurial instincts. You will show your successor how you sense and respond to shifts in your market, see and seize opportunities and run day-to-day operations.

If your business transition is to be successful, you'll need to learn to:

1. Teach your successor how you do things, step by step, and communicate your entrepreneurial insight.

2. Step back and, without interfering, let your successor succeed and fail occasionally.

3. Get out of the way.

Learning to stand back and watch can be a challenge but will also bring great rewards. Among them is the free time you gain as your successor takes over your role. You can devote that time and your energy, creativity and drive to developing your life after business ownership.

You may feel the same excitement and trepidation as you step into the unknown as your successor does when stepping into your shoes. That's normal. These feelings are just part of change. As you know from experience, change often motivates and puts the fun in life.

A business succession involves managing multiple relationships and making far-reaching decisions, but it doesn't have to be overwhelming or complicated. If you put in time and effort to create a Transition Roadmap, you set up yourself, your family, your successor and your business for success.

If you do not take the lead in creating a Transition Roadmap:

- You jeopardize your relationships and the future performance of your company.

- Your successor, management team and business will likely be unprepared to succeed without you.

If you take the lead in creating a Transition Roadmap:

- You give everyone involved time to learn new skills and take on new roles, putting the odds in their favor of being able to succeed without you.

- You provide guidance, direction and a framework for the journey ahead while you create your Next Adventure—the life you will lead after you leave your business.

POINT OF INTEREST

When you look at yourself and your situation, how ready are you to create a Transition Roadmap?

Even if you are not clear on the details of the transfer of your business (successor, timing, method of transfer, etc.), please respond as best you can to the following prompts.

1. What thoughts or feelings *hold you back* from creating a Transition Roadmap today?

Mindsets Regarding My Transition That Hold Me Back

Thoughts or feelings that hold me back from creating a Roadmap today	The reasons why this thought/feeling holds me back include:

2. What thoughts or feelings *energize* you when you imagine a successful transfer of your business to a successor?

Mindsets Regarding My Transition That Energize Me

Thought or feeling that ENERGIZES me...	The reasons why this thought/feeling energizes me include:

CHAPTER FIVE

THE BENEFITS OF COMMUNICATING WELL

The single biggest problem in communication is the illusion that it has taken place.

George Bernard Shaw, Irish playwright

How, what, when and with whom we communicate can enhance relationships and maximize the chances of a successful outcome, no matter the topic. Great communication is absolutely critical when the topic is as important, and often as emotional, as a business transition and the people involved are those you've spent a lifetime caring for.

One of the common threads we see when owners fail to transition a business successfully to new owners is a lack of communication or poor communication between the two parties. Typically that lack of communication involves owners assuming their successors either know nothing or know everything about running the business. Either assumption can doom even the most successful businesses to failure in the hands of the next generation of owners.

Over the course of a business transition (from conception to completion), you will communicate relevant information with a number of parties at the proper time and in the proper way. At least, we hope you will!

The Family Business Institute cites a 2005 Canadian Federation of Independent Business survey that found that "...while 74% of the senior generation leaders report that there is a clearly communicated [succession] plan, 78% of successors report that there isn't!"* In our experience this disconnect persists.

---

*"Family Business in Transition: Data and Analysis," Family Business Institute, 2016, Part 2 (of 3), page 6.
 https://www.familybusinessinstitute.com/wp-content/uploads/2019/01/Family-Business-Succession-Planning-White-Paper.pdf

Communicating that you have created a plan is critical, so our goal is to help you to communicate productively. To us, productive communication involves selecting the optimal time for your conversations and controlling the content. You thoughtfully determine with whom and how you communicate your plan.

For example:

- **When:** Owners talk about their transition ideas with their spouses before speaking with successors or employees.

- **Who:** Owners should, and generally do, solicit opinions and counsel from their spouses and trusted advisors rather than from talking with their possible successors.

- **How:** The way in which owners approach or present a topic or course of action that they are *considering* is far different from how they present the same topic once they've *committed* to it.

- **What:** We encourage owners to remember that the prime concern of the person they are speaking with is what's in it for them. Owners can still be transparent in their communication—as long as they are discreet and use "the need to know" as a filter.

Communicating At The Right Time

Throughout the transition process, owners consult with others and integrate the best thinking into their own. As owners begin to think about their Next Adventures, they may read a few books or attend a webinar or two and begin to formulate their thoughts. They may then broach the topic with their spouses, accountants or attorneys. By the time owners approach us, most have already talked with a select group of people and are either overwhelmed or see the vague outline of a plan but don't know how best to achieve their goals. All know they will eventually communicate with potential successors, but few are prepared for those conversations and most have some level of concern about potential reactions.

Of course, owners communicate their desires, visions, plans and hopes with their spouses, successors and advisors *before* they communicate with employees, customers, vendors and others outside the company. We help owners create a timeline to schedule conversations with all of these parties—timelines tailored to the date owners wish to complete the transition of their businesses. (Please see Chapter Twenty-Three for a more complete discussion of Transition Timelines.) For example, we'll work with owners to identify their objectives for the transfer before we bring in other advisors to discuss transfer options. Once an owner chooses an option (perhaps six months after our initial meeting), they will share their plans with their intended successor. It may take another 6 to 12 months to transfer key responsibilities to that successor, during which time owner and successor craft the story they will share first with others who may be on the executive team and then with employees, vendors and customers.

It is important for owners to invite spouses, advisors, successors and others who support them into their journeys—*when the time is right*. We suggest the right time is not before owners have, at a minimum, established their objectives for the transfer and identified the objectives they will not sacrifice.

Ideally, owners achieve greater success communicating with possible successors when:

- They can be confident and clear because they have developed their Transition Compass™ and Transition Roadmap (see Sections II and III, respectively).

- They can share what they know with regard to their Transition Roadmaps and answers to their Big 6 questions. (We'll introduce you to those important questions in Section II.)

- They recognize that successors want to know what's in it for them.

- They are comfortable disclosing that there are some unknowns in their plans. For example, in the early stages Transition Roadmaps lack a detailed curriculum designed to prepare the successor(s) for leadership and do not include a strategy to grow the business to the value necessary to support the transition. These are not yet available because both require successor input.

We know it is far better for owners to communicate with others along the way—if that is possible—than it is to create plans in a vacuum and hope everything turns out well. But the timing of that communication matters! If there is already a high level of conflict or great potential to injure relationships, operating alone until information must be shared may be an owner's best option. In general, however, communication uncovers roadblocks and detours that are best managed as early in the process as possible.

Communicating With The Right People

Most owners share their thoughts about the transition out of their businesses with very few people or no one at all because they have too many unanswered questions and know the future of their businesses has a significant impact on the lives of so many people. Owners realize that until they can be clear, the people they lead will respond to a mention of a future transition with questions and anxiety. Owners correctly suspect some people will have strong feelings about owners' visions. In addition, owners know that those emotions can quickly escalate into disengagement, disagreement and conflict. For these reasons, most owners are very careful not to open this can of worms with the wrong audience.

When the topic is business succession, everyone—especially those closest to you—will have an opinion about whether a choice you have made is fair. Children, partners and longtime employees can react very emotionally to even the most well-crafted and carefully delivered messages because these individuals have a long history with you. They can't help but hear what you say through their own long-lived filters.

If you are a parent, you know that at times—and despite your best intentions—a child can completely misinterpret what you say. The more you explain yourself, the deeper the hole you dig. For example, imagine lovingly explaining to one son the very valid reasons you chose his younger brother to be CEO. This older son, who has *never* expressed any interest in the position, doesn't even try to hide his disgust as he tells you that he should have expected as much. He informs you that you have finally admitted what he long suspected: You love his brother more than you love him. As you wonder at the turn the conversation has taken, he reminds you that you sent his brother to sleepaway camp and denied him that experience. Sleepaway camp? How could this conversation about the future possibly be related to your sons' elementary school years?

Rather than remind your son that *his doctor recommended* he attend a day camp close to home due to his extreme allergic reactions to a long list of plants and some foods (and begin to describe the possibly lethal consequences of unknowingly eating a single peanut), perhaps you should consider recruiting an objective third party for conversations like these. Our memories are long, and we tend to have intractable filters.

How To Communicate

The way owners communicate during the early stages of a transition journey is far different than how they communicate near the end. At the outset, communication resembles fishing. Near the end of the process, however, the owner's plan is clear, so successors can evaluate that plan and whether to accept the owner's invitation to join the transition journey.

The Early Stages

When owners are fishing (or testing the waters to see who bites), they say something like "I've been thinking lately about my future and that of the company. I'm interested to hear what direction you see the company going in the future as I get older."

To learn what possible successors are thinking, owners might say, "In the past, we've talked in general about you taking over the business. Are you still thinking about whether you want to do that and how that might look?"

To a child who works in the company but hasn't mentioned taking over, an owner might say, "You seem happy with your job and your work/life balance. Have you thought about whether you want to be more active in the company as your children get older? Is that something that you'd find fulfilling as the demands on your time at home begin to shift?"

During the early stages of transition planning and throughout the process, owners should follow four important rules:

Rule 1: Prepare for these conversations. Understand what information you are fishing for. Decide what you will and will not share. Try to anticipate what the other person may think or feel and determine how you might best respond.

Rule 2: Be honest and appropriately transparent.

Rule 3: Make no promises.

Rule 4: Do not try to persuade anyone to do something they don't want to do.

The purpose of a fishing expedition is to gather information. Rather than throw out specific ideas, ask questions and test your assumptions.

Later In The Journey

The conversations that occur after owners have "gone fishing" and created Roadmaps based on what they've learned are similar to those that occur in the early stage in that they adhere to the four basic rules. They are, however, quite different in content because once owners have done the work to create their Roadmaps, they:

- Can paint an accurate picture of the path ahead so others can see how the business transition process will work and how the process and planned outcomes align with their own objectives. Only then can others make informed choices about whether to join.

- Realize that it is possible to integrate some of a successor's objectives into their Roadmap and still honor their own objectives.

During the creation of a Roadmap, owners learn some important information about their successors, specifically that successors also have objectives they will not sacrifice. Successors want to know why owners are choosing a particular path, how they navigated dilemmas and what their primary objectives are. Keep in mind that successors must absorb a great deal of information, so listen carefully to feedback and thoughtfully answer their questions.

Near the end of the journey, when owners announce their transition plans to those beyond their successors, the four basic rules of communication continue to apply. In addition, we strongly recommend that owners and successors agree to "sing from the same hymnbook." If owners and successors do not relate the same positive story, opinions multiply and rumors begin to fly.

Communicating The Appropriate Information

Have you ever noticed how fishermen brag about the size of their catch *after* they are off the water but don't make grandiose predictions *before* they go fishing? For many reasons, owners (like fishermen) should make no predictions or promises when discussing the transition out of their companies. Instead, they should methodically build strategies designed to take themselves and the people who are important to them to the best possible destination.

Communicating From A Position of Gratitude

At times owners can view communication as the opportunity to defend their positions. Some believe that if it takes subtle, or even not-so-subtle, persuasion to convince others to go along with their plans, so be it. These owners tell us a good defense and persuasive offense is the only way to manage their many, many what-ifs. The most common what-ifs include:

- What if someone doesn't like my plan or something about it offends them and they say no?

- What if my plan doesn't meet someone's expectations?

- What if someone thinks my plan is unfair or misconstrues it as my chance to pick a favorite?

- What if my plan for someone isn't part of their plan for themselves?

Far more successful are owners who operate from gratitude and abundance. They recognize they have created valuable businesses that contribute to their purpose in life. When they pass their businesses to someone else, they provide a valuable opportunity. They see that they are not losing something; instead, they are giving to themselves and to those they care about.

Communicating With Successors

Owners typically choose successors who care about the health of the business and its employees and customers. These successors hope your transition plan works for you, but their first concern is whether it's going to work for them (also known as WIFM or what's in it for me). Anticipating and addressing a successor's concerns help combat the negative speculation that often results from a premature dissemination of half-baked information.

Communicating With Confidence

When owners are grounded in and positive about their reasons for transitioning out of their businesses, they:

- Can respond confidently to questions about their transition plans and address any conflicts that may arise.

- Reassure successors and others (e.g., employees, vendors, customers and any additional people whom owners may choose to include) who wonder whether and when owners will move on and how that change will affect them.

- Show that they have a plan that is designed to take care of themselves, their successors and their businesses.

When owners share the reasons behind their choices, they demonstrate how they have worked to meet as many other people's needs as possible and wrestled with the tough decisions. When others understand the choices you make, they may not agree with those choices, but they see your reasoning and find it easier to join your journey. Most owners are relieved when others join them, because the process keeps moving forward.

> *People do things for their reasons, not our reasons.*
> Dan Sullivan, Founder and president of The Strategic Coach

The Ideal Vs. The Reality

Conversations rarely go as planned. Sometimes they go as badly as owners fear they will. When that happens, some owners are tempted to stop in their tracks. They believe it is impossible to navigate through or around all of the obstacles, or they hope the obstacles will magically disappear.

We have seen that even the most difficult conversations yield critical information that validates an owner's assumptions or causes them to recalibrate their plans. As a result of difficult conversations, owners see the road ahead with greater clarity and can continue to move toward their Next Adventures. We remind them that obstacles don't disappear when ignored and explain that they must keep moving toward the ultimate goal: transferring with grace their businesses from their own watchful hands to someone else's.

Their Dream, Not Yours

Inviting someone to become a business owner is an exciting and wonderful part of the business transition process. We celebrate this part *as long as the owner's dream aligns with the successor's dream.*

Ownership is not easy, nor is it for everyone. It is a financial and emotional commitment many people are not willing to make. Owners can justifiably worry that offering ownership could ruin the life of a successor who feels pressured to accept it. A second-generation potential successor once told us, "I want to make sure that ownership is my dream and not just my parents' dream for me."

The only way to know whether a possible successor truly wants to become an owner is to ask and then really listen to the response. Communication does not end there because even successors whose dream and intent it is to assume ownership may be unable to handle the challenge. After they agree to the milestones an owner sets for the journey to ownership, successors may learn that they are unable to meet them or find they have signed up for more than they imagined. When that happens, owners must rethink their choice of successor or recalibrate their Transition Roadmaps.

The most successful business transitions are led by owners who communicate the right information with the right parties at the right times in the right ways. Great communication creates cohesive teams that journey forward in the same direction.

If you communicate poorly:

- You cause the people who matter to you to wonder and worry about their future.

- You turn what should be a wonderful journey into a one-person slog to an uncertain finish line.

If you communicate well:

- You will likely feel great relief when your questions are converted into a plan to move forward and you bring others on board. When you invite others into your journey at the right time and in the right way, you enable them to make informed decisions about their roles in the business and transition plan.

- Others understand the reasoning behind your decisions and see your efforts to craft a transition plan that benefits your company, successor and everyone involved. They see that you have a plan to move the company forward, see how they fit into the future picture, and feel honored to be engaged in a wonderful transition journey.

POINT OF INTEREST

Create a list of the people with whom you have communicated and those you want to communicate with regarding your transition. Make sure to include advisors, friends, spouse, family members, employees, customers and vendors. If it makes sense, create groups of people. Indicate whether you will communicate with individuals or groups early in the process, in the middle, or late in the process. This exercise will help clarify your thinking. Your list of people will most likely change as you follow your Transition Roadmap, as may the timing of your conversations.

Communication Timing

Person/Group	Communication in Progress	Early Journey	Mid Journey	Late Journey

CHAPTER SIX

NO TRANSITION IS PERFECT

PRINCIPLE 3

Be decisive. Right or wrong, make a decision. The road of life is paved with flat squirrels who could not make a decision.

Unknown

Most of us feel some anxiety when we attempt something new or encounter the unknown, so it's natural to feel anxious about transferring your company into the hands of a new owner. The stakes are high for you, your business, your customers and the people you care about. The route you will travel isn't clear (not yet anyway), the obstacles you'll need to overcome are hidden, and the outcome for all concerned is a little cloudy. High stakes, unmarked paths, concealed obstacles and a murky vision of the future are enough to give any owner pause, but please don't add to your anxiety by equating a successful transfer with a perfect transfer. *There are no perfect business transfers.*

WARNING: You will encounter multiple dilemmas on your journey to your Next Adventure. Every owner does. Some dilemmas will be difficult to resolve, and your solution to one may affect the solution to another. Transitioning a business is not for the faint of heart!

Let's begin with a definition.

Dilemma: A situation in which a choice must be made among competing options. All options yield outcomes deciders want or do not want or outcomes they fear or don't think will work.

At the end of Section I, you'll find a Business Owner Transition Confidence Survey where you can rate how confident you are as you think about 11 of the most common dilemmas owners face during this early stage of their transition journeys. First, however, we're going to show you how to establish your lines in the sand and organize possible dilemmas into manageable categories.

The Art Of Resolving Dilemmas

In the face of a dilemma, too many owners get stuck because resolving it involves some level of the unknown. These owners suspect that they could take an action expecting one result only to find that the action elicited a response (possibly negative) that they did not anticipate. They don't know whether an action will or will not precipitate an unwanted response, but just the possibility that the action might keeps them frozen in place. We remind owners that the process of choosing always involves some outcomes they cannot anticipate. That's the reason we ask owners to identify their boundaries (or Deal Breakers) at the beginning of the Transition Roadmap Development Process.

Deal Breakers: Your Lines In The Sand

Before we discuss some common dilemmas (or forks in the road) that many owners encounter on their journeys to their Next Adventure, let's talk for a moment about defining the objectives that you will not sacrifice, your Deal Breakers. These objectives are so important to you that unless the decision you make leads to them, you will not go forward.

A Deal Breaker for you might be that you will not leave your company until it is worth $X or you have $Y in the bank. Or perhaps you will abandon the transition path you've chosen once you learn that the person who has been with you since the start and instrumental in your success will not keep their job at the end of the road. Your Deal Breaker might be that you will not go down a road that destroys family relationships or that the transfer you design must give your brother a shot at becoming a leader.

Basically your Deal Breakers are outcomes so important to you that they put lines in the sand beyond which you will not go. Identifying your Deal Breakers reduces the number of options you must analyze and consequently prevents you from wasting valuable time and energy.

If you define your Deal Breakers and make decisions based on respect for yourself and your important relationships, you put the odds in your favor of achieving a transition that gives you most of the outcomes you want.

We'll show you how to set your Deal Breakers in Chapter Ten.

ORGANIZING DILEMMAS

The most common dilemmas owners encounter on their journeys to put their companies in the hands of successors fall into three basic categories: 1) those related to their personal well-being, 2) those related to the well-being of their companies and 3) those related to their families.

Considering possible dilemmas in advance will help owners decide which direction to travel on their transition journey.

Of course, no one encounters every dilemma we address in this chapter, because the path to a Next Adventure is different for each owner.

Our goal is to help you gain some clarity about the dilemmas you anticipate, not overwhelm you by introducing more issues than you ever imagined! As you read through each dilemma, keep in mind that The Transition Roadmap Developer Process gives you tools to manage those dilemmas you do encounter. When you use the seven principles and your Deal Breakers to guide you, your Transition Roadmap will deliver most of your objectives. Notice we did not say "all of your objectives."

On your journey you may have to give up some objectives that are less important to you than others, because every successful business transfer is the product of negotiation. At the end of the day, neither owners nor successors get everything they want. The beauty of The Transition Roadmap Developer Process is that it tremendously improves the odds that everyone will achieve the objectives that are most important to them.

With some flexibility, open-mindedness and creativity on your part, you should be able to align most of your dilemmas so you can set your direction to your Next Adventure.

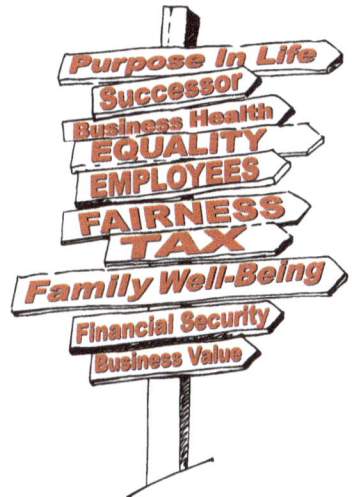

Personal Well-Being Dilemmas

Dilemmas related to your personal well-being come in three basic varieties. All three involve stepping into the unknown and experiencing some type or degree of loss to achieve a greater goal.

1. In transferring your business to a new owner, you may lose the *purpose* that motivates you today. That can be uncomfortable until you find a new purpose to replace it.

2. In moving to your Next Adventure, you will inevitably turn over *leadership* of your business to someone else.

3. After you leave your company, you will no longer earn *income* from it, at least in the way you are accustomed to earning it.

Purpose

Today some engaging and energizing reason gets you out of bed each morning. Most owners wonder what that reason will be when they are no longer involved in the strategic direction and day-to-day management of their companies. Not knowing what comes next can create anxiety, especially for owners considering transition and at relatively younger ages. Whether younger or more mature, we suggest that you ask yourself a few questions:

- As your successor assumes responsibility for an increasing number of tasks that were once yours and after you leave your company, what will you do with the gift of time?

- Have you envisioned a Next Adventure that REALLY excites you?

- If you would like to stay involved with your business on a limited basis once your successor is in place, will doing so be good for you, your successor and the business?

Leadership

On your way to your Next Adventure, you turn over leadership to a successor. That can be difficult for those of us who are used to making decisions and leading others. Some of us suffer from FOLG (Fear of Letting Go), and most find letting go of financial decisions to be especially difficult.

Setting the stage for your successor to succeed can be a challenge not only because you will gradually be allowing someone else to lead, but also because you must learn new skills to let your successor fly on their own.

- Are you adept at delegating?

- How skilled are you at being an effective teacher and mentor?

- How well have you transferred the knowledge in your head into documented systems and procedures that others can follow?

- If you have set a date to begin your Next Adventure, will you meet that deadline if you sell or merge your business with the successor you have in mind?

- Will your successor be ready to step up when you are ready to step away?

Income

It is very common to be concerned about making the transition from income-generator to savings-spender, although with the right diversified investments, you will arguably have income through other sources. That being said, many owners experience anxiety about living on a "fixed income," even if that income is more than they ever made in a year.

- Are you prepared to climb the steep learning curve from making money and plowing it back into your company to investing in other types of assets?

- Are you comfortable investing in assets over which (unlike your business) you have little or no control, e.g., the stock market, private equity, real estate, etc.?

All owners want to leave with the financial resources necessary to support the lifestyle they desire.

- Have you and your spouse defined your future lifestyle? Will it be the same as or different from the one you enjoy today?

Your lifestyle during your Next Adventure will likely be affected by the proceeds from the sale of your business.

- Is your business worth enough to support your Next Adventure?

  ~ Do you know how much money and what level of return you need to support this Next Adventure along with your other goals and needs for the rest of your life?

~ Do you really know what your business is worth? Valuing a business is an art that delivers various results depending on the purpose of the valuation.

~ If the value of your business isn't where you want it to be, how long will it take to grow the business to the level that will support your Next Adventure?

Finally, you've dedicated your life to your company, so it's natural that you want to be rewarded financially for your investment of time, energy and cash.

• Will your transition plan accomplish the financial goals you've set for yourself and your family?

Business Well-Being Dilemmas

Cash Flow

Before you embark on your journey to your Next Adventure, your company's cash flow has supported operations and growth. Included in operations is your salary. At some point during the process of transitioning your company to a successor, the company's cash flow will also have to support the salary of that successor. Typically, that person is a high-level performer who requires a high-level salary. Either over time or in a one-time event, your successor must also pay you for your business interest. Unless your successor is a fully financed, outside third party, the source of that payment (either in full or in part) is excess operating cash flow.

If your company is throwing off 15 to 20 percent profit each year, has no debt and there is only one successor, great! It may not be a problem for the company to fund operations, growth, your successor salary and your buyout. If, on the other hand, your company's profit margin is far slimmer (say 2 to 3 percent), there are several successors or successors have minimal resources, you've got a possible dilemma on your hands.

• In these situations, can your company afford to buy you out and remain financially viable?

• What will the tax impact be and how will it be optimized?

• When the cash funding your buyout is unavailable for operations and growth, how will that affect the company?

• If your buyout will jeopardize the future growth of your company, will you decrease the amount of proceeds you want or consider a different path?

These questions may keep you up at night. Answering them is something that you will explore and address with your advisors as you navigate your Transition Roadmap.

Financial Strength

You have a track record of proven financial performance, so your company's financial commitments (e.g., bonding, lines of credit) likely depend on you.

Will it be possible to shift these commitments to your successors? If so, what hurdles will your successors have to clear?

Successor Selection

The successor you choose plays a huge role in the ongoing financial and operational viability of your company. Consider the following two situations:

1. You have an employee who makes good decisions and is completely capable of running your company successfully. Your daughter is working in the business and has more to learn before she is ready to lead the company. You always dreamed that a family member would succeed you, but that capable employee is not family. You are ready to leave sooner rather than later.

2. You are ready to leave, yet there is no one in your company who could run it successfully without you. You have a longtime employee who would like to be considered for ownership, but you know it would be a big stretch and risk for them to be able to afford the purchase. In your heart you are concerned the company may not go forward well under their ownership. Or perhaps you are concerned that this person does not have the personality or skills to run the company (e.g., the ability to make tough decisions, take the required risk or lead people).

- Can these dilemmas be resolved in a way that maximizes your company's odds of success, keeps the peace, and honors your desires and relationships?

- How will you harvest your investment while simultaneously supporting your successor's ability to financially invest in the business as needed?

- What happens if you have no successor and cannot attract a buyer? This happens!

Company Practices

As you prepare your successor to assume ownership, you will also prepare your company. For example, you will document guidelines related to how you financially manage the company, identifying the amount of cash to be kept in reserve, how you determine salaries, and what you look for while reviewing financials. You will explain why the ranges you set for various financial metrics are key to your company's success. You will also solidify the culture and work to enhance the efficiency and profitability of your business. Your focus will be on documenting the company practices that are foundational to the business's well-being and then putting that documentation into other team members' hands.

- How will you simultaneously identify and transition the company knowledge only you have while running the business day to day, when your available time is limited?

- To whom will you transfer knowledge, especially that related to the tasks you believe are so important that you have never shared them with anyone?

Employee Reaction

Have you thought about whether after you leave employees will stay engaged and willingly make the shift from your leadership to your successor's? How will you prepare your employees to trust and look to a successor for leadership, when that successor is likely younger than you and may be related to you? Some employees may not agree with your choice of successor, or they may want to leave when you do. If these employees are important to the company's success, their discontentment or departure may significantly impact the business's health.

- If you suspect that your successor may face a mutiny, how can you plan for and mitigate it?

- Do you want to reward any family or nonfamily employees for their contributions to your company's success?

Culture

It is likely the culture you created contributes to your company's success. The great unknown is what happens to it after you leave.

- Is it important to you that your successor maintains the culture you established?

- Is it important to you that your successor retains the employees who were part of that longtime culture?

Family Well-Being Dilemmas

Whose Vision Is It Anyway?

Remember, the transition to your Next Adventure may or may not be consistent with the Next Adventures of the people who will be affected by your departure.

- Do you know how your spouse or significant other envisions their Next Adventure? Do they want to do (or have) things that are not currently "within your means"? Put another way, will you have the money to live the life you both dream of?

- If there is a successor (or more than one) available within the business or the family, is it your dream or theirs that they take over the business?

- Do your children (those active in the business and not) even want ownership or to be involved?

Maintaining Relationships

If you are considering family members as successors, fumbling the transition of a family business can damage both business and family. Creating a thoughtful plan to execute that transition can draw your family even closer together.

With so much at stake and without a clear path (yet) to your transition objectives, how do you approach the topic with your family? Talking business at the dinner table is one thing; talking business transition is a whole different animal. There is a danger of making promises that you may not be able to keep, and there is the unwanted prospect that issues such as fairness and entitlement may arise. When you make decisions designed to sustain the success of your business, feelings can get hurt and relationships damaged.

- How will you address your family members' concerns about what's fair in a way that is fair to you, your business and all concerned? Your belief systems and the dynamics that are specific to your family and business determine how you define "fair." We'll talk more about this issue in Chapter Seventeen.

- Will you require all family members to be actively involved in the business if they are to have ownership? If not, will non-active owners and active owners have an equal voice in decision-making?

If you fail to acknowledge and address dilemmas:

- They do not disappear. You simply lose control over when and how to resolve them.

- Sleepless nights continue and the clock keeps ticking because of the anxiety that results when you know the dilemmas exist, but you don't know how to resolve them.

If you acknowledge and address dilemmas:

- You realize some dilemmas will resolve as you test assumptions, and you discover that those that appeared insurmountable are surprisingly easier to navigate than you thought.

- You gain confidence about the journey ahead because you know you can handle issues as they pop up.

POINT OF INTEREST

Please make a list of your dilemmas related to your personal, business and family well-being. If you have dilemmas that don't fit into these categories, list them here as well. Then, please allocate a percentage to each category. The purpose of this exercise is to gain awareness of the dilemmas you face today.

My Dilemmas

	Personal Well-Being	Business Well-being	Family Well-being	Other
Related percentage	%	%	%	%
Primary dilemmas				

CHAPTER SEVEN

IT'S YOUR NEXT ADVENTURE™: GO FOR IT!

PRINCIPLE 4

Wherever you go, go with all your heart.

Confucius, Chinese philosopher

So far we have talked about moving out of your role of business owner and out of your business. But as you move *away* from your business, what are you moving *toward?* What is your Next Adventure?

Most of our clients have found it far easier to engage in The Transition Roadmap Developer Process when they truly understand that their transition is the beginning of a new chapter in their lives.

One of the byproducts of creating a Transition Roadmap that transfers responsibilities to your successor is that it frees up time to plan for your post-transition future, or Next Adventure.

Crafting Your Next Adventure

Put relationships first. This rule of the road should sound familiar by now, but this time we suggest you apply it to your Next Adventure. In other words, what do you want to gain from the transfer of your business? Consider your relationship with yourself and decide how you want to treat yourself as you go through this shift in time and purpose. Many owners' priorities are family, business, friends and community, and they either forget or struggle to make themselves a priority.

Family

For many years, your business consumed much, if not most, of your time and energy. Once your successor has assumed responsibility for the ownership and leadership of your company, you'll have more opportunities to spend time with family.

There's a bumper sticker that makes us laugh and cringe at the same time because it contains a kernel of truth: *Retirement: Twice the spouse, half the income!*

Will you hang around the house with your spouse? If both you and your spouse are transitioning out of ownership, will hanging out be okay with you? with your spouse? Realize that just being around each other for longer periods of time may be one of many big changes for both of you.

Many owners do not take time to communicate with their spouse when they begin to envision their Next Adventures. It is fun to explore what your Next Adventure might look like for the two of you as a couple.

Many years ago a great mentor and teacher Dr. Mel Wernimont brought clarity to the concept of individuals as a couple. It is both simple and deep: I am ME, you are YOU, and we are US. When you think about life with a partner, it is important that each of you gets to be themselves and together you get to be us. Understanding that there are two individuals as well as a couple makes achieving what "all three" want incredibly rewarding!

Friends

While your roster of family members doesn't change from your "business life" to your Next Adventure, you may find that your friend roster shifts and grows. Leaving your business is a major life event, and like others (the birth of a first child, divorce or the death of a spouse) it can affect your friend group. Once you cash out, you may have the time and funds to travel to fun or unique places, but your friends may not. On the other hand, you may have time to golf every day, so you will likely make new friends who enjoy the game as much as you do.

The prospect of spending more time with family or changing your friend roster may appeal to you, but it is likely a bit of an unknown for you. Keep in mind that family and friends are experiencing the same unknown. Exploring it is part of the journey we've been talking about. Along the way, you will figure out what you need to do to maintain the quality of the relationships that are important to you.

Community

By providing jobs and supporting the economy, you have contributed to your community. You may have also given money and time to local causes or organizations.

- Will you disengage or stay engaged in these causes once you leave your business?
- Will you take on new roles in these groups?
- Will you join other organizations and take on new challenges?

Yourself

Part of your post-transition "job" will be to act as a good steward of your financial investments as you shift from building wealth to preserving it. The other part—and we'd argue the far more exciting part—is to continue to live a life that is meaningful to you. Your Next Adventure might include exotic things like sailing to incredible harbors, spending months volunteering in a medical clinic in a third-world country, climbing Mount Kilimanjaro or building an airplane. It may also include developing new hobbies, spending more time on your health and deepening relationships.

Don't limit yourself as you consider your Next Adventure; imagine anything is possible and open yourself up to abundance. Later we will assess what resources you will need to support your Next Adventure, but at this point open your mind, heart and imagination.

Whatever your Next Adventure may be, it is important that you are able to emotionally invest in it. If you devote energy and time to it, you will make your Next Adventure a fulfilling and wonderful next stage of your life.

If you ignore your Next Adventure and focus only on what you are leaving:

- You won't leave! You won't intentionally and actively make the transition out of your current role. Without something engaging to move toward, it is difficult to leave what you have and are doing today.

- You enter the next phase of your life with no focus for your energy and enthusiasm.

If you clearly envision and fully embrace your Next Adventure:

- You are motivated to take action and prepare for the future.

- You are prepared and excited to bring your energy and contributions to your family, community and future pursuits.

- You are ready to step out of your business and into your Next Adventure without missing a beat.

POINT OF INTEREST

As you envision yourself out of your business and no longer experiencing the risk and reward of ownership, what do you believe will be most fulfilling to you in your Next Adventure?

Take a moment to think about people, places, relationships, events, experiences and activities that have given you joy in the past and those you believe will give you joy in the future.

Write 10 things that come to mind. Don't overthink this.

My Next Adventure Top 10 List

1.

2.

3.

4.

5.

6.

7.

8.

9.

10.

Now write the top 10 things that you expect to miss most.

What I Will Miss Most During My Next Adventure Top 10 List

1.

2.

3.

4.

5.

6.

7.

8.

9.

10.

CHAPTER EIGHT

CHOOSE YOUR DESTINATION WITH INTENTION

PRINCIPLE 5

Indecision becomes decision with time.
Anonymous

A s a business owner, you already know there are risks in life and business. Risk comes in all sizes—big and small—and in all degrees—crucial and not so essential.

No matter which industry we are in, it's easy to focus our attention on the day-to-day business risks we are used to and ignore the risk an unplanned transition creates for our families and businesses. We entrepreneurs are experienced and adept when managing daily risks but may have little to no experience managing the risks associated with a business transfer.

We can ignore the inevitable transition out of ownership or postpone thinking about it, but avoidance won't eliminate the risk to our families or our businesses. Unless you create a Roadmap to manage your transition out of your business and into your Next Adventure, situations could arise that leave others to make decisions—without your guidance or involvement—that affect your family and your business.

Owners who ignore their inevitable transitions out of their companies, are too overwhelmed to take action, or simply don't know there's a process to help them achieve the successful outcome they desire (for themselves, their companies and the people they care about), take a huge risk.

The Problem Of Inertia

Inertia means continuing on as you always have: moving forward in your straight line until an external force (such as a health issue) moves you off that line. Consider how "Joe's" inertia put his family and business at risk when he failed to acknowledge his mortality.

Joe had spent decades pouring time and energy into his business. With thousands of clients and millions of dollars in revenue, he had achieved success far beyond his expectations. Joe's wife, "Martha," dedicated her time to raising their daughter, "Heather," and taking care of their home and family.

Heather started working full-time in the business directly out of college. After just a few years, Heather's hard work told Joe that she would have a successful career with the business. Joe's dream of having his daughter take over the business looked more and more realistic, so Joe transferred 20 percent of his equity to her. Not getting around to acting on the advice from his business attorney, Joe never created a buy/sell agreement to control the disposition of the company's stock in the event of any lifetime events (disability, divorce, termination of employment, etc.) or the death of either father or daughter. As the majority shareholder, Joe applied for life insurance in an amount that would fund the transfer of the business to Heather if something happened to him and provide cash equal to the value of Joe's interest in the company to Martha.

Joe was disappointed when his application was denied for health reasons. He had run into a roadblock, but he told no one, just as he had told no one about his desire to ultimately transfer the business to his daughter.

Several years later, Joe died suddenly. There was no insurance to fund Heather's purchase of Joe's stock, so there was no source of funding for Martha's financial security. The bulk of Joe's assets (his ownership in his company) were illiquid. He had never communicated to either Heather or Martha what he wanted each to receive—— namely, the business to Heather and the value of Joe's ownership to Martha.

Martha reacted to Joe's death, his leaving an illiquid business in her hands, and her "new job" as the 80 percent owner of the business as one might expect: with fear. When she closed her eyes at night and woke each morning, the same questions swirled in her head: Will I be okay? Where will the money come from to live my life the way we planned? What will I do with the business?

Despite her complete lack of experience in the business, Martha decided her only option was to run it. As the new majority owner, she dug in and took charge. She challenged employees about the way they did things, and she made financial decisions that far exceeded what the business could afford. Complaints skyrocketed as customers failed to receive the level of service they expected. Revenues and employee morale declined.

Meanwhile, Heather, who had justifiably expected to one day take over the business she loved and had invested in, became angry. She had always intended to take care of her mother in the way she knew her father would have wanted, but she had had enough of her mother's "leadership."

After butting heads with her mother for months, Heather took the only route she could see: She filed suit against her business partner—her mother—to purchase her mother's shares and remove her from the business before it failed.

Three valuations and tens of thousands of dollars in legal bills later, mother and daughter agreed on a value and Heather bought her mother's stock.

This long and acrimonious process damaged the mother-daughter relationship and the company, but both survived. In fact, once Heather and Martha each got what they needed, they were able to mend their relationship.

Joe's story is a sad one because of the damage done to both his family and business. More than that, it's tragic because *it didn't have to happen!* If Joe had created a Transition Roadmap and communicated that plan to both his wife and daughter, it's likely his business and family would have thrived. Instead, Joe just kept his head down and did what he did best, which was to run a successful business. Joe's failure to act and communicate his wishes had consequences long after he died.

Not everyone has the luxury of time to lead the successful transition of a business. That's why it's important to act now. Putting off decisions because you feel no sense of urgency or don't see a way to balance competing objectives (e.g., the health of your family relationships vs. the health of your business) reduces your runway and, as a result, your number of good options. Without adequate time to plan, you may not be able achieve your goal of leaving your company in the hands of a successor you know. Instead you might have to sell to a third party you don't know or liquidate your company.

Know that as years pass and you continue business as usual, the people around you are wondering what is going to happen to them and to your company. The longer you wait to create a plan to transfer your business to a successor, the greater the risk something could happen to you (death or disability) or to your desired successor (they become so frustrated with your unwillingness to turn over the reins that they leave). The longer you wait, the less time you have to plan and lead your transition and the fewer options you have.

The sooner you begin to tackle dilemmas and make your decisions, the more time you have to enjoy the journey and navigate the risks. Time tilts the odds of success in your favor. When you create a Transition Roadmap to guide you, *you* lead the journey.

If you don't take action to address your inevitable exit from your business:

- You run a higher risk of leaving your family and your business in the lurch, as your absence is very likely to create a leadership and talent void.

- As your five-year retirement plan becomes a rolling five-year retirement plan (resulting in no definite date of departure), over time tensions increase while the number of choices decreases.

- Through the simple law of inertia, your transition journey transforms into an event, one that strains relationships and burdens those most important to you.

If you take action and plan your transition out of your business:

- You protect your business and your family.

- You handle difficult conversations and resolve issues with grace and ease because you understand your priorities.

- You help those whom you invite into your journey work through their fears and achieve more.

POINT OF INTEREST

Take a moment to think about how prepared your family and your team are to take on the business or sell it if tomorrow you were not available. Circle the value that is most representative for each.

How ready is my family to take on the business or the sale of the business without me?

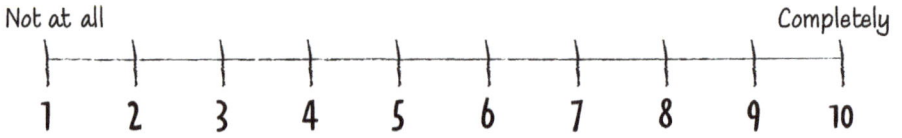

Not at all   Completely

1   2   3   4   5   6   7   8   9   10

How ready is my team to take on the business or the sale of the business without me?

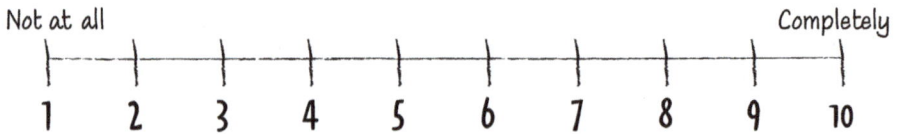

Not at all   Completely

1   2   3   4   5   6   7   8   9   10

Now think about how prepared specific family members and specific team members are to run or sell your business if you were unavailable. List those people and rate their preparedness on a scale of 1 to 10. Make a note of what you think or feel (e.g., encouraged, disappointed, concerned) as you look at your ratings.

Family/Team Readiness

	Preparedness to run or sell the business 1 = not at all 10 = completely, without question	Thoughts or feelings regarding each rating
Family Members		
Team Members		

CHAPTER NINE

STEP AWAY FROM MUTUAL DEPENDENCY

PRINCIPLE 6

If the company depends entirely on you—your creativity, ingenuity, inspiration, salesmanship or charisma—nobody will want to buy it. The risk and the dependency are too great.

Margaret Heffernan, Documentarian, serial CEO and author

We've worked with many owners and their companies over the years, all of whom were, in varying degrees, dependent on each other. This two-way, or mutual, dependency—business dependent on owner, and owner dependent on business—is completely understandable. Many owners have founded their businesses and/or played an integral role in them for years. Most have put on many hats: employee motivator, rainmaker, operations supervisor, idea generator, financial backer, reputation booster, bookkeeper, PR agent, leader and more.

As owners begin to think about their Next Adventures, we ask them to look at their reliance on their companies and their companies' reliance on them. Why? Because mutual dependency must end if owners are to successfully move on to their Next Adventures and their companies are to succeed after they leave.

To accomplish a successful transition, we help owners reframe both sides of the dependency equation: 1) eliminate the owner's dependence on the business for income, personal fulfillment, identity, social engagement and stature in the community; and 2) eliminate a company's dependence on its owner for knowledge, talent, rainmaking, business relationships, financial strength and identity. The measure of our success is the happiness of our client-owners after they leave their companies, and the continued success of the companies they leave behind.

The Ties That Bind Owner To Business

Income

For the majority of owners, compensation (in the form of salary, benefits, distributions and dividends) from their companies is their major source of income. Most have spent years investing in their companies and want to reap the rewards of those investments through the transfer of business ownership. Whether owners receive proceeds from the sale of their business all at once or over time, those proceeds often finance their Next Adventures.

Happiness/Fulfillment

Not all owners who are considering their Next Adventure derive the level of happiness they once did from their companies, but almost all still feel connected to and fulfilled by their businesses. They know they've built successful enterprises that have supported their families, employees and communities well. It is natural that many owners wonder what will fulfill them once they no longer own and run their companies.

Relationships With Their Teams And Communities

Owners of successful businesses often play important roles in their communities. As owners, we sometimes spend more time with members of our management teams than we do with members of our own families. Owners and the members of their teams may belong to multiple charitable and business organizations and often will support causes and sponsor events that are important to them, their community and customers. Work relationships can be richly rewarding and community activities result in friendships and social engagement opportunities. When business owners move on, however, their strong ties to people both inside and outside of the business can loosen or disappear.

The Ties That Bind Business To Owner

By definition, a successful business transition is one in which all parties—former owner, successor and company—thrive after the transition is complete. To accomplish that result, owners must end their dependence on their companies, and they must also sever their companies' dependence on them.

Businesses are typically dependent on their owners for:

- Knowledge/talent
- Rainmaking
- Business relationships
- Financial strength
- Identity

Knowledge/Talent

How will your business replace your knowledge and talent contribution? In Chapter Twenty-Eight we will discuss how owners must transfer tasks and wisdom to their successors. Because there's never an exact match between an owner's and successor's areas of expertise, you may need to do some hiring to fill the gaps. This type of investment of time and resources is key to unwinding a company's dependence on the owner.

Rainmaking

The founder or longtime owner is very often the source of sales and the driver of new revenue initiatives. To ensure the continued growth and success of a company this torch must be passed!

Business Relationships

Companies are always dependent on an owner's relationships with customers, key vendors and strategic alliances. These relationships are based on the trust that comes from a long history of working together. For example, suppliers may routinely extend handshake deals or variable payment schedules to owners they know and trust but may be less likely to do so with new owners they don't yet know. The earlier you begin to involve your successor in these trust-based relationships, the more time you give yourself to properly transfer these relationships to your successor.

Financial Strength

Intrinsic to business operations are obligations that often depend on relationships owners forge with various financial institutions. For example, a bank's willingness to extend a line of credit or finance a loan (collateralized or uncollateralized) may depend on its trust in the credit worthiness and financial stability of the soon-to-be former owner. Similarly, an insurance company may extend bonding due to a longstanding relationship with the owner. The bottom line is this: Transferring debt obligations and financial commitments is one of the hardest and last things to be transitioned in an internal transaction simply because new owners typically do not start out with sufficient financial resources.

Identity

In some businesses, the customers, vendors and members of the community make no distinction between the business and the family that owns it. In these situations, owners must begin to separate their names (or that of their families) from the names of their companies.

We recommend that owners craft detailed plans to create a clear delineation between owners/families and their companies. These should include internal and external communications, updated marketing programs, press releases and extensive networking. To change the perception of customers and key constituencies we suggest owners conduct a three-stage meeting strategy involving their successors:

Stage 1: Owners run meetings with various parties while successors observe.

Stage 2: Successors run meetings while owners observe.

Stage 3: Successors run meetings without owners present.

Knowledge, talent, rainmaking, business and financial relationships, and an intertwined identity are the common ties owners must think about—and work to transfer to their successors—before they hand over the keys. In Chapter Eighteen we discuss timing for the transfer of these ties.

Think for a moment about your business.

- What talents, knowledge and relationships of yours does your business depend on?

- Are you the primary rainmaker?

- What business and financial relationships must you transfer to your successor if your company is to grow under their leadership?

- Do vendors, customers and your community view you and your business as one and the same?

Think for a moment about yourself.

- How will you replace your current income? Will the sale of your ownership interest result in the return you seek on your investment in your company or provide the financial resources you need to support your Next Adventure?

- What will replace your business as the source of your happiness and sense of fulfillment?

- Once your roles are no longer "business owner" in your community and "owner/leader" in your company, what will they be? What will you be doing that is wonderfully fulfilling?

If your business remains dependent on you and you remain dependent on your business:

- You leave your successor and team unprepared (and likely unable in the case of financial relationships) to run the company successfully. As a result, customers and employees suffer.

- If your payout and financial future are dependent on the continued success of the business, you may not receive the funds you need to live the life you planned.

- You will likely be continually pulled back into the businesses, robbing you of the freedom of time necessary to fully experience your Next Adventure.

If you take action to reduce your company's dependence on you and your dependence on your business:

- Your successor and team acquire critical knowledge and benefit from the relationships that are necessary to lead the company successfully into the future.

- You move closer to your Next Adventure.

- If you decide to choose a third party as your successor, your company is more salable and likely will bring a higher value.

As you look at your business and your life, think about how dependent your business is on you and how dependent you are on your business.

List ways in which your business is dependent on you, and estimate (on a scale of 1 to 10) how difficult it would be to alleviate that dependency.

Business Dependency

Area/Item for which my business depends on me	To alleviate this dependency would be 1 = No Problem 5 = Somewhat Difficult 10 = Highly Difficult

List ways in which you are dependent on your business, and estimate (on a scale of 1 to 10) how difficult it will be to shift that dependency. Remember to consider both the function of making a shift, and the emotion involved in doing so.

Owner Dependency

Area/Item that I depend on my business to provide	To alleviate this dependency would be 1 = No Problem 5 = Somewhat Difficult 10 = Highly Difficult

CHAPTER TEN

YOUR TRANSITION ROADMAP IS INDISPENSABLE

PRINCIPLE 7

A map is the greatest of all epic poems. Its lines and colors show the realization of great dreams.

Gilbert H. Grosvenor, First full-time editor of National Geographic magazine

A Transition Roadmap is indispensable to a successful transfer of a business. It identifies and organizes all of the activities and events owners must consider and tasks they and their successors must complete. It includes timelines that schedule when tasks will begin and end for both owner and successor and when equity will change hands. In short, a Transition Roadmap organizes all of the thoughts running through your head about whom you want to succeed you as owner, what will you transfer, when and how that process will happen and how much you will be paid.

Of course, there isn't a straight line from where you are today to your Next Adventure. Along the road are detours, roadblocks and opportunities—all in the form of internal and external events that may require you to adjust course. Your Transition Roadmap keeps you heading in the right direction.

Imagine, for example, you want to travel from Denver to Canada, and you choose the province of Alberta as a destination. After you gather some information about Alberta, measure the distance, and check out the average temperatures, you decide to see Yellowstone National Park and Glacier National Park on your way to Calgary and to begin your trip in early fall. After digging into the character of neighborhoods in Calgary, you choose one that appeals to you. After more research, you choose a bed-and-breakfast there.

A Transition Roadmap organizes more than just your route, and it requires you to know where you are starting and understand the direction in which you want to go. As you make decisions about your direction, how you will get where you want to go and when, your route becomes clearer and clearer. You are able to make educated guesses about when you'll arrive at various points along the way. If circumstances force you to find a new route, you've got your map to remind you of your destination and how lucky you are to be taking this trip.

Fictional owners "Wally" and "Don" provide a great illustration of how a Transition Roadmap:

- Charts a path to the destination you choose.

- Organizes a transition in a way that preserves the relationships that are important to owners.

- Guides you and those who will take this journey with you.

- Motivates your successor and your team to work together, because it clearly lays out the route you will take.

- Adapts as necessary so no matter what happens, you increase the odds of reaching your Next Adventure successfully.

W*ally and Don had spent years assembling a great management team and building a fabulous enterprise. As they reached their mid-60s, they began to talk about a succession plan, one which would take care of their employees and the members of their executive team they so valued. One of their biggest concerns was how their business would be able to support their buyout.*

In an effort to answer this question, the business partners met with multiple advisors who shared so much information and offered so many opinions that the two were overwhelmed. There were so many choices to make that Wally and Don could not envision a path that would lead to the result they wanted.

Wally (the dreamer) was anxious to move on to the activities he and his wife had put off for years. Don (the problem solver) still found fulfillment in his role as co-owner and was determined to figure out a way to transition out of the business in a way that would work for both of them. Each began to ask friends who had transitioned out of their companies for input. One of those former owners introduced Don and Wally to us.

As we always do, we suggested the partners table the question of how they would structure the sale of their ownership equity until we could understand why they wanted to transition to the next phase of their lives. They agreed and each completed an Objectives Matrix, a tool that we will introduce you to in Chapters Thirteen and Fourteen.

When we asked the two owners whom they envisioned as their successors, they weren't really sure. They didn't know if their key employees would want to buy the company or if those employees could pay what Don and Wally thought it was worth, so the two owners were open to the idea of other successors. They were, however, in complete agreement that if a transition plan did not honor the employees who had helped them build the company, the plan was a nonstarter.

There was some misalignment between the two men related to when they wanted to make the transition from owner to former owner. Wally was tired and no longer really enjoyed the work. In addition, now that their team was doing so much of "his work," Wally had the bittersweet experience of knowing he'd trained them well on the one hand and wondering what current value he brought to the team on the other. Don, however, was still very much engaged. He enjoyed both the interaction and the work, and he felt he played a key role in the company's success. Unlike Wally, he was energized and not ready to give up his role. To resolve this misalignment, we developed a great strategy that kept Don in his position as CEO for several years so he could continue doing work he found meaningful, while Wally could move on immediately to his Next Adventure.

Now that we understood what each partner wished to accomplish and when they wanted to take off on their Next Adventures, we worked with each to determine what financial resources they had and what resources they'd need to live their Next Adventures. We then suggested several strategies they could use to close the gap between the two amounts. When Don and Wally learned that the financial gap between where they were and where they wanted to be was not as large as they had feared, they began to believe they really could transfer their company to employees in a way that would satisfy everyone's objectives.

At this point Don and Wally were equipped to tackle the question of the method they would use to transfer ownership to their successors in a way that would enable the two men to live their Next Adventures and position their successors and their company to succeed without them. Only then did we assemble their accountant, attorney, banker and personal financial advisors to give input and approve the tax efficiency, legality and financial viability of their succession plan.

Don and Wally created a Transition Roadmap that ultimately put their business in the capable hands of people they trusted. They could confidently begin their Next Adventures and continue to support the people they cared about. Not only that, they maintained the great relationships with their employees that had taken years to create.

What great results, all thanks to a Transition Roadmap.

If you try to transfer your business to a successor without a Transition Roadmap:

- You waste time and energy traveling to dead ends or even become lost in a series of dilemmas, while the number of nights you wake up wondering and worrying about what you will do with your company increases.

- You do your best to resolve conflicts on the fly without an understanding of how they fit into your overall transition.

- Your successors can't see a clear path to ownership, and they begin to develop their own contingency plans which do not involve you or your company.

If you create a Transition Roadmap to guide you on your journey to your Next Adventure:

- You design a functional and effective strategy to get from where you are today to where you want to be, on your schedule and in a way that achieves the objectives you set for yourself, your business and those you care about.

- You and your successors work as a team toward the successful transfer of a business that is important to all of you, navigating and resolving the dilemmas that have long concerned you and perhaps held you stuck in place.

- You are able to nimbly switch to alternate routes when either detours or dilemmas arise or conditions are better than anticipated (e.g., your business grows faster in value than expected) because your Roadmap is a living navigational tool.

POINT OF
INTEREST

We pause here to allow you to take a deep dive into your thinking about your journey to your Next Adventure.

Have you been thinking about the transfer of your business to a successor as a journey or as an event?

Look at the various aspects of your transition. Is it fun and energizing to think about these aspects? Which aspects seem difficult (or almost impossible) to accomplish? Use the table below to outline all the aspects, indicate whether each is energizing or not, and note how accomplishable you believe it to be.

Transition Energy Assessment

Aspect of Transition	Energizing? Yes/ No	Accomplishable? Absolutely, Difficult or Not Likely

Acknowledging how you view the journey ahead, as a whole and in parts, indicates how likely you are to begin it. If you envision a long, hard road full of difficulties, it is likely that you will hesitate and possibly become stuck. If, on the other hand, you look at the broader picture and see how this journey can create a win for everyone involved, you can jump in with both feet and engage with enthusiasm.

SURVEY

The Business Owner Transition Confidence Survey™

At this point we hope you have a better idea of what's involved in your journey to your Next Adventure and you understand the principles that will keep you on the path you choose. Before we ask you to set the six points on your Transition Compass that will set your direction, we encourage you to take stock of how confident you are as you think about 11 of the most common concerns or dilemmas that owners have at this stage of their transition journeys.

Please rate your confidence level on a scale of 1 to 9.

1. Next Adventure: I am confident in my Next Adventure and excited to live it.

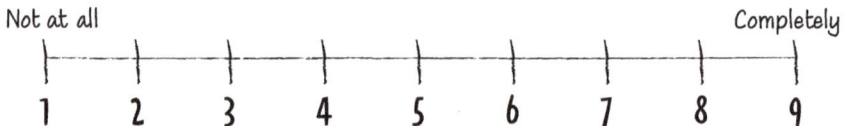

Not at all   Completely

1   2   3   4   5   6   7   8   9

2. Successor: I am confident in my successor. I have chosen the best leader to take the business forward.

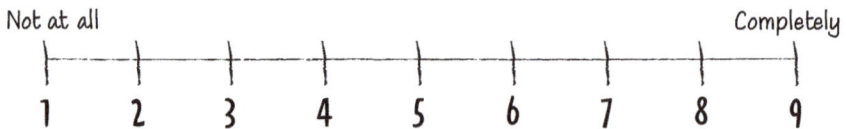

Not at all   Completely

1   2   3   4   5   6   7   8   9

3. Financial ROI: I am confident I will harvest my investment (get the money I desire) from the transition of my business.

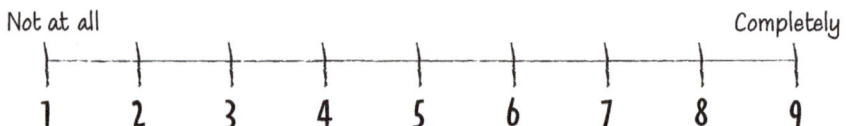

Not at all   Completely

1   2   3   4   5   6   7   8   9

4. Financial Freedom: I am confident I will have the money necessary to live my Next Adventure the way I desire.

Not at all   Completely

$$1 \quad 2 \quad 3 \quad 4 \quad 5 \quad 6 \quad 7 \quad 8 \quad 9$$

5. Optimal Tax Strategy: I am confident the tax strategy I have planned for the transaction will yield the outcome I desire.

Not at all   Completely

$$1 \quad 2 \quad 3 \quad 4 \quad 5 \quad 6 \quad 7 \quad 8 \quad 9$$

6. Business Resources: I am confident my business has and can generate the resources needed (including cash flow) to support the additional expenses that will be incurred throughout the transition.

Not at all   Completely

$$1 \quad 2 \quad 3 \quad 4 \quad 5 \quad 6 \quad 7 \quad 8 \quad 9$$

7. Fairness and Equality: I am confident I have tackled fairness and equality and that they will not be issues for me or for my family, partners or employees.

Not at all   Completely

$$1 \quad 2 \quad 3 \quad 4 \quad 5 \quad 6 \quad 7 \quad 8 \quad 9$$

8. Financial Commitments: I am confident the financial institutions that support my company's operations will accept my successor as a guarantor of those obligations.

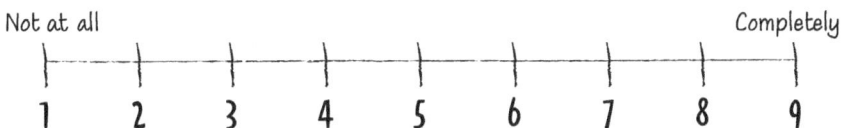

Not at all   Completely

$$1 \quad 2 \quad 3 \quad 4 \quad 5 \quad 6 \quad 7 \quad 8 \quad 9$$

9. Leadership: I am confident in my ability to lead my successor, team and family through my business transition.

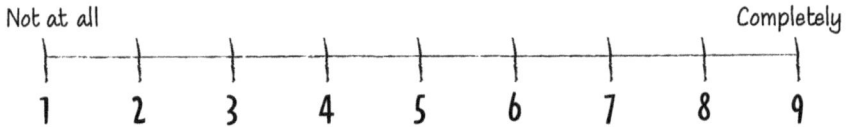

Not at all   Completely

1   2   3   4   5   6   7   8   9

10. Relationships: I am confident the succession plan I envision will protect and support the relationships that I value.

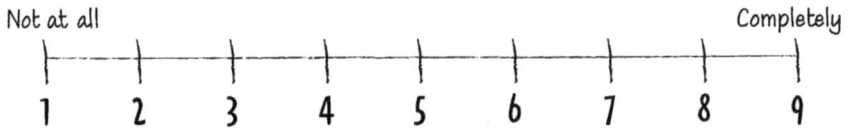

Not at all   Completely

1   2   3   4   5   6   7   8   9

11. Time Freedom: I am confident I will gain choice of time as I go forward in my transition journey and will meet my transition timetable.

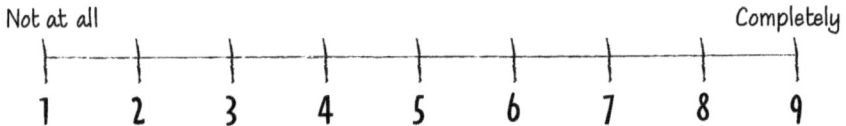

Not at all   Completely

1   2   3   4   5   6   7   8   9

Please plot your rating from each scale as a point on the Business Owner Transition Confidence Spider Graph on the following page, and then connect the points.

The Business Owner Transition Confidence Spider Graph

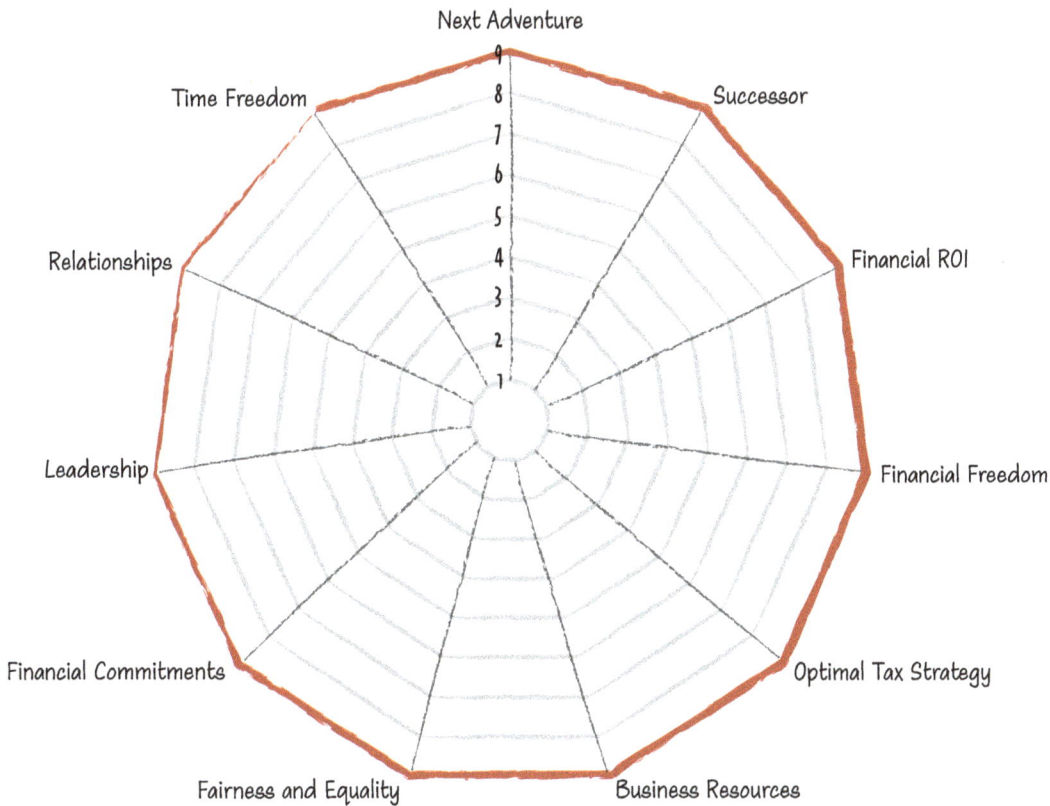

Overall Rating: Looking at your Business Owner Transition Confidence Spider Graph, how clear and confident are you in your business transition?

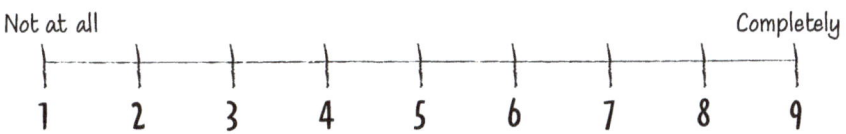

Not at all — Completely

1   2   3   4   5   6   7   8   9

We encourage you to return to this Survey after you finish this book. You may find, as most owners do, that once you establish your goals and think about transition issues in the order we recommend, your confidence grows exponentially. If you'd like additional copies of this Survey, please go to *www.TheSuccessionPlanningBook.com/Tools.*

SECTION II

Set the Points on Your Compass

In Section I we suggested you think of the transfer of your business to a successor as you would a driver changing places with a front-seat passenger. In both scenarios, you make a series of decisions necessary to create a plan. In a business transition, however, there is no gas pedal or steering wheel to control the forward movement. Instead, you must communicate your knowledge and wisdom to your successors if you want them to be able to run your company as successfully as you did.

We also introduced you to our seven guiding principles, or rules of the road, that improve odds that the business transfer you envision is the one you will achieve.

Principle 1: Put relationships first. A business transfer is successful only if it protects or enhances your relationships with the people who are important to you.

Principle 2: You are in charge of your journey. As the owner of your business, you pick the destination, create the map and drive the car. You lead the transition in a way that optimizes success for all involved. To arrive safely at your destination means that you are able to enjoy your Next Adventure, your successor is prepared to run the company, and your company succeeds under your successor's leadership.

Principle 3: No transition is perfect or provides everything you want. If crafted properly, however, your transition should provide what is most important to you.

Principle 4: It's your Next Adventure: Go for it! If you devote time to planning your Next Adventure, your life after business ownership will be another meaningful and fulfilling experience.

Principle 5: Choose your destination with intention. If you do not lead the transition out of your business, what happens to your business and family will be the result of others' choices, not yours.

Principle 6: Step away from mutual dependency. You must let go of your dependence on your business and sever your company's reliance on you.

Principle 7: Your Transition Roadmap is indispensable. It charts the route to your destination, motivates you and your successor and adapts to changing circumstances

Six Questions To Guide You On The Journey To Your Next Adventure

In Section II we will dive into the six points on your Transition Compass that steer you in the direction you want to go. We present these points as six questions, a group we call The Big 6™: *Why, What, Who, When, How,* and *How Much.* We will show you how to use these points at the beginning of and throughout your journey.

If you do not have all the answers to these six questions at this point in your journey, that's okay. You will know the answers to some, but may be unsure of answers to others. As you create your Transition Roadmap and share your vision, it is entirely possible that your answers to The Big 6 will change or become clear.

In Section II you will learn to:

- Identify the motives or objectives that will guide you through tough decisions and motivate you to complete your journey.

- Determine exactly what you will (and possibly will not) transfer to successors.

- Choose a successor while keeping in mind fairness for those involved.

- Use your departure date as a tool to protect yourself, your successor and your company.

- Explore how much you need in order to live and to finance your Next Adventure, and how much your business can afford to pay you for your ownership and remain successful.

- Evaluate multiple transfer options.

Now that you understand the rules of the road, it's time to embark on your journey!

CHAPTER ELEVEN

START WITH THE RIGHT QUESTIONS

Before you start some work, always ask yourself three questions: Why am I doing it, What the results might be and Will I be successful. Only when you think deeply and find satisfactory answers to these questions, go ahead.

Chanakya, Ancient Indian teacher and political advisor

As soon as most owners begin to think about business succession, they jump immediately to questions about business value (*How Much*) and transaction strategies (*How*). They have far more questions than answers as they wonder:

1. *How Much...*

   • *How Much* is my business worth?

   • Does its value need to increase to support my Next Adventure? If so, how am I going to do that?

   • *How Much* will I get from the sale once everything is settled and paid?

2. *How...*

   • *How* will the transaction work?

   • Will the transaction be structured as a sale, a gift or some combination of the two?

   • *How* will I minimize taxes on the proceeds?

Most entrepreneurs are independent problem solvers and self-sufficient. That's likely how you live and how you run your business. It's natural to be interested in—even focused on—your return on a lifetime of work, and it's very tempting to immediately formulate tactics designed to answer the compelling questions of *How Much* and *How*, but please be patient!

We agree that *How Much* and *How* are important questions, but we find owners who dive into them first usually become hopelessly tangled in a web of endless options. When they become completely overwhelmed, owners procrastinate or—unable to see a way through the web—get stuck and give up altogether.

A participant in one of our recent workshops provides a great example of the questions of *How Much* and *How* immobilizing both owners and successors.

During the casual coffee and pastry time that preceded one of our presentations, a young man took us aside. "I'm not sure what to expect today," he started, "but I hope you talk about how to restart conversations about transfers, not just how to start them." This was an unusual request, so we asked a few questions. We learned he had worked in his father's manufacturing business for the past 10 years. He told us that at least two years earlier he and his father had talked about his father's transition out of the business and the son's transition into ownership.

When we asked why he wanted to know how to restart a conversation he was already having, he laughed and said, "We haven't gotten near the topic in two years! Once we started talking about how we might structure the transaction, how much he'd get, how much he might give me, how we would create fairness for my sister, and how we would tackle taxes and financing the deal, it got so complicated that we just stopped talking. That's why I'm here today: I want to know how to restart this conversation!"

These aren't the only owners and successors stuck in the web of *How Much* and *How*. Those are two complex questions that can and do stop many transition conversations when owners tackle them before asking four other just-as-important questions.

The Big 6

It can be overwhelming to figure out how to transfer your business in a way that:

- Fulfills both your emotional and material needs.
- Honors the relationships that are important to you.
- Positions your successor to be as (or more) successful as you were.

• Positions your company to be as (or more) successful under new ownership as it was under yours.

• Launches you into your Next Adventure.

Overwhelming? Yes. Impossible? Definitely not. When we work with owners to craft transitions that achieve these objectives, we ask them to consider, *in order*, six critical questions—a group we call The Big 6.

The first four questions are:

1. *Why?*

2. *What?*

3. *Who?*

4. *When?*

The last two questions are:

5. *How Much?*

6. *How?*

Answers to the first four questions (*Why, What, Who, When*) make finding the answers to *How Much* and *How* far less likely to leave you caught in a web like the web that our seminar participant and his father had lived in for the past two years. Believe it or not, once you explore the first four questions in order, *How Much* and *How* fall right into place.

The Measure Of A Successful Business Transfer

The measure of success in transferring a business is not whether you get *everything* you want. The goal is to get *what you need* as well as *what's most important to you*. The genius of The Big 6 is that by working through them in order, you:

• Maximize your chances of achieving great outcomes for you, your family, your successor and your business.

• Begin to see how answers to some questions affect and can conflict with answers to others.

• Discover what you know, don't know or are unsure about.

• Appreciate how each of The Big 6 questions has both emotional and logistical components.

No owner has a clear picture of where they are going before they start their journey. They may have a preliminary list of Deal Breakers (objectives that they will not compromise), but the direction of a journey eventually becomes clear and that clarity comes from wrestling with The Big 6.

If the first questions you ask when thinking about your business transfer are *How Much* and *How*:

- You will likely get caught in a web of confusion. Without an understanding of *Why* you are undertaking the transfer of your business, it is impossible to assess all the possible ways you can accomplish it.

- Without a foundation on which to base your decisions, you are likely to make choices in reaction to new information rather than as a result of your plan.

If you begin thinking about your business transfer by asking The Big 6 questions in the order we recommend:

- With your *Why, What, Who* and *When* as your foundation, you will more easily identify which *How Much* and *How* options are best for you.

- You will narrow your number of options and then consider each one in the context of the objectives that are most important to you.

POINT OF INTEREST

Take a moment to write the story of your ideal transfer as if you've finished the journey. For example, you might begin with "Here's the story of my amazing business transition. Here's how we all ended up happy, fulfilled, engaged and financially healthy. And we did it all while keeping our relationships intact and business thriving."

Include in your story your feelings, your vision of how The Big 6 questions played out and as many details as possible. Have some fun with this Point of Interest, and don't allow whatever you believe won't work or can't happen to get in your way of your dream. Go for it!

My Ideal Transition Story:

CHAPTER TWELVE

THE BIG 6™: THE POINTS ON YOUR TRANSITION COMPASS™

Directions are instructions given to explain how.
Direction is a vision offered to explain why.

Simon Sinek, Best-selling author

To maximize the chances that you will join that elite group of 100 percenters, who have successfully reached their Next Adventures, please don't begin—as so many owners do—by trying to answer the questions of *How Much* you will be paid and *How* you will transfer your equity. These two questions bog down most owners—those that aren't stopped dead in their tracks.

Full disclosure: Even if you tackle other questions first (*Why, What, Who* and *When*), you will likely encounter speed bumps along your journey, but as you'll see, we will give you the tools necessary to travel safely over those bumps and make the choices you must in order to create your own Transition Roadmap.

The Big 6 In Order

1. *Why.* Your *Why* consists of the forces that drive you—your most important objectives—that will guide you through tough decisions and motivate you to complete your journey.

2. *What.* The *What* is the content of the transfer. Are you selling the whole company or a part of it? Are you selling intellectual property, real estate, infrastructure and/ or other assets?

3. ***Who.*** The *Who* is your successor. Will you transfer your business to a family member, partner, key employee or third-party outsider? Do you have a successor in mind, or do you need to find one?

4. ***When.*** The *When* is your timeline. Do you want to leave your role as owner immediately, next year, in five years? How much runway do you have to prepare for this transition?

5. ***How Much.*** The *How Much* is about the return on your investment and financing your Next Adventure. Do you know how much money you need to live and finance your Next Adventure? How much can the business afford to pay you for your ownership and remain successful?

6. ***How.*** The *How* is the logistics of the transfer. Will you gift or sell your ownership? Will you walk away after a one-time liquidity event or receive payment over a period of time? Will it be an asset or equity transfer? How will the transition and transaction be structured?

Question 1: *Why*

The *first* question you will ask as you begin your business transition journey is *Why*. Your *Why* is the collection of objectives that motivate you to do the work necessary to create a business transition that is a success for everyone involved.

Have you thought about *Why* you want to transfer your business? Your reasons will include those that motivate you to leave your business as well as those that attract you to your Next Adventure. For example, is there a new business or long-delayed passion that you are ready to pursue? Are you tired of being responsible for the welfare of all of your employees and their families? Do you want to leave with enough time to really get to know your grandchildren? Is it your spouse's turn to pursue their dream?

Your reasons for planning to transfer your business will likely include benefits to you, your company, family members, business partners, employees and others who are important to you.

Among the objectives that make up your *Why* will be a few Deal Breakers, those objectives that you will not sacrifice. In Chapter Fourteen, we describe the tool you need to list, prioritize and articulate the reasons you want to transition into your Next Adventure.

Of course, others will have *Whys* too. Your successor will have reasons for wanting to assume ownership of your company. Your spouse will have objectives they want your departure from ownership to achieve, as will your successor's spouse and perhaps some of your employees. Of course, you will not be able to meet everyone's objectives. You want to honor your most important relationships, however, as you move through this journey you will eventually uncover and take the *Whys* of those people into consideration.

Question 2: *What*

Once you've explored and documented your reasons for making a transition, we suggest that you move on to the question of *What*.

- *What* do you have to sell (e.g., processes, materials, inventory, clients, intellectual property, real estate, goodwill)?
- *What* do you want to sell?
- *What* do you want to keep (e.g., trademarks, patents, specific product lines, buildings)?

Thinking of your business as a set of components helps you see exactly what you have available to sell or transfer and may open a new set of options. For example, you could choose to sell or transfer a particular component at one point in your transition journey and another component later in your journey. Once you see *What* you have to transfer, you may decide to transfer different parts of your business to different people.

Question 3: *Who*

The third of The Big 6 questions is a close cousin to Principle 1: Put relationships first.

- *Who* will be your successor: a family member, employee or outside third party?
- Can you treat everyone involved fairly?
- *Who* are the stakeholders who will be affected by the transfer?
- *Who* has to buy in to your transition in order for you to maintain your important relationships?

When choosing one successor over another, owners justifiably worry how their choice will affect their relationships.

Question 4: *When*

- *When* do you think you will be ready to begin your journey to your Next Adventure?

- *When* will you transfer to your successor the numerous responsibilities that prepare them to assume ownership and leadership?

  ~ Will your successor be prepared to take over when you are ready to leave?

- After a lifetime of building and running this business, *When* will you be able to emotionally let go of your role as owner?

- *When* will you transfer each responsibility and portions of equity?

- Do external causes affect your choice of *When*?

- *When* will your employees, clients and all stakeholders be ready to support your successor?

- *When* will you prepare yourself for your Next Adventure?

- If you are transferring your business to successors of different ages or from different branches of the family, *When* (and in what stages) will each receive ownership?

Time can be your best friend, because the more of it you have, the more options you give yourself. The more options you have, the more deliberately you can make decisions, and the more precisely you can craft your results.

The last two questions: *How Much* and *How*

As we discussed earlier, the final two important transition questions you should ask are *How Much* and *How*.

The good news is that the information you gathered during your search for answers to the first four questions will make answering *How Much* and *How* far easier than had you started with them. It will be far easier because the foundation you begin to build by answering the first four keeps you out of the sticky web of confusion. Despite that, the *How Much* and *How* questions can be intimidating.

How Much?

- *How Much* wealth do you want or need to support your Next Adventure?

- *How Much* of your financial security depends on the proceeds you'll take from the transaction, or do you already have enough other assets in place?

- *How Much* is your business worth?

- Do you need to increase the value of your business before you transfer it? If so, by *How Much*?

When you leave your business, you want the financial independence to fund your current and future living expenses, and, ideally, to give you the ability to live the life you envision (your Next Adventure). Unless your financial plan includes a projection of the assets and income necessary to support your Next Adventure, how do you know you will have enough?

How?

- *How* will you transfer equity?

- *How* will the transfer of equity be structured?

  ~ Sale, gift or partial gift?

- *How* will you minimize taxes to lighten the burden on your company and successor while maximizing your return?

- *How* do tax- and estate-related issues affect the timing of a successful transfer of equity?

Answering the question of *How* requires input from a team of tax, legal and financial planning professionals because the method you use to transfer equity has a huge financial impact on you and your successor. There are pros and cons related to every tax, legal and financial planning decision, and your pros and cons are not the same as your successor's. Due to the complexity and financial impact of these decisions and the number of people involved, attempting to answer the *How* question before you've answered the first five is a recipe for inertia. That inertia will cause you to continue on as you always have: moving forward in your straight line until an external force moves you off that line.

The Big 6 And Your Transition Compass

We know that answering The Big 6 can seem overwhelming, so we've created The Transition Compass™, a tool to help you organize your thoughts as you consider each of these important questions. As you can see on the Transition Compass template (Figure 12.1) each of The Big 6 questions is followed by categories to consider or questions to answer. For example, after *Why*, you'll see how you would list objectives and note which objectives are Deal Breakers. (It is important to identify which of your

Figure 12.1

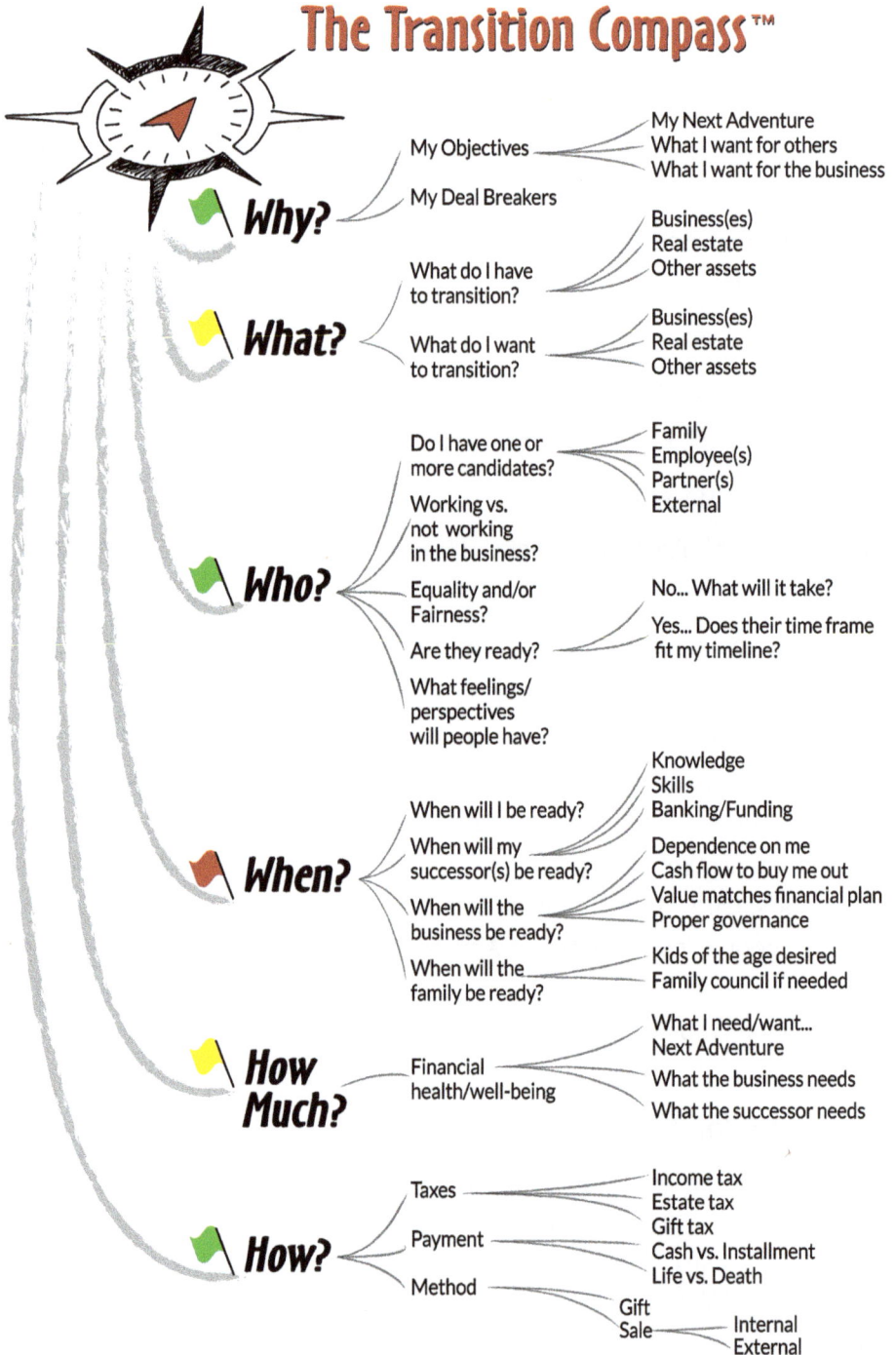

The Transition Compass™

- **Why?**
  - My Objectives
    - My Next Adventure
    - What I want for others
    - What I want for the business
  - My Deal Breakers

- **What?**
  - What do I have to transition?
    - Business(es)
    - Real estate
    - Other assets
  - What do I want to transition?
    - Business(es)
    - Real estate
    - Other assets

- **Who?**
  - Do I have one or more candidates?
    - Family
    - Employee(s)
    - Partner(s)
    - External
  - Working vs. not working in the business?
  - Equality and/or Fairness?
    - No... What will it take?
    - Yes... Does their time frame fit my timeline?
  - Are they ready?
  - What feelings/ perspectives will people have?

- **When?**
  - When will I be ready?
    - Knowledge
    - Skills
    - Banking/Funding
  - When will my successor(s) be ready?
    - Dependence on me
    - Cash flow to buy me out
    - Value matches financial plan
    - Proper governance
  - When will the business be ready?
  - When will the family be ready?
    - Kids of the age desired
    - Family council if needed

- **How Much?**
  - Financial health/well-being
    - What I need/want... Next Adventure
    - What the business needs
    - What the successor needs

- **How?**
  - Taxes
    - Income tax
    - Estate tax
    - Gift tax
  - Payment
    - Cash vs. Installment
    - Life vs. Death
  - Method
    - Gift
    - Sale
      - Internal
      - External

objectives are Deal Breakers because you will return to them again and again as you craft your Transition Roadmap.) Your remaining objectives are divided into those you want to achieve for yourself, those you want for others and those you want for your business.

As we work with owners to create their Transition Compasses, we supplement each of The Big 6 questions with issues and questions that are unique to an owner's situation. For example, after the question "*What* do I have to transition?" this owner includes "real estate" because they own the property on which the company operates. There may be other types of assets you do or do not wish to sell. The Transition Compass is a great template to use to spur your thinking and organize your thoughts.

You will note that next to each of The Big 6 questions is a red, yellow or green flag. The color of each flag on your Compass indicates a level of certainty. A green flag means one already knows the answer or is as confident as one can be at this point. A yellow flag indicates that one is fairly certain about the answer. A red flag indicates not yet knowing the answer.

We will examine each of The Big 6 questions in detail in the next several chapters and look at a fictional owner's completed Transition Compass in Chapter Twenty-Two.

If you fail to organize all of the questions you have about your business transfer:

- You may jump from question to question and make one-off decisions that initially make sense only to find later they have unanticipated negative effects that don't optimize your opportunities or outcomes.

- You wander into uncharted territory, take the wrong roads and encounter more detours than necessary.

- Your successor and others involved end up confused and reluctant (or even unwilling) to join you on the journey you envision.

If you organize all your questions into The Big 6 format:

- You will have a framework that points you in the direction you want to go.

- Your confidence and clarity will increase as you address and answer each question.

At this moment, how would you answer The Big 6 questions? If you are like most owners, you know answers to some, have thoughts about a few and don't yet have answers to several. That's normal. Transitioning out of your business is an iterative process, one in which new and additional information usually prompts course adjustments.

Use the following Transition Compass to indicate your thinking about your answers to The Big 6 questions. (This form is available at *www. TheSuccessionPlanningBook.com/Tools.*) Circle the flag that best indicates your current thinking.

- A green flag means you already know the answer or are as confident as you can be at this point.

- A yellow flag indicates you are fairly certain about your answer.

- A red flag indicates you don't yet know the answer.

CHAPTER THIRTEEN

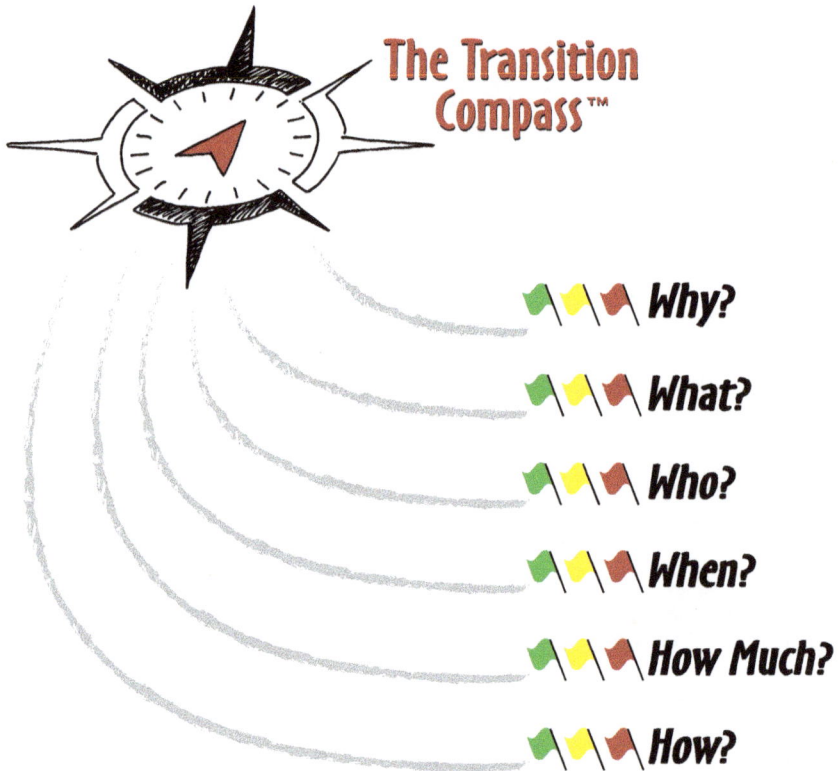

THE *WHY*: THE FIRST OF THE BIG 6 QUESTIONS AND YOUR TRUE NORTH

If a man knows not to which port he sails, no wind is favorable.

Seneca the Younger, Roman philosopher

As a business owner you have dedicated years, even decades, to your business. In return, it has supported you and your family, your employees and their families, and, by extension, your customers and community. With so much history and responsibility, it can be difficult for some owners to imagine the future of their businesses without them, and their own futures without their businesses.

All of the owners we work with share the common goal of leaving ownership and beginning their Next Adventures in a way that is not only personally satisfying, but also leaves their companies and important relationships healthy. When we first tell owners that we've developed a process to transfer ownership in a way that can meet their criteria, the typical response is "That sounds too good to be true." Well, it's not, as Tom Kirk, one of our 100 percenters, explains:

> I reached out to Elizabeth for some help regarding my transition out of my business several years after we had worked together on projects related to growing my business. When I called her, I'd already done my homework on succession planning. I'd read about the pros and cons of multiple ownership transfer strategies, but I was always left wondering how I could make a particular method of transfer fit my business. The Transition Roadmap Developer Process took a radically different approach. It started with me rather than my business. Elizabeth first asked why I wanted to leave and what I wanted the transfer to accomplish for me, my family, my successor and my company—and then she fit a method of transfer to me.

We suggest you begin at the same point Tom did: establishing your True North, or your *Why*. As we define it, an owner's *Why*:

- Informs every decision they will make.

- Motivates them to focus on and move toward the exciting Next Adventures they anticipate rather than solely on what they are leaving.

- Answers these questions: What will make them happy and matters most in their lives? What will their *ikigai* (reason for being) be? What will motivate them to spring out of bed, ready to face each day?

Why: The Foundation For A Successful Business Transfer

Your *Why* is the very backbone of your transition strategy. Once you define your *Why*, you will make decisions that align with this focus. When a conflict or dilemma arises—and we promise you it will—you return to your *Why*. Does the solution to the conflict or dilemma move you closer to or further from your *Why*? If a particular option does not serve your *Why*, you can in good conscience kick it to the curb!

Let's imagine that one element of your *Why* is you want your company to continue to protect and support your employees because you care about them and their families. One day a large national chain makes an offer to acquire your company. The timing is good because it meets your objective of getting out of the business immediately. The offer matches the proceeds you need from the sale to support your Next Adventure. You learn, however, that this buyer plans to provide shared services from one centralized location in another state. Logically, you suspect the buyer will replace your management team, and most of your employees will lose their jobs. You look to your *Why*, which includes protecting your employees and community, and decide this buyer is not one you will consider.

This very simple example illustrates that had you not done the work to define your *Why*, you might have traveled a road and spent time and money on a successor choice that ultimately would have violated one of your key objectives.

You would also look to your *Why* if an employee, partner or one of your children wanted ownership but could not pay you the amount you want for your company. In this case, you don't change your *Why*, but you might change your *How* and possibly your *What, Who, When* or *How Much*.

Using Your *Why* For Yourself And Those You Care About

The process of listing objectives is an intensely personal exercise in which owners set objectives for themselves first. We recommend they begin by listing the good things they wish to continue (such as remaining in good health and spending time in a second home), before listing the goals they wish to achieve (such as starting a charitable foundation or achieving financial independence). We also remind owners to consider objectives they may have for themselves that involve sharing time, experiences or activities with the people who are important to them. For example, you may want to go on the expedition to Mount Kilimanjaro you and a friend have talked about for years. You may want to pay for your grandchildren's education, teach your spouse to fly an airplane, spend more time with your children and grandchildren, or sail with old college friends through the Caribbean. The driving question we ask each owner is "What matters most to *you?*"

We request that owners document *all* of their objectives, no matter how far-fetched they may seem. Proceeding as if all things were possible is the best way to start your journey. Let's focus the types of personal objectives owners set for themselves alone and then those that involve others.

Some Thoughts As You Begin To List Your Objectives

- Include any objectives you may have already attained but are not willing to give up.

- If you have already planned activities to enjoy later in life with your spouse, family or friends, include them on your list.

- Write your objectives in the present tense. Doing so helps you think about these life goals as if you are living them and paints a brilliant picture in your mind of your desired life. For example, "I visit my grandchildren in Europe three times each year."

- Be as specific as possible. In the example above, the owner included the location of the grandchildren and the number of visits per year.

- For now, do NOT think about how you will achieve an objective. That is a completely different exercise. The goal at this point is simply to draw a detailed word picture of your Next Adventure.

- Take as much time as you need to imagine your ideal outcomes and your ideal activities.

- Think about what you do want, not what you don't want. When objectives are clear and fulfilling, you can emotionally connect to them. Positive emotions increase the odds that you'll achieve your objectives!

THE PERSONAL DIMENSIONS OF EVERY OWNER

Every person is a composite of multiple dimensions. Of course, we don't divide our lives or pursuits into separate silos, but categorizing objectives by dimension makes it far easier to draw a complete picture of a Next Adventure.

When we work with owners, we ask them to think about 10 dimensions:

1. Spiritual

2. Life Purpose/Direction

3. Professional/Intellectual

4. Financial

5. Time Freedom

6. Peace/Groundedness

7. Relationships/Love/Connectedness

8. Play/Fun

9. Physical Mobility/Health

10. Environment

How you categorize your objectives is up to you. You might put "Live in Spain for 12 months" in the Environment category, while someone else might put it in the Play/Fun or Time Freedom category. Where you put your descriptions is not critical. Describing your life during your Next Adventure as completely as possible is.

We give owners a tool we call The Objectives Matrix™ to help them organize all of their objectives. (See Figure 13.2.) In this chapter we provide sample objectives for each of the 10 dimensions. In the next chapter, we'll show you how many of the objectives appear on an Objectives Matrix.

1. Spiritual

Most people are spiritual beings in one way or another, whether we believe in a higher power, world energy or God. Think about the role spirituality plays in your life. Consider whether you are happy with that role and want it to continue as is, or if you'd like to grow spiritually or do something you have never had the time to do. For example:

- I am active in my church and give $10,000 annually.

- No matter where I am, I pray every day and am connected to "my higher being."

- Each year I study one religion to better understand the world and its people.

- We enjoy and are active in a couples' Bible study group that meets once each week.

- We continue to build and support orphanages in Kenya during mission trips.

Figure 13.1 illustrates how this fictional owner's spiritual objectives would appear on an Objectives Matrix.

Figure 13.1

The Objectives Matrix ™

Owner/ Entity	Objectives	Time Frame			Deal Breaker
		Continue	Short-Term	Long-Term	
Me	I am active in my church and give $10,000 annually.	X			
	No matter where I am, I pray every day and am connected to "my higher being."	X			
	Each year I study one religion to better understand the world and its people.			X	
Us	We enjoy and are active in a couples' Bible study group that meets once each week.		X		
	We continue to build and support orphanages in Kenya during mission trips.			X	

NOTE: You would address each of the 10 dimensions as you complete your Objectives Matrix. In the following chapter, (Figure 14.3), you'll see a sample Objectives Matrix that includes many types of objectives.

2. Life Purpose/Direction

If you have worked in your business for many years, your company may have been your life's focus—at least up until now. Perhaps you have not had time to do or explore other activities that interest you. For example, you may love to golf and want to play more often but as owners often tell us, "I can only play X days per week!"

What do you envision your life will be like without the responsibilities of your business and with plenty of time to do what you want to do? Owners whose businesses have dictated how they use their time can find this question very difficult to answer. Ask yourself what will satisfy your need for fulfillment. The Japanese term for one's reason for being or for having a direction is *ikigai*. What is your reason for getting out of bed in the morning? That's your *ikigai*. Some objectives in this category might include:

- I serve on two nonprofit boards for organizations that make a difference by motivating students to finish high school and get a positive start in life.

- My wife and I enjoy spending time together checking off items on our bucket list: a two-week raft trip through the Grand Canyon, a summer living in Italy's wine country, heli-skiing in Peru, and traveling the United States for a year in a motor home.

- With my help, my grandchildren are learning to play golf. They enjoy spending time with me on the course. I feel good that I am teaching them to play a sport they can enjoy for the rest of their lives.

3. Professional/Intellectual

Owner/entrepreneurs are typically constant learners, problem solvers and leaders. Once you embark on your Next Adventure, consider what you want to learn, what problems you will solve, and whether you will continue to exercise your leadership skills. Here are some sample professional/intellectual objectives:

- I go into the office only to see/support my kids, develop business and take clients to lunch. I am free from day-to-day responsibilities and the corner office. Instead, I am happy splitting my "work time" between my home office and the space I use in the company's conference room.

- I am still active, engaged and paid well for my contribution to the company. I am valued both monetarily and personally for my thoughtful and experience-based input.

- I serve on a political committee to support the presidential candidate of my choice.

- My son and my CFO are partners and run the business with my guidance.

- My employees are able to support themselves and their families, and the culture makes the business a great place to work and earn money.

- The business thrives without me, and the business relationships that I have valued over the years are well cared for.

4. Financial

The unpredictability of legislation and economic ebbs and flows make thinking about your financial future "interesting." In this dimension think about how much money you may need to fully retire and live the life your objectives describe. We will focus on the importance of developing a financial plan to support these objectives later (in the *How Much* question). For now, simply list your financial objectives. Are any of the following objectives on your list?

- I sleep well at night knowing we are financially set for the life we enjoy both today and in the future.

- We have paid for our childrens' college education, so they are debt free at graduation.

- We have a net worth of $10 million, so we live well until we are 100 years old.

- We are debt free. Our two homes and all loans are paid off.

- Every other year we enjoy a family trip overseas with our children and their families.

5. Time Freedom

Time freedom (or choice of time) is having the time to do remarkable and meaningful things you enjoy. Imagine being able to live a life that has many fewer "should dos" than "want to dos." Here are some sample objectives:

- I surf when the surf is up! If the tide is right, no matter the day or time, I have the flexibility to take full advantage of it.

- I have the time to learn a second language or take classes necessary to become an artist and pilot.

- I enjoy seeing the grandchildren every quarter and staying for as long as my children will let me spoil their children.

6. Peace/Groundedness

For most of us, reducing anxiety and stress is a goal. What will it take to live in peaceful abundance and wake up each day grateful and ready to engage the world? Some owners might identify the following objectives:

- As part of my morning routine, I reenergize through my yoga practice in my beautiful home studio.

- During spring, summer and fall, I enjoy walks and hikes at least weekly. Weather permitting, my spouse and I walk the golf course to watch the sun set. During the winter, we ski.

- At the end of each day, I easily find at least three things to record in my gratefulness journal.

7. Relationships/Love/Connectedness

Throughout your life and career, you have served so many people that you likely have numerous objectives related to the relationships that have been the foundation of your life. You want to continue to create opportunities for others to do well during your Next Adventure. You may decide you want to honor some of those who have supported you in the past in a particular way. Objectives of this kind might include:

- My spouse finds fulfillment through art and volunteer activities.

- My spouse and I have a great relationship: I am me, you are you, and we are us! We support each other as individuals and in what each of us chooses to do. We have fun doing things that strengthen our relationship.

- Each year I attend at least one activity each grandchild is involved in, because it's important to me they know I care enough to show up.

- I am engaged in the lives of my brother, nieces and nephews. I connect with them—in person—at least every month.

- My former partner and I are untangling our ownership relationship so well that we are still friends.

- Employees are happy and confident about the future of the business and the continuation of the culture we worked so hard to create.

- The business remains a source of connection for members of my family, rather than an anchor that weighs us down. I have great relationships with my children (those in and out of the business). We have wonderful Christmases together!

- Customers continue to rely on my company's ability to deliver outstanding services. We have great vendor/supplier/manufacturer contracts, and we maintain and strengthen our historical competitive advantages.

8. Play/Fun

Play and fun definitely deserve their own dimension. As you identify your objectives related to the previous dimensions, you may list activities that are fun for you. In this dimension take a deeper dive to uncover activities that simply bring you joy. Has it been a long time since you let loose? How did you let loose in the past? What do you want to do to bring yourself joy during your Next Adventure? Here are some sample play/fun objectives:

- So that I can sail my boat from New York through the Great Lakes, I study to become a captain and I buy a boat. This is an adventure I have always dreamed of.

- I enjoy flying my stunt plane. Over time, I become skilled enough to place well in aerobatic competition events.

- I ski 30 days each winter and enjoy time with friends at our mountain home.

- We go to a concert in Las Vegas each fall just for fun.

- Every October or November we spend a week in New York City to see a Broadway show, enjoy great food and wine, and do a little Christmas shopping. This trip is a new tradition for us.

9. Physical Mobility/Health

Whether you wish to take hour-long daily walks during your Next Adventure, or your goal is to run six marathons each year, you will require the physical mobility to engage in the activities you choose. Focusing on good health and mobility frees you to live the life you want to live. Here are sample objectives that address some aspects of good physical mobility and health:

- I am active, strong, flexible, pain free and able to participate in the activities I choose.

- Each day I enjoy at least 30 minutes outdoors either working in the yard, skiing, golfing, bike riding, or taking walks or short runs.

- I work with a personal trainer twice each week and have a massage every other week.

- I sleep well for at least eight hours each night and have a bedtime routine that supports rejuvenating rest.

- We fuel our bodies with great nutritious foods, and we feel great.

10. Environment

Your environment includes many aspects of your physical home: its type (single family, apartment, condominium, etc.), location (an adult community, close enough to your children that your grandchildren can ride their bikes to visit, warm in the winter, etc.), and amenities (an office, studio, etc.). Imagine an environment in which you are happy and healthy and you enjoy the people and activities that are important to you. Here are some examples:

- I live in Colorado, one hour from my favorite ski area.

- I have a "cave" where I do what I want (read, keep my train collection). I don't have to keep it clean or picked up for anyone but me.

- My spouse and I enjoy being in Florida to be close to the grandchildren.

- We have a small lock-and-leave condo in Florida, where we live during spring and fall. We come and go as we please.

- Our home is large enough (three bedrooms) for our children and grandchildren to visit and be together for fun holidays and events.

OBJECTIVES FOR OTHERS

Owners usually set objectives involving more than just themselves and their immediate and extended family members. Specifically, they often create objectives that focus on their companies, business partners, employees who helped them get where they are, successors and/or philanthropic causes they desire to support. For example, some owners wish to help their successors create wealth or want to help a partner achieve his or her objectives.

Our purpose in raising the issue of objectives for others is that the broader an owner's vision is, the more emotionally engaged they are with their Next Adventures.

Better a diamond with a flaw than a pebble without.

Confucius, Chinese philosopher

No Perfect Objectives List

Has any owner ever achieved every transition objective without making a single trade-off? We're confident the answer is no. None of us completely controls our environment, the actions of others or even our own health. Owners can, however, commit to using their objectives to make the best possible decisions on their business transition journeys.

If you fail to create your foundational *Why* for the transfer of your business:

- You can easily lose your way when dilemmas or conflicting wants, wishes and needs muddle your thinking and impair your ability to make sound decisions.

- You are likely to become stuck thinking about *How* or end up in a Next Adventure that does not give you a sense of purpose or make you happy.

If you begin your journey by first establishing *Why* you want to transfer ownership of your business:

- The picture of what you are moving toward (your Next Adventure) becomes nearly as clear as what you are moving away from (your Current Adventure).

- Your path flows forward, and your *Why* grounds, drives and guides you through the difficult choices you will make.

POINT OF INTEREST

The fun really begins when you begin to complete your own Objectives Matrix! See Figure 13.2 or download a Matrix at *www.TheSuccessionPlanningBook.com/Tools*.

As you list your objectives, be creative, bold and imaginative. Write in the present tense, as though each objective is real and you are living it now. This should be a very enjoyable exercise as you create the story of your perfect Next Adventure: doing what you love, enjoying and spending time with others, making a difference in the world, and being healthy and happy.

Figure 13.2

The Objectives Matrix™

Owner/ Entity	Objectives	Time Frame			Deal Breaker
		Continue	Short-Term	Long-Term	
Me					
My Spouse/ Significant Other					
Us					
Our Family					
Our Extended Family					
My Partners					
Employees/ Successors					
The Business					

CHAPTER FOURTEEN

USE THE OBJECTIVES MATRIX™ TO GET WHAT YOU WANT

The most important thing to do in solving a problem is to begin.

Frank Tyger, American cartoonist and columnist

In the prior chapter we addressed what objectives are, whom owners consider when writing them, and 10 dimensions objectives can address. The purpose of identifying and organizing your objectives is to paint as vivid a picture as possible of your Next Adventure. The ability to see your Next Adventure is critical because it is the touchstone you will refer to when you have to make tough choices, and it is the fuel that propels you toward a meaningful and exciting future. The tool we use to paint that picture is The Objectives Matrix.

THE OBJECTIVES MATRIX

The Big Picture

It is helpful to approach your Objectives Matrix with an attitude of gratitude and abundance. It is your hard work that has given you the opportunity to walk the road to the transition of your successful business. It is an extraordinary gift to lead a transition process that affects the rest of your life and all of the people you care about.

The Objectives Matrix helps you organize your objectives according to whom the objectives apply. The Matrix also provides space to identify which objectives are Deal Breakers and to assign a time frame to each objective.

Deal Breakers: Your Lines In The Sand

A Deal Breaker is an objective that is so important to you that if a particular transition scenario will not achieve it, you will abandon that path and switch to a new one. As we start to use The Objectives Matrix to help owners develop and evaluate possible pathways or options, we recommend they be as careful and complete as possible when identifying the objectives that are Deal Breakers for them. Establishing Deal Breakers:

1. Is freeing and brings clarity to their *Why*.

2. Makes it easier to say no to people and strategies that violate the Deal Breakers.

3. Creates a clearer picture of:

   - *Who* will be a successor.

   - *When* owners will begin and end their journey to their Next Adventures.

   - *What* they will transfer and *What* (if anything) they will keep.

   - *How Much* cash and/or income they want to realize from the transaction.

   - *How* the transaction will be designed.

Setting A Time Frame For Each Objective

The Objectives Matrix asks you to assign a time frame to each objective by noting whether it is long-term, short-term or an objective you have already achieved and want to continue into the future. A long-term goal is one that will take a year or more to achieve, and a short-term goal can be achieved in less than a year. Figure 14.1 shows examples of objectives in each of these categories. It isn't necessary to pick a time frame right away, but assigning one to each objective eventually is important. As you begin to communicate with others and build your timelines, a general scope of time frame helps you and others understand which goals you plan to accomplish within months and which are further down the road.

Figure 14.1

Objectives	Expected Time Frame
Transition the business to my daughter.	Long-term—ownership transfer over 3 years
Have $10M personally invested.	Long-term—2 years
Transfer business equity, keep real estate.	Long-term—3 years
Create a charitable foundation.	Short-term—8 months
Maintain health and be active.	Continue
Live in Barbados three months annually.	Long-term—3 years

Let's return to our fictional owner's spiritual objectives from Chapter Thirteen, shown again in Figure 14.2. This owner has already met (and will continue to meet) two objectives. The owner's remaining objectives are designated short- or long-term. This owner has not designated any spiritual objective as a Deal Breaker. Had they done so, and the transition could not deliver that objective, the owner would adjust course and travel another path to their Next Adventure.

Figure 14.2

The Objectives Matrix™

Owner/ Entity	Objectives	Time Frame			Deal Breaker
		Continue	Short-Term	Long-Term	
Me	I am active in my church and give $10,000 annually.	X			
	No matter where I am, I pray every day and am connected to "my higher being."	X			
	Each year I study one religion to better understand the world and its people.			X	
Us	We enjoy and are active in a couples' Bible study group that meets once each week.		X		
	We continue to build and support orphanages in Kenya during mission trips.			X	

One Owner's Objectives Matrix

Figure 14.3 shows a sample of a completed Objectives Matrix and provides you with helpful examples of the various types of objectives. The objectives shown are representative of the many objectives our owners have created.

Note that this fictional owner set achieving a net worth of $10 million as a long-term goal. At this early stage in the process, we encourage owners to make their best guesses related to time frames. Best guesses give owners a starting data point and indicate the direction in which they want to move.

Notice also this owner only had eight Deal Breakers. As he thought about which objectives were Deal Breakers, he began to appreciate that not all of them were. You too will see that not all of your objectives are Deal Breakers.

No Transition Is Perfect

Establishing Deal Breakers and setting realistic time frames often shines a spotlight on objectives that compete and cannot be accomplished simultaneously. Competing objectives have the power to confound so completely that owners become stuck and risk becoming passive participants in, rather than leaders of, the inevitable transition out of their businesses.

When owners run into competing objectives, we remind them that it is often not possible to accomplish all of one's Deal Breakers exactly as originally envisioned. If giving up a Deal Breaker is *the best or only way forward*, we help owners to reschedule, reprioritize or redefine the Deal Breaker. "Greg" and "Lisa," a father-daughter team in a family business, provide a great yet simple example.

Greg decided he wanted to leave his business completely within 18 months. Lisa, his daughter, was committed to her father's plan, but after some reflection, felt she was not ready to become CEO. She believed that an MBA would better position her to take on that role. The problem was timing: The degree program that she preferred required a two-year commitment.

Lisa proposed to Greg that after completing her degree she would return to the business, and work with him for a year before he left the company. Greg agreed. He changed his timeline so Lisa could get the degree from the school she desired.

Once Lisa returned to work, she and Greg had one of the best years of their lives. Lisa reinvigorated Greg with new ideas for the company, and he felt great knowing that his company was in the hands of someone well prepared to take the business to the next level.

Figure 14.3

The Objectives Matrix™

Owner/ Entity	Objectives	Time Frame			Deal Breaker
		Continue	Short-Term	Long-Term	
Me	I am free from day-to-day responsibilities and the corner office.		X		
	I am paid well for my contribution to the company. I am valued both monetarily and personally for my thoughtful and experience-based input.	X			X
	I am active in my church and give $10,000 annually.	X			
	Each year I study one religion to better understand the world and its people.			X	
	I serve on two nonprofit boards for organizations that make a difference by motivating students to finish high school and get a positive start in life.			X	
	I sleep well at night knowing we are financially set for the life we enjoy, both today and in the future.			X	
	At the end of each day, I easily find at least three things to record in my gratitude journal.	X			
	I ski 30 days each winter, enjoying time with our friends at our mountain home.		X		
	I am active, strong, flexible, pain free and able to participate in the activities I choose.	X			
My Spouse / Significant Other	My spouse finds fulfillment through art and volunteer activities.	X			
	My spouse enjoys being in Florida to be close to the grandchildren.	X			X
Us	We enjoy and are active in a couples' Bible study group that meets once each week.		X		
	My wife and I enjoy spending time together checking off items on our bucket list: a two-week raft trip through the Grand Canyon, a summer living in Italy's wine country, heli-skiing in Peru, and traveling the United States for a year in a motor home.			X	
	We have a net worth of $10 million and are debt free, so we are able to live our Next Adventure as we envision.			X	X
	My spouse and I have a great relationship. I am me, you are you, and we are us! We support each other as individuals and in what each of us chooses to do. We have fun doing things that strengthen our relationship.	X			X
	We fuel our bodies with great nutritious foods, and we feel great.	X			

continued

The Objectives Matrix™ - *continued from prior page*

Owner/ Entity	Objectives	Time Frame			Deal Breaker
		Continue	Short-Term	Long-Term	
Our Family	With my help, my grandchildren are learning to play golf. They enjoy spending time with me on the course. I am teaching them to play a sport they can enjoy for the rest of their lives.		X		
	Every other year we enjoy a family trip overseas with our children and their families.		X		
	Each year I attend at least one activity each grandchild is involved in, because it's important to me that they know I care enough to show up.		X		
Our Extended Family	I am engaged in the lives of my brother and nieces and nephews. I connect with them—in person—at least every month.		X		
Employees/ Successors	My employees are able to support themselves and their families, and the culture makes the business a great place to work and earn money.	X			X
	My son and CFO are partners and run the business with my guidance.		X		X
The Business	The business thrives without me, and the business relationships that I have valued over the years are well cared for.			X	X
	The business remains a source of connection for members of my family, rather than an anchor that weighs us down. I have great relationships with my children (those in and out of the business). We have wonderful Christmases together!	X			X

When owners give up a Deal Breaker as Greg did, they often realize what they gave up really wasn't a Deal Breaker. We recommend that owners only abandon Deal Breakers intentionally and with good reason.

Few of us have ever undertaken a significant project and achieved every single outcome that we desired. The same is true of the business succession process. All owners adjust or discard at least one Deal Breaker on the road to a successful business transfer, and they add, subtract and/or refine their objectives when unexpected events occur.

There are no perfect transitions, but there are many, many former owners who are living Next Adventures that (in most aspects) they described on their Objective Matrices. There are just as many successors living their dreams of being business owners and just as many companies that are succeeding under new ownership. We know because we've worked with many of them.

If you fail to identify all of your objectives, do not note which are Deal Breakers and omit time frames:

- It is difficult—if not impossible—to appreciate when your objectives are inconsistent or cannot be accomplished simultaneously. Owners who work to achieve inconsistent objectives not only waste time and money, but they also jeopardize their important relationships.

- Other people will not understand which objectives you plan to accomplish immediately and which you have set for the long term.

If you use The Objectives Matrix to establish objectives, assign time frames and identify Deal Breakers:

- You collect and organize many types of objectives into one comprehensive tool.

- You begin to appreciate which objectives are so important to you that you will not move forward unless you can achieve them (Deal Breakers), while you are able to discard or consolidate some objectives as you analyze and revise them.

POINT OF INTEREST

Look at your Objectives Matrix from Chapter Thirteen. (If you didn't complete that Point of Interest, please do so now.) As you review what you've written, add any new objectives you have and, if necessary, refine others. Write an X in the appropriate Time Frame column for each objective. Think about which objectives are Deal Breakers for you, mark them accordingly and ask yourself if you overlooked any.

Specifically, consider whether there are any additional items or situations that would cause you to stop the transition or change course. If so, add those items or situations to your Objectives Matrix and mark them as Deal Breakers.

Download The Objectives Matrix at *www.TheSuccessionPlanningBook.com/Tools*.

As you add detail to your Objectives Matrix, you may wish to have some fun conversations about the future with your spouse or, depending on your situation, with others you would like to include at this time. Talking about the future may remind you of an objective you missed or help others think of objectives they'd like to add for themselves.

This finalized Objectives Matrix is your foundational *Why*!

CHAPTER FIFTEEN

THE *WHAT*: WHAT DO YOU HAVE TO TRANSFER?

I would rather have a mind opened by wonder than one closed by belief.

Gerry Spence, Attorney and writer

Now that you've set your objectives and know your *Why*, the next question to ask is *What*. *What* are you transitioning?

Put simply, your *What* is your business. But is it that simple?

Your business is made up of various segments, such as individual business lines, assets, functions, processes and departments. There isn't just one moving part—there are literally dozens of them that involve products, sales, production, intellectual property, infrastructure and more.

If you think about your business as a compilation of separate units, the *What* question can have many, many answers. There are a multitude of ways to define what you wish to transfer. There is no rule that says you have to treat your business as a singular entity to be transferred intact in a single event.

There are countless ways of defining What *you are transferring.*

Transitioning your business as one entity may be the best solution for you. Or it may not.

Company Assets

Each of your company's assets (real estate, intellectual property or digital assets, territories and lines of business, inventory, A/R, etc.) has value. When you consider each asset separately, you may see your *Who, When, How Much,* and *How* from an entirely new perspective.

If you have multiple businesses that interact with one another, such as one entity leasing assets to another entity that provides services, the level of complication increases but so do the possibilities.

Consider the question of *What* for each entity, and remember you need not transfer all of your assets at one time. You have multiple possibilities.

The Power Of Inclusive Thinking

You're a successful entrepreneur, so it is likely you have solved numerous problems by thinking outside the box or using what is known as inclusive thinking. Inclusive thinking puts disparate elements together, often in unexpected ways. As a simple example, you might have successors purchase segments of your business over a period of time (rather than at once) so they can afford to pay you and take on less debt. That strategy would be worth pursuing *only if* it does not somehow violate one of your Deal Breakers or create undue risk.

When we look at our businesses from only one perspective, it can be difficult to apply inclusive thinking to transferring them in a way that will meet our objectives and maintain our important relationships. "Jerry" and "Julia" are examples of owners who couldn't design a path to the outcome they desired until we helped them see their company in a new way.

If you look at your business from a new perspective, you may see new paths that lead to the outcome you desire.

Thanks to years of hard work, Jerry and Julia had created a successful, family-owned nursery business. As they began to think about transitioning to their Next Adventure, one of their objectives was to keep their business thriving and prosperous.

The couple had two sons, both of whom had expressed interest in taking over the business. Jerry and Julia were extremely concerned that if they chose one son over the other, family relationships would be irreparably damaged. They couldn't see a solution but weren't willing to give up their Next Adventure. That's when we met them.

We quickly learned that although the business functioned as a whole, there were two large greenhouses that produced most of the nursery's plants. When we first suggested that Jerry and Julia separate the greenhouses and gift one to each son, they had several objections and questions, including "If we split the company in two, each company will need its own computer system, bank account and contracts with vendors! Since we've always attributed our administrative overhead to both greenhouses, will these expenses double?"

As we addressed their concerns and answered their questions, Jerry and Julia were able to envision an exciting new path to transitioning out of their company in a way that achieved their two primary objectives: keep their family intact and position the business for ongoing success. The cost of separating the two greenhouses was minimal compared to the price their family would pay if they chose one son over the other. As a bonus, splitting the company enabled the couple to leave each son a substantial legacy. By segmenting their business, Jerry and Julia achieved their Why *and moved on to their Next Adventure.*

If you don't look at your *What* from various perspectives:

- You may not see all of the elements that make up your business and how each might fit into the achievement of your objectives.

- You may overlook paths that would lead to achieving your objectives.

If you use inclusive thinking to answer your *What*:

- You may recognize that there are multiple paths you can take to reach the outcome you desire.

- You may see new ways to overcome financial, tax and a host of other obstacles on the journey to your Next Adventure.

POINT OF INTEREST

Use the following table to list the segments of your business that could be transitioned separately—even if ultimately it does not make sense to do so. Then indicate whether or not you want to transition each segment. Use inclusive thinking! The purpose of this exercise is to broaden your thinking and help you begin to see your business as a collection of parts.

Segments to Transition

Business Segment to Transition	Want to Transition?

CHAPTER SIXTEEN

THE *WHO*: CHOOSING YOUR SUCCESSOR

And human resources are like natural resources; they're often buried deep. You have to go looking for them, they're not just lying around on the surface. You have to create the circumstances where they show themselves.

Sir Ken Robinson, Ph. D., Author

Identifying your *Who*—your successor—is the answer to another critical Big 6 question. No one knows your business like you do, so how can you find a successor with the skills, knowledge, risk tolerance, ingenuity and other entrepreneurial characteristics to take over where you leave off, much less lead the company forward?

CHOOSING A SUCCESSOR

It can be difficult to find the right successor because not just anyone will do. When you wonder who could possibly replace you, remember: *Everyone* is replaceable. *EVERYONE! Even you!*

Someone You Know

Choosing your *Who* is not easy, but it can be even more difficult if the successor you are considering is someone you know, such as a business partner, family member(s), or friend. Transitions to business partners or family members can be complicated.

- No matter how the deal turns out, good or bad, you have an ongoing relationship with family members. Thanksgiving dinners could get uncomfortable!

- In many cases your partners and family members won't have sufficient access to capital or adequate funding to cash you out fully at the time of sale. This situation presents a cash flow problem for you and carries more risk than a sale to a third party.

- You will likely be an ongoing mentor to a successor you know and have a very personal, and possibly a financial, interest in their success.

Despite these issues, putting your business in the hands of someone you know and care about can be one of the most rewarding paths you can take.

The Qualifying Questions

As you think about possible successor candidates, ask yourself:

1. Does this person want to be an entrepreneur/owner?

2. Has this person demonstrated the qualities of entrepreneurship that they will need to be successful?

3. Is this person capable of learning how to do what you do to lead a successful business? (And are you capable of teaching them?)

4. Does this person's time frame for ownership match yours?

You will notice there's a question that does not appear on this list, namely, will this person do everything precisely the way you would? It is not on the list because the answer is simple and applies universally: They won't. The "right" successors have their own skills, plans and, quite likely, their own definitions of success. Once they understand how to do what you do (drawing upon your knowledge, wisdom and practices), they will be able to drive the business forward and build on your success. They will surround themselves with key people who complement their abilities, not yours as the following case study involving "Giselle" and "Gordon" illustrates. Pushing for exact replication of your skills, ideas and methods will not work. Recognizing your successor's abilities and building on them does.

G iselle was a brilliant engineer who started her radio company shortly after graduating from college. She anticipated the explosion in cellular communication and began to construct radio towers and antennae. Thirty-five years later, she had a nice asset in her radio and cellular towers and one of the best reputations in the radio industry.

Giselle's son, Gordon, did not follow his mother's footsteps into the hard sciences. Instead, he put his gift for numbers to work in finance and accounting. He became a CPA and then went on to become the CFO of a furniture manufacturing company. When he indicated to Giselle that he was interested in running the company, she was thrilled. She was also uncertain because she could not imagine how anyone but an engineer could run the company successfully.

Giselle was sitting on the horns of that dilemma when we met her. After assessing her situation, we encouraged Giselle to do some inclusive thinking: If she were to sell to a third party, especially a private equity group, would it install an engineer in her place? Not likely. She could expect to see a CEO with leadership and financial skills as well as some knowledge of the industry. She realized this description fit Gordon to a T.

As a result, Giselle decided to mentor Gordon in industry-related topics and practices, and she helped him hire an engineer who could replace her expertise. She also offered her input as Gordon hired a management team that filled his skills gap just as she had once hired a team to fill hers.

Today Gordon has used his financial acumen to make several profitable acquisitions. The company has evolved from a regional company to a national powerhouse. Giselle is off on her Next Adventure, and Gordon is running a multimillion-dollar company.

The Curse Of Knowledge

Giselle became stuck on her journey to her Next Adventure when she assumed her company could not succeed under the leadership of anyone but an engineer. Another sticking point crops up when owners think about how they will teach successors to do what the owners do "naturally." They know so well what they do—and how they do it—that they have trouble teaching their successors. "Janine" is a great example.

The Knowledge Curse: Owners don't know what they know, and successors don't know what they don't know.

W*e met Janine, the owner and president of a retail business, when she was four months pregnant with her second child. Janine had kept her business moving forward during the early months of caring for her first child. With her second, however, she wanted to enjoy two months off with few or no business distractions. She asked us to design a plan that would prepare her* *employees so well that they would not need to call her during her maternity leave.*

Once we helped Janine develop a comprehensive list of the tasks that she performed to run her company day to day, we created a timeline and strategy to transfer each process/task to a designated employee or group of employees.

Janine started teaching and transferring the least complex items on her list and moved to increasingly complex tasks until she reached the last: merchandising. When we asked her which employee was best suited to take over merchandising, Janine said, "I can't transition it." That belief presented Janine with a choice: Option A - give up her maternity leave, or Option B - allow the store to run out of merchandise until she returned.

It was no surprise that Janine rejected both options, and she argued that even if she could give up merchandising, she was unable to explain to anyone exactly how she did it. "I don't know how I decide whether to order more of an item or replace an item with something else," she explained.

She had a problem, but hardly an insurmountable one. We asked Janine to observe herself making merchandising decisions over the next 10 days. When she returned, she had gained insight into a task she did so naturally that she'd never considered how she did it. We built a step-by-step decision matrix based on the information Janine gave us about her decision-making process. Using that matrix, she taught two employees how to merchandise. Four weeks later she delivered her second child and began her relaxing, uninterrupted special time with her family.

Curriculum Development

Developing a plan to transfer your skills, knowledge and wisdom to a successor is a lot like developing a college curriculum. In college, students move through four years of successively more difficult courses. In a business transition, the goal is to move through four developmental stages:

1. Owner makes decisions while the successor watches.

2. Owner and successor make decisions together.

3. Successor makes decisions while the owner watches.

4. Successor makes decisions without the owner's involvement.

Gaining expertise and taking on critical responsibilities is a sequential process. Students start at a basic level and progress through increasingly difficult levels. For example, they take chemistry classes to learn the basic elements and study reactions before professors turn them loose in the lab! A business transition also begins at the basic level then progresses: Owners begin by transferring the least complex tasks to successors before the more complicated. Using this method allows you to assess whether successors are capable of increasing levels of complexity and equip them with the tools they need to succeed.

In college the curriculum is designed to generate a degree in four years. In a business transition, the owner's *When* sets the time frame for completion. If a successor takes longer to complete the "required courses," you will need to extend the time frame. If the successor masters tasks more quickly than expected, you may be able to compress the time frame.

A four-year college curriculum includes a variety of courses that deliver a comprehensive grasp of an area of study. When developing a successor, you will also transfer your knowledge about a variety of areas, e.g., business development, financial management, leadership and tasks specific to your business (as merchandising was to Janine's).

To extend this metaphor just a little further, think about your own college experience. You likely entered with a major in mind, based not on experience but expectations. Perhaps you changed your major once you discovered what interested you or where your skills were sharpest. In a business transition, we give successors a similar opportunity: Once they gain some experience, they may find that business ownership is—or is not—something they want to take on. They may discover that a particular role they thought would be perfect for them within the business is not right. Consequently, they will move toward another role that is more fitting.

Your successor will not be your clone but instead will have their own abilities. (See Gordon and Giselle earlier in this chapter.) Your knowledge-transfer plan will be unique to the two of you. Common to all plans is that they reduce the business's dependency on you. That's something that ultimately must happen whether your *Who* is someone you know or someone you do not.

Whose Dream Is It Anyway?

It is important to understand that the person you identify as your *Who* has their own dreams and goals. What you view as a golden opportunity they might view as a complicated, impossible burden. You have already defined your *Why*. Chances are, your successor has not.

If you are to build a bridge between you and your successor, there has to be open and clear communication. Only by communicating will you learn whether your *Who* even wants to lead and own your company.

Choosing your Who *may be the most challenging element of The Big 6.*

Ready Or Not?

Assuming your chosen successor wants to step into your shoes, what happens if they aren't quite ready due to a lack of skills or cash? Or what happens if your willing successor is ready to take the reins but you aren't ready to ride off into your Next Adventure?

In either case, you have a decision to make:

1. If your *When* is more important to you than your *Who*, you can shift to another *Who*.

Or

2. If your *Who* is more important to you than your *When*, you postpone the beginning of your Next Adventure until your chosen successor is ready to step into your shoes.

Choosing a *Who* requires you to identify a successor who:

1. Is willing and eager to assume ownership.

2. Has demonstrated the entrepreneurial characteristics necessary to lead a company to future success.

3. Is capable of learning how to do what you do in overseeing and leading the business.

4. Fits with your timetable and you with theirs.

If one of these four characteristics is absent, you have a dilemma and will need to address the issue. This may mean reconsidering your choice and possibly choosing a different successor, or determining if adjustments can be made to help you and your successor engage. A successful journey requires open communication and meeting each other along the way.

A successor may possess all of these characteristics and show interest when initially presented with the prospect of business ownership, but then realize somewhere along the line that they no longer want the Next Adventure they thought they wanted (ownership of a business and all that comes with it). Maybe they don't want the risk, even though they initially thought they did. Maybe they thought the role of owner would be more glamorous and not as difficult as they find out that it is. Maybe their spouse wasn't willing to take the necessary risk for an uncertain reward.

One of the reasons we encourage owners to chart their journeys as soon as they begin to think about moving on to their Next Adventures is to give possible successors time to confirm that business ownership is indeed *their* dream. There is no shame in the decision to decline the opportunity to become a business owner. If your *Who* decides to do so, you will adjust your path to your Next Adventure. Your Plan B might be to invite a different person to join you on this journey or to prepare your company for a third-party sale.

If you fail to choose your *Who:*

- You allow Father Time to take control of your business transition, a non-strategy that jeopardizes your company's odds of future success.

- As you become overwhelmed by the difficulty of choosing your *Who*, your stress increases.

- A sale to an outside third party begins to look like the best path even though it may not be the best option for you, your family, your employees or your business.

If you choose your *Who:*

- You keep moving toward your Next Adventure.

- You show people how much you care about them. By designing the next steps for your company, you honor your people and honor the intentions you have for your business.

- The curriculum you create for your successor lessens your company's dependence on you. That makes your company more valuable to any type of successor.

POINT OF
INTEREST

Use the Potential Successors table to list successors you'd like to consider. Remember there are many successor variations: one or more individuals and one or more companies.

What are your thoughts on each potential successor? Consider the potential or known positives for each possible successor as well as the potential or known drawbacks, barriers or obstacles.

The purpose of this exercise is to gain insight into your thoughts and feelings about each possible successor. You may even find there are other options or combinations of successors you may not have considered before. Explore!

Potential Successors

Potential Successor (or Combination of Successors)	Potential or Known Positives	Potential or Known Drawbacks, Barriers or Obstacles

CHAPTER SEVENTEEN

DECIDING WHAT'S FAIR WHEN CHOOSING YOUR *WHO*

You cannot be fair to others without first being fair to yourself.
Vera Nazarian, Author and artist

Choosing a successor can be a very challenging dilemma. If you choose one employee, how will other employees react? If you choose your child, how will your other children, your business partner, or your business partner's children react—not to mention your employees?

Back in Chapter Six we talked about three types of interrelated dilemmas: personal well-being, business well-being and family well-being. In the process of choosing your *Who*, you will encounter these dilemmas and make some hard choices. Recall that, by definition, working through a dilemma means no matter which choice you make, you will get what's most important to you but perhaps not everything you want. The purpose of this chapter is to show you how to work through the dilemmas related to the issue of what's fair when choosing your *Who*.

You likely have anticipated that family members, employees and business partners will have opinions about whether the successor choice you make is fair—to them or to others. In the face of "public opinion," some owners begin to wonder if it's better to sell their companies to outside third parties or maybe just keep working until they wear out or have the amount of money they want or need to retire. It's not too surprising that, when confronted by what seems to be an insurmountable challenge, owners are tempted to abandon their ideal successor.

Overwhelmed owners may assume that, in selling to a third party, they eliminate the risk of ruining any relationships. A sale to an unrelated third party can certainly be a first option or may serve as an owner's Plan B, but it is not always a means to avoid damaging relationships. Consider the child who has worked in the business for years and assumed they would one day own the company. Will that parent-child relationship deepen if you sell to a third party? If you have a long-term employee who is key to your company's success, is capable of running it and wants to do so, will they congratulate you or walk out the door when you choose an outsider as your successor?

More than one owner has told us they'd rather die with their boots on than wade into the dangerous waters of picking a Who *that will disrupt their most important relationships.*

We agree that the waters of choosing a *Who* are dangerous *if you have no plan or map to navigate them*. If you chart your path as we've outlined so far, however, you have the points on your compass necessary to navigate. You have set the objectives that establish your True North (your *Why*), and you've identified the Deal Breakers that will keep you from taking a turn that leaves you completely lost. Now we share the step-by-step process we designed to help you achieve your goal of choosing a family or nonfamily successor without destroying your relationships.

Entitlement Vs. Fair

Entitlement is the feeling that one deserves something. When you choose a successor, that feeling may be validated in your successor and aggravated in those you do not choose. For example, if you have children and choose only one (or less than all) as your successor, the issue of entitlement almost always raises its ugly head. Or if you choose just one among several partners or employees, entitlement may come into play. Nonfamily employees may have expected you to fast-track your children to the top, but it doesn't mean they will be thrilled when you do.

Fair is not the same as entitlement. We may or may not feel entitled to something, but at an early age all of us develop a sense of what's fair. Researchers find that infants as young as 12 months expect items to be divided equally. As they mature, children will object if they receive less, intervene when they perceive someone is treated unfairly, and punish those who are unfair.*

---

*McAuliffe, Katherine et al, "Do Kids Have a Fundamental Sense of Fairness?" *Scientific American*, 23 Aug. 2017, https://blogs.scientificamerican. com/observations/do-kids-have-a-fundamental-sense-of-fairness/ Site last visited 11.19.20

Fairness: A Matter of Perspective

When we meet with owners, we start every discussion of fairness by reminding them that each of us has a unique sense of what's fair, based on our values and past experience. If you were ever treated unfairly or watched someone in your family be treated unfairly, your priority may be to never do the same to others. Someone else who has never had that experience may not share that priority.

Fair: Not The Same As Equal

When you taught your children to share, did you ask one child to split something in half and allow the other to choose a half first? That strategy works well for cookies and bags of pretzels. Unfortunately, it does not typically work for ownership of a family business.

Consider two parents who decide that in order to be fair, they will gift 20 percent of their business to each of their five children. Three work in the business, and the other two have successful careers outside the business. The two "outside" children are creating wealth for themselves and their families. Under the parents' plan, any wealth the three children inside the business create will be shared with their two siblings outside of the business. The parents thought it fair to allow all of their children to benefit equally. The children inside the business see things differently. They question why their siblings outside of the business should benefit from their own careers as well as the labor of those working in the business. That's a great—and solvable—question that this family could resolve using the steps we describe in this chapter.

Before we dive into those steps, a few important reminders:

1. There are no perfect solutions to dilemmas related to what is fair. Every person and every situation is unique. As you choose your *Who*, you can only be expected to do the best you can to maintain your important relationships and achieve most of your objectives. Remember, not all of your objectives may be attainable, but you navigate which ones take priority over others and which you may have to shift.

2. You must make decisions without a crystal ball when determining what is fair. You cannot possibly anticipate every possible outcome, so please keep this in mind as you work to find the best solution.

3. Expect to do some rigorous thinking about how your successor perceives what you are offering. Before you make a choice, ask yourself whether a potential

successor will view ownership as a fabulous opportunity to pursue a great career and generate wealth (through ownership and profits of a business) or as the denial of an opportunity to pursue a great career and generate wealth outside of the business. The choice of a successor may either fulfill or deny the lifetime dream of your successor, a business partner, other children or other employees. Looking at ownership from a successor's point of view tests your assumptions and gives you a broader and more realistic perspective of the ownership you are offering.

4. If you are married, clarifying fair as it relates to the choice of a successor is typically a joint project. Once you think through the many facets of fair, does your spouse (whether active in the business or not) agree? If you aren't sure, we recommend that you ask. Even long-married couples can have differing opinions about what's fair.

Clarify What's Fair In Four Steps

To clarify how you think about what's fair, we suggest you use a four-step process that applies to successors whether they are family members or not.

Step 1: Revisit your objectives.

Step 2: Consider the many facets of fairness (or think beyond 50/50).

Step 3: Test your fairness assumptions and adjust.

Step 4: Be clear and communicate well.

Step 1: Revisit Your Objectives.

Everyone has an opinion about what's fair in a business transition. But again, we begin with you: how will you clarify in your mind what's fair? The first step is to look back at your Objectives Matrix. Your goals and Deal Breakers help you chart your course to fairness. For example, perhaps your goals include having your daughter take over the business and somehow "compensate" your other children. Perhaps one goal that is a Deal Breaker is any action that would damage your relationship with your business partner. Revisiting your objectives—especially your Deal Breakers—reminds you of what you want the transition to achieve.

Step 2: Consider The Many Facets Of Fairness (Or Think Beyond 50/50).

When we help owners clarify their idea of fairness in the context of their *Who*, we ask them to consider many factors that affect what's fair. These include:

- Perspective
- Sweat equity and/or tenure
- Risk
- Timing
- Tools in your toolbox

Facet 1: Perspective

Perspective is a critical facet of fairness because opinions of what is fair can vary dramatically between spouses and among family members and employees. We counsel owners to establish clarity about their own idea of what's fair first because clarity is your rock when every person—directly or indirectly involved with the business—views your choice of successor from their own set of beliefs and experiences.

As preparation for these conversations—and possibly debates—about what is fair, work through your own thinking and dilemmas first. For example, as you contemplate one person as a successor, ask yourself whether that person is a good choice or whether someone else would be a better one.

It can be difficult to stay the course when a chorus of voices plants the seeds of doubt in you. As the chorus grows louder and more insistent, you may choose to assess its opinions to see if they contain any important information. If not, your job is to get ready to communicate confidently your vision of what's fair.

Facet 2: Sweat Equity and/or Tenure

When they calculate fairness, it is not unusual for owners to consider possible successors' contribution to the company's success (sweat equity) or time spent working in the company (tenure). It can be difficult for owners to compare one successor candidate who has dedicated themselves to the business (possibly for years) against another candidate who has better skills, potential for leadership and entrepreneurial focus.

Facet 3: Risk

No matter the choice of successor, there is risk in business ownership. Keep in mind that as you are working to reduce your risk, your successor is diving headfirst into it. You know risk well and have lived with it for years. Your successor has not. Nor does your successor have a crystal ball. Neither of you can predict whether the risks to your successor will include:

People who have not been owners cannot fully appreciate the risk of business ownership.

- A weak economy.
- The appearance of a well-financed competitor who swoops into the market with a similar product or service.
- A legislative, regulatory or tax change that will affect the business.

When owners consider these possibilities, some wonder whether the transition they contemplate will ruin their successor's life.

Facet 4: Timing

A crystal ball would come in handy when it comes to considering timing as it relates to fairness.

If, for example, you are considering a younger partner as your successor but he or she is not yet prepared to lead, is it fair *to you* to wait to begin your Next Adventure until that partner is ready to begin theirs? Is it fair for you to assume that your partner can run your company when they have never done so?

Imagine instead that you want one of your three children to succeed you. Two have expressed interest in taking over the company, but one is too young to have even worked in the business. Is it fair *to you* to wait years for your youngest child to know whether they want to become an owner? Is that wait fair *to your older children*? Will the fact that you are all waiting on your youngest child to make a decision put undue pressure on that child?

To wait or not is a solvable dilemma, but, as is true of any dilemma, you may have to give up something to get what you want.

Facet 5: Tools In Your Toolbox

As you consider the fairness tools available to you, remember three of your goals: 1) to create the Next Adventure you want to live, 2) to maintain your important relationships, and 3) to set up your business to succeed.

There are at least two tools you can use to be fair to children inside and outside of ownership: your estate plan and/or promissory notes. While these tools don't change the fact that not all of your children will become owners, the tools are consistent with

Principle 1: Put relationships first. You can use your estate plan and/or promissory notes to demonstrate your commitment to making children who are not owners feel as important and valued as the children who are.

Making others feel valued is just as important if your successor is one of several partners or employees. The tools in your toolbox for nonfamily successors, however, are different. They include phantom stock plans, sizable bonuses for staying with the company for a period of time after you leave, and nonqualified deferred compensation plans. When owners do not make employees or partners not named as successors feel valued, those people often head straight for the exit.

Step 3: Test Your Fairness Assumptions And Adjust.

As you think about possible successors, do you know whether it is their dream to be a business owner? Before you assume it is, ask!

As we discussed in Chapter Five, asking about or testing assumptions is not the same as firing a string of direct questions. It better resembles a fishing expedition to see what others think of your bait. We often coach owners on how to conduct fairness fishing expeditions that yield important information rather than knee-jerk emotional reactions.

When you test your assumptions, you learn whether there is alignment between what you want and what others want. If two perspectives are out of alignment—and there is always some misalignment between what owners want and what others want—you make an adjustment that is consistent with your objectives.

Step 4: Be Clear And Communicate Well.

Once you have reviewed your objectives, considered fairness, tested your assumptions, and made any necessary adjustments, you will be able to confidently respond to those who may question your choices. You will be able to explain that you took into consideration what was best for not only yourself, but for your family, company and employees as well.

Pinch Hitters

As you may suspect, when it comes to perceptions about what's fair, communicating your decisions—especially with children—can be fraught with emotion. Longtime partners or employees who have worked years for ownership can also react strongly—

even if your message is well-crafted and carefully delivered—because message recipients hear senders through filters that they have had in place for years. For example, imagine telling a daughter who wanted to be CEO that you've chosen her brother instead. Through her filter her reaction is "Of course, my brother gets to be CEO! He always got the new bike, and I got his hand-me-downs." Rather than defend yourself for long-forgotten choices made years ago, recruit a pinch hitter. Take yourself out of the batter's box, and bring in a person who doesn't have a long relationship with the other players.

In our practice, we have a great deal of experience in "tough conversations." Recipients of the messages we deliver don't have the same filters when we speak as they do when their parents, bosses or business partners speak. We come to conversations prepared to present an alternative better suited to the receiver's talents or Next Adventure. In the case of the CEO brother and long-waiting sister, we might suggest the sister would be happier or more successful in another role (perhaps as chair of the family council—which may be a much more important role than CEO as the family moves ahead) because in that position she truly steps into her father's shoes as the keeper of the family legacy— something she has always wanted to do.

No matter who your successor is, you are in a unique position to help others recognize and even attain their own Next Adventures. Just remember, Next Adventures can happen both inside the business (as an owner, employee or director) and outside the business (in other fulfilling careers and pursuits).

Choosing your *Who* comes with dilemmas, but they are dilemmas you can work through. We know this because you are a resilient, successful business owner. If you have ever resolved a situation with a difficult employee, managed a product recall, or found a reasonable solution to a profound disagreement with a partner, you have the skills to navigate fairness issues. You've got this.

If you fail to consider the many facets of fairness when choosing a successor:

- Perceptions about whether you have treated people fairly can fester and become ticking bombs that can damage and possibly destroy employee teams and/or families.

- You can damage your relationships with those who are most important to you. You will find it challenging to communicate to others how you incorporated equality and fairness into your decisions because you didn't.

When choosing a successor, if you consider the many facets of fairness and ground yourself in your definition of fair:

- You help others understand the choices and opportunities you are offering them, and you are able to explain your thinking and decision process.

- You minimize friction and smooth the path to retaining your most important relationships.

- You set up your successor for success and position your company to succeed under the best possible leadership.

- You honor the unique talents and desires of everyone involved.

POINT OF INTEREST

Here we ask that you take time to reflect on two of the greatest roadblocks many owners anticipate: equality and fairness. These two issues prevent numerous owners from even embarking on their transition journeys.

Please describe the concerns you have related to equality and fairness. Does the concern raise issues of entitlement, of equality, of fairness or another issue? Also, how much of an impact could each issue have on the transition you envision and your Next Adventure?

Equality and Fairness

My Concern	Is it entitlement, equality, fairness or other?	Size of the Potential Impact on Your Envisioned Transition and Next Adventure

THE *WHEN*: USE IT TO PRESERVE YOUR RELATIONSHIPS, NEXT ADVENTURE™, FINANCIAL SECURITY AND LEGACY

The two most powerful warriors are patience and time.
Leo Tolstoy, Russian author

One of the truths we eventually learn in business and in life is that no matter how powerful, wealthy or large our empire is, Father Time will transition us out of it...if we don't beat him to the punch. Tom Kirk (the real, not fictional, owner whom we met in Chapter Thirteen) describes how just the possibility of a meeting with Father Time ignited an unexpected desire to move on to his Next Adventure.

I am like most owners in that I did not develop a business succession plan until a personal event gave me a strong push. Near the end of a visit with my doctor to discuss the results of some tests, he dropped a bomb into the conversation: "I strongly suggest you take the necessary steps to get your affairs in order." A comment like that is a surefire attention-getter!

Once I accepted the fact that I'd be undergoing a second heart surgery that was clearly more serious than I had thought, I began to imagine what would happen to my business if I was away from it for a time. What would happen if it took me 30 to 90 days—or even 6 to 12 months—to recover?

I assembled my team, and we assessed which parts of the business would remain successful and which would not in each time frame. We then put into place resources and contingency plans to address our firm's weak areas; for the first time, I had a written business continuation plan. In my absence, this plan would take care of my family (because income would continue), my team and clients.

With confidence that the important people would be taken care of during my recovery, I began to wonder if a similar plan would work for a future transition out of ownership of my business entirely. If it did, that would be a positive and proactive move toward the next phase of my life.

As most owners do, I began to think about how a transition would work and quickly realized I was going nowhere fast. I had more questions than answers— important questions such as: Why do I want to transition my business? What do I want this transition to accomplish for myself and for others? Who will the next owners be? Will the decisions I make damage or destroy my relationships with people who are important to me? When do I want this transition to occur? How much do I need to receive for my current business ownership?

Without answers to these questions, I could not assemble my team to talk about a "permanent" transition, and I was unable to find the perfect solution on my own. So I did what many owners do: I looked at a number of "business exit" programs and found they focused almost exclusively on various methods of selling a business. I was familiar with these methods; what I needed was a way to make decisions consistent with my desire both to keep the relationships I valued intact and receive a fair return on my investment.

I finally found a program that put people first and showed me how I could create a roadmap to take me to the outcome I wanted. That program was the one Laura (my successor) and Elizabeth are describing in this book: The Transition Roadmap Developer Process.

Today my—well, Laura's—business is thriving, and I am living a life beyond what I imagined.

A life event or health event might give you an unavoidable push to plan your transition, but whatever the motivation, thinking through when you want to transition out of your business is a process that can take time and is usually loaded with emotion. After all, you are putting an expiration date on what may have been your life's work. At the same time, however, you are establishing your legacy and setting a start date for your Next Adventure. Setting start and end dates can be daunting and frightening, but it can—and should!—be satisfying and joyful as well.

As we help owners identify their *Whens*, or establish milestones for their journeys, we offer three perspectives that most owners never consider.

1. ***When* can be a valuable shield.** The dates owners choose to begin and complete their transition journeys can protect their own (and their families') financial security, their relationships and Next Adventures, their successors, their companies and their legacies.

2. **Many elements contribute to a *When*.** Setting dates requires owners to balance: 1) their own financial reward, personal agendas and desires, 2) their successors' preparedness and thirst for ownership, 3) their company's ability to succeed under new leadership and 4) external conditions and events.

3. **There is more than one *When*.** Rather than a single date, owners set multiple dates, usually over years, as they prepare their successors to assume ownership and their new role.

Perspective 1: Your *When* Can Serve As A Shield

Ideally, the dates you choose to begin and finish your journey protect you, your family, your successor and your company.

- Your *When* should protect you by:
  - ~ Improving your ability to reach your objectives.
  - ~ Safeguarding your financial security (and by extension that of your family) by taking you off the hook for any financial obligations related to the company.
  - ~ Retaining important relationships by lining up with the timing that your spouse (and others) expects or you have promised.
- Your *When* should protect your successor by:
  - ~ Coinciding with their desire to assume ownership.
  - ~ Giving them time to prepare to lead successfully.
- Your *When* should protect your business by placing it in the hands of a leader fully capable of running it.

That's a lot to ask from dates, but we've helped owners use their *Whens* to protect themselves, objectives, families, successors and businesses. To accomplish this, we use a number of strategies (tailored to each situation, of course), such as managing the release of ownership control and structuring a successor's financial commitment.

Control

This is the guiding principle that we use when considering ownership control: As long as owners retain a controlling interest in their companies, they retain the ability and authority to guide and structure decisions. That principle is important for two reasons:

1. As long as you are on the financial hook for business obligations, you should retain ultimate authority over all major financial decisions, such as whether to secure an additional line of credit, make an acquisition, restructure or expand your company, or renew contracts with vendors.

2. Until you realize the financial objective you desire or the financial resources necessary to support your Next Adventure, you should maintain a controlling interest in your business.

By "controlling interest" we mean greater than 50 percent of the voting rights. Even if your controlling interest drops below 50 percent, you can contractually set boundaries related to specific actions so that your successor cannot take these actions without your approval.

Control and Business Financial Obligations

Typically, as owners transition controlling interest to their successors, and banks agree to finance these successors, owners can remove themselves from the financing/banking agreements (and other obligations) that tie their financial well-being to their companies. Extracting owners from financial obligations for companies they do not control is an essential step in the transition journey, but one that usually occurs near its end.

Control and Personal Financial Security

Understandably, owners are more confident in moving forward on their transition journeys once they have met—or are well on the way to meeting—their personal financial objectives.

Successor Financial Commitment

If your successor can fully compensate you for your ownership interest all at once, that's great. When a successor is an employee or family member, however, they typically do not have the funds to cash out owners in a single event. What then?

As you think about your situation, consider first whether your successor is willing and able to assume ownership. If so, have they backed up that commitment with their own cash or bank financing, or by satisfying all requirements necessary for you to accept a promissory note?

If not, here are many solutions to this dilemma, including:

1. Employee or family successors purchase the business interest via a promissory note or other contractual agreement.

2. Employees or family successors earn equity annually as part of their compensation.

3. An owner establishes a deferred compensation plan that helps successors purchase equity in the future.

Note: While a deferred compensation plan can help a successor to purchase equity in the future (by providing funds for an initial down payment), it may not be an ideal solution. A company is taxed on its profits and in a typical plan, it commits a portion of those profits to the successor. The company only receives a tax deduction when that successor receives the compensation (at which time the successor is taxed on their income). Keep in mind that a deferred compensation plan legally obligates a company to pay the compensation at a future date. Because tax regulations are constantly changing and each situation is unique, *you should review all the pros and cons of these plans with your legal and tax advisors, who can help design a plan to meet your particular needs.*

If successors cannot qualify for bank financing or satisfy an owner's requirements for a promissory note, the transition journey need not come to a screeching halt. There are numerous possible solutions to this dilemma. For example, an owner could restructure the transfer by adjusting the *When* to give a successor time to become bank worthy. As is true of most dilemmas, the sooner it is tackled, the more options are available.

Resolving the payment issue is not always the insurmountable obstacle some owners assume it is. Figuring out how to address it successfully requires some inclusive thinking and some balancing among the other five of The Big 6 questions. Given time to make adjustments, however, owners find they have multiple options that still enable them to reach their desired outcomes.

Every owner must find the balance between their financial needs and the company's ability to generate the cash successors need both to run the business and provide owners the return on their investment that they want for their ownership (or pay the bank that financed the successor).

Perspective 2: The Many Elements Of A *When*

Setting a date on which you'd like to start your Next Adventure isn't quite as easy as picking a date on a calendar. If it were, fewer owners would maintain their continual rolling five-year exit dates. Owners typically end up with a series of rolling exit dates when they don't know how to balance all of the owner-, successor- and company-related factors that go into their *Whens*.

Owner-related elements to be balanced include:

• Financial reward.

• Personal agenda.

Owners must also balance several successor-related elements, including their:

• Preparedness.

• Thirst for leadership.

The critical company-related element is its ability to succeed under new leadership.

Finally, there are external conditions and events to consider.

Let's look at each of these four elements.

Owner-Related Elements

Owner's Financial Reward

If owners need business proceeds to support their Next Adventures, they must estimate when their businesses will be valuable enough to transfer. Even owners who do not need the proceeds of a sale to finance their Next Adventures but want to receive a fair price for their lives' work must estimate when their companies can sell for that "fair price."

We note here that a temporary loss in business value, such as one caused by an economic slowdown, can help some owners who do not need top-of-market value to achieve their goals. For example, when business value falls, it can be the perfect time for owners who wish to gift ownership to children or sell to successors at a lower value to do so.

Owner's Personal Agenda

Owners often have objectives on their personal agendas for their current adventure, such as building the company to a certain value or position in the industry. They may also have objectives related to their Next Adventure. Is there a particular age or event that will influence the timing of your *When*?

Successor-Related Elements

Successor's Preparedness

No owner wants to leave a company in the hands of an unprepared successor, and only foolish or uninformed successors want to lead before they are prepared. When will a successor be prepared to run your company successfully?

Successor's Thirst For Leadership

Many owners do not consider the possibility that successors who were once eager and energetic can grow frustrated when owners don't "get out of the way." When owners hang on too long, they can lose their best successors and unnecessarily narrow their options.

Company-Related Element

Company's Ability to Succeed Under New Leadership

Before setting a date to begin their Next Adventure, an owner should be sure the company is healthy enough to withstand the shift to new ownership. In this context, healthy means that:

- Key employees will continue to trust and perform under new ownership.

- Key customers, primary vendors, and business advisors will confidently transfer their relationships to the new owner.

- Contracts with vendors and customers will not only remain in place, but the company's ability to perform makes renewal likely.

- The business is healthy enough to generate adequate cash flow to support the transition.

External Conditions and Events

Owners who have been in business for any length of time know the economy is a continuous, but unpredictable, cycle of ups and downs and, therefore, current financial success is no guarantee of future success. Owners must balance their desire to leave on a specific date with the risk that a transfer can become difficult—if not impossible—during an economic downturn. Without a crystal ball, the *When* owners choose may jeopardize many, if not all, of their objectives.

The good news is that if the economy falters (as it did during the Covid-19 pandemic), if access to debt becomes difficult or the government changes regulations, owners have established their compass points and direction. They have the option to shift, accelerate or delay their departure, because the foundation for the transition is in place.

PERSPECTIVE 3: MORE THAN ONE *WHEN*

Business succession is a process, so a *When* is not a single calendar date. Instead, it often consists of multiple dates spread over years as owners prepare their successors for leadership and ownership. A one- to five-year process is not uncommon, and we've created timelines that span as many as 10 years. If your company has more than one owner, it is likely each owner has his or her own *When*, and each person's *When* involves multiple dates.

Multiple dates are not at all unusual, because preparing a successor to assume ownership involves a sequence of events or series of stages that you can extend or collapse as you go along. For example, owners set dates to transfer tasks to their successors. (See Chapter Twenty-Three.) Each task transfer may take less or more time than you anticipate, and many of them trigger actions as you step away from your current positions and into new (or maybe even former) ones. For example, you might choose to work in product development (your favorite job of all time in the business but one you haven't been able to do as CEO) or become the chairman of the board (a new position for you) while you mentor your successor as CEO.

These three perspectives (that *When* can be a shield, that there are many elements of a *When* and that there is more than one *When*) help owners set time frames and dates to transition out of ownership that maximize the odds of successfully reaching their Next Adventures.

Shifts Are Inevitable.

As is true of all of The Big 6, developing a *When* is an iterative process and adjustments to the answer to one of The Big 6 questions can affect answers to others. For example,

- Once owners reach the questions of *How* and *How Much*, they often refine their *Whens*.

- If an owner's chosen departure date clashes directly with a Deal Breaker, or the date puts an important relationship in jeopardy, owners are fully aware of the collision *before* it happens. If they wish, they can then avoid that collision by adjusting a *When*.

- Conversely, if an owner chooses to adjust a Deal Breaker in favor of their desired departure date (as emotional and difficult as that is), they do so with full knowledge of what they are giving up.

Making adjustments to transition strategies and/or timing is just one way that owners demonstrate their ability to give and take. (The same is true of successors.) The goal is always for you and your successor to work together and move the process forward.

As you work to develop your Transition Roadmap in Section III, your *When* may also shift once you see it fully integrated with your objectives and the objectives of those who you will invite into this transition journey.

If you ignore all of the elements that go into the choice of your *When*:

- You work under a rolling retirement plan and dream about the day you will no longer work in the business. That day never gets any nearer, and your successors continue to wonder when they will get the chance to run a business that you have not prepared them to run.

- As you age, your successors' frustration with your inaction grows. As it does, the risk that they will choose to go elsewhere to pursue their Next Adventures increases.

If you choose a *When* that protects yourself, your family, successor and company:

- You are the strong leader, the protector not only of your Next Adventure and family's financial security, but also of your relationships, successor and company.

- You gain the clarity and confidence necessary to tackle the questions of *How* and *How Much*.

- You help all involved reach the majority of their objectives, and is doing so minimize the detours on the road to your Next Adventure.

POINT OF INTEREST

When is a great question to ponder! Considering the question may bring up many thoughts and feelings: some exciting and some not; some reassuring and some unsettling.

On the "Understanding My *When*" chart, list your ideal *Whens* even if you are not yet confident about the perfect timing of each.

For example:

- *When* would you like to begin transferring equity to a successor?
- *When* will you begin training your successor to become CEO?
- *When* will you give up your position as CEO?
- *When* will your successor join the company's board of directors?
- *When* will you complete the transfer of equity to your successor?
- *When* will you no longer be active in the company's operations?
- *When* will your successor finish paying you for your equity?

List the qualities that make each *When* ideal, and then list the related obstacles that you (or others) may encounter. The goal of this exercise is to put something on paper—even if just in pencil—so you can evaluate what attracts you to a particular *When* as well as identify any reservations you have or barriers that may stand in your way. Once you complete the exercise for each *When*, you can compare the pros and cons of various timing options and thus broaden your thinking about the possibilities.

Understanding My *When*

Ideal *When*	Positives	Possible Obstacles

CHAPTER NINETEEN

THE *HOW MUCH:* YOUR PEACE-OF-MIND NUMBER

Financial freedom is less about financials and more about freedom.
Manoj Arora, Author

When owners begin to think about leaving their companies, it's almost automatic for them to look for answers to the questions of *How* and *How Much* long before they consider their *Why*. That's unfortunate because it's nearly impossible to know *How Much* one needs or wants from the transfer of a business until and unless one knows *Why* one wants or needs it! If you have followed The Transition Roadmap Developer Process to this point, you have at least explored—and may possibly have fully identified—your *Why* or Next Adventure. Congratulations!

In this chapter, we introduce you to two tools that we've created for you to use to answer the all-important question: Can you get what you want? Or, in other words, will you have "enough" to move successfully through the transition you envision and live the Next Adventure you desire?

We will look first at how we determine the amount of financial resources you will need to support your Next Adventure, and then we will turn to how to assess whether your business is capable of generating those resources while remaining healthy.

Peace Of Mind Is Priceless. Objectives Require Cash.

Financial plans for individuals typically show the projected future value of a nest egg based on variations in the rate of inflation and rate of return. You are a business owner, so one of your assets is your business. For that reason, we have a few questions:

- If your financial plan lists the value of your business as an asset, what is the basis for that value?

- If you have not put a price tag on your Next Adventure, does your financial plan tell you whether you are prepared for the future you desire?

It is rare to find a business owner's financial plan that takes a deep dive into business value or transition scenarios. If your plan does include the value of your business, it likely assigns it a static value.

Two Sources Of Funds For A Next Adventure

Some of the objectives on your Objectives Matrix describe what you need during your Next Adventure (e.g., health insurance, a comfortable home), and others describe what you want (e.g., to buy a home in Spain, to become an angel investor). Whether a want or a need, all objectives have a price. So just for a moment think of *How Much* not in terms of the proceeds you want or need from your business, but expand your thinking to consider *How Much* it will take to make your Next Adventure a reality.

The expanded question recognizes that a successful Next Adventure may require a combination of your personal funds and income you will earn during and at the conclusion of your business transition. Or it may not. Some owners do not need one dime from the sale of their companies to support their Next Adventures. Others require piles and piles and piles of dimes from the sale. Most fall somewhere in-between. The question we explore in this chapter is: How do you know which group you are in?

Note that we used the word "know." We do so very intentionally because we "know" from long experience that your confidence and financial security, as well as your family's financial security and the future of your business, is in jeopardy unless you have a data-based, comprehensive estimate of all of the following:

1. Your personal financial resources.

2. The cost of your Next Adventure.

We have found most business owners' financial plans lack a clear, motivating vision and documentation of their Next Adventure. Without this vision, how can they determine whether they are financially prepared for the future they desire?

3. The resources you can harvest from your business.

One of the primary benefits of The Transition Roadmap Developer Process is priceless: peace of mind. When you answer your *How Much* question, you not only establish another crucial point on your Transition Compass, but you also gain confidence in the financial feasibility of your Next Adventure. In addition, you create a credible basis for the financial proposal you will make to your successor.

FIXING THE *How Much* POINT ON YOUR TRANSITION COMPASS

When we help owners to determine *How Much* they need to achieve their Next Adventure, we use two tools. The first is The Future Wealth Projection™. It projects the value of an owner's personal financial resources. The second is The Wealth Development Worksheet™. It projects the value of an owner's business equity along with salary and distributions the owner will receive before transferring all equity to a successor. We then use these tools to first determine whether owners can achieve their goals. With that information, we can then test a host of variables (related to timing, business growth, salaries, distributions, etc.) to come up with a solution that does.

Let's look first at the process we use to establish whether an owner's existing personal financial resources will support a Next Adventure.

The Personal Component: The Future Wealth Projection™

To set the *How Much* point on an owner's Transition Compass, we begin with what most financial planners do: an estimate of your personal financial resources. Then we do what other planners do not: We put everything into the context of your objectives (described on The Objectives Matrix).

Many business owners don't have up-to-date financial plans, so often we begin by gathering high-level data related to what they are currently earning, their current expenses, the number of years they wish to work, what they think their business equity is worth and what nonbusiness financial resources they already have. This gives us a starting point for The Future Wealth Projection.

In the course of creating The Future Wealth Projection, we 1) establish a benchmark, 2) do the analysis necessary to estimate sticker prices for each objective, and

3) determine the length of your runway: the number of years before you will need those resources.

The benchmark is an accurate summary of where you are now: the current value of your assets, liabilities and expenses. Most owners have an idea of what their assets (except possibly their companies) are worth and a good handle on their liabilities. Far fewer have a crystal clear picture of their current living expenses. Those who enjoy perks and benefits related to their business expenses (e.g., health insurance and business travel) as most owners do, may have an even muddier picture. To achieve clarity, we help our clients gather, coordinate and consolidate the information necessary to accurately assess and document their current assets, liabilities and expenses.

Once we've established a benchmark, we do the analysis necessary to make realistic estimates of the cost of each objective on The Objectives Matrix. For each goal that requires money to achieve it (e.g., add to your vintage car collection or put three grandchildren through college), we must estimate, in today's dollars, how much it will take to accomplish that objective and then we adjust that number for inflation over the life of the plan.

At this point in the process, we ask spouses to talk to us about their objectives (as a couple and as individuals) and the importance they assign to each. Our purpose is to identify and put into writing what gives our clients joy and purpose, and to paint a word picture of the Next Adventure that they envision. We find putting price tags on objectives encourages and energizes owners because it 1) provides a solid rationale for the strategies we will recommend to reach the objectives, and 2) illustrates whether and which additional advisors (such as estate planning or other attorneys, insurance or real estate professionals) can help them reach those goals.

During these powerful discussions with owners and their spouses, they often identify new objectives together and add to their Objectives Matrix. We use this more complete list of joint objectives to build a financial plan that assigns a cost to each objective and builds a strategy to reach them all. As a result, each individual begins to see that the integration of their personal financial plan and business Transition Roadmap fuels their journey to a shared Next Adventure.

You may recall that you assigned a time frame (continue, short-term and long-term) to each objective on your Objectives Matrix. When we work to establish your *How*

Much, we ask you to estimate more precisely the actual dates by which you want to accomplish each specific objective.

We find that when we help owners assign specific dates to their objectives, the theoretical moves much closer to reality. Setting dates can reveal goals that spouses may not have fully considered when they completed their Objectives Matrix. It's also not uncommon for spouses to surprise each other with goals and time expectations. For example, before moving to that mountaintop retreat, one spouse may want to complete a board of directors term and finish a passion project with a local charitable organization. It is very enlightening (or some might say "interesting") when one spouse envisions a certain event happening during the first week of a Next Adventure and then learns that the other imagines that event occurring 10 years in the future. "Brad" and "Suzanne" discovered they had different timelines for an objective on their Objectives Matrix.

> B rad and Suzanne had included a second home on their Objective Matrix and had classified it as a long-term objective. When we asked Brad to tell us when they planned to buy that home, he answered, "I've got my eye on a few places, so it could happen at any time."
>
> Suzanne, on the other hand, planned to start looking for a second home only once their youngest child finished school. "She's waiting for her acceptance to medical school right now," Suzanne explained, "so we won't even start looking for another four years."
>
> This discussion provided a great opportunity for Brad and Suzanne to share and understand each other's visions of their future in detail.

Establishing dates for accomplishing objectives is more than an alignment-between-spouses exercise, however. Dates tell us how much time is available to grow financial assets.

Once we know where you currently are financially and we have worked with you to establish realistic price tags and time frames for your objectives, your Future Wealth Projection is complete, and we have what we need to project whether your personal resources are capable of supporting your Next Adventure. If they cannot, it enables us to see how much your business must contribute. Your Future Wealth Projection may even provide the information and confidence you need to add new objectives, such as take an extended trip around the world and build a new dream home.

With the personal financial element complete, we move on to the business element of your *How Much*.

The Business Component: The Wealth Development Worksheet™

For most owners, financial security depends (to greater or lesser extent) on the financial state of their companies. Similarly, the income-generating power of their companies plays a role in the feasibility of their Next Adventures. That's why we make a host of careful projections about annual excess business cash flow and the anticipated shifts, including the growth (or contraction) of the value of a business, between the present and the day that owners begin their Next Adventure.

After studying the historical data of a company, in the simplest models we project:

- Annual revenue.

- Cost of goods sold.

- Operating expenses.

- Net profit.

- Estimated value of the business.

- Timing of and payment for equity transfers.

We use these projections to provide insight into five questions:

1. How much excess cash flow from operations do we expect the business can produce?

2. What is the estimated value of the business at various points during the anticipated equity transfer time frame?

3. During the transition, how much income does the owner expect to be able to harvest from a combination of financial streams, including salary, distributions (based on the percentage of equity owned), consulting agreements and eventual sale proceeds?

4. During the transition, how much income may be provided for the successor from a combination

When you answer your How Much question, you not only establish another crucial point on your Transition Compass, but you also gain confidence in the financial feasibility of your Next Adventure. In addition, you create a credible basis for the financial proposal you will make to a successor.

of salary and distributions (based on the percentage of equity owned), when applicable?

5. Will the "deal" work financially? Will it enable the owner to get out with the value the owner and successor agree on and support the successor while maintaining the company's profitability?

We capture all of this business-related data on a tool we call The Wealth Development Worksheet. We then use that tool to illustrate the ability of a business to contribute to an owner's financial goal, which we determined when completing their Future Wealth Projection. Just as we do on The Future Wealth Projection, we can adjust any of the variables (e.g., timing, business performance, operating expenses, compensation, equity liquidity events) to create a variety of scenarios to consider.

The Power Of Information

When we combine the data from an owner's Future Wealth Projection with that of the owner's Wealth Development Worksheet, we can tell whether there is a gap between the amount of personal and business resources the owner is likely to have as they navigate toward their Next Adventures and the amount they will need. Owners who will have more than they will need (from both personal and business resources) to support their Next Adventures have a positive gap. Those who have less than they will need face a negative gap. Once owners know whether their gap is positive or negative, they then have a host of options and additional questions to answer.

If, for example, you learn you will not have the resources necessary to support your Next Adventure (a negative gap), we would ask you to consider the following questions:

- Will you earn more, spend less, invest more aggressively or some combination of all three?

    ~ How much more do you need to earn? (We can use our tools to answer that question.)

    ~ Will you need to adjust your current lifestyle to meet your future objectives? (If so, we can help you determine how large that adjustment must be.)

    ~ What types of investments will generate the growth and income you need at a level of risk that you can tolerate? (We can offer a variety of suggestions.)

- Will you consider an adjustment to your *When* by staying active in your business longer and pushing back your departure date?

- Will you increase the sale price of your business (your *How Much*)? If so, how will you do it?

- Will you revisit your *Who* because you need a higher purchase price for your business than a child, employee or partner is able to pay, and then sell instead to a better financed third party? You might if that path aligns with your *Why* and does not violate one of your Deal Breakers.

- If you had planned to sell the real estate on which your business operates to a successor, will you adjust your *What* by installing a long-term lease with the successor so you can create an income stream and allow the value of the real estate to increase over time?

If you are an owner whose gap is positive, you would also have options and questions to answer.

- Do you want to change your *When* and move up the date of your departure? (We can plug various dates into our tools to help you pick a date.)

- Will you revise your *How* by carrying a note (despite the risk) to help your successor?

- Will you adjust your *How Much* by decreasing your sale price or considering larger gifts of equity to your successor? (Again, we can insert various sale prices and gift amounts into our tools so you can make the best determination for you and your successor.)

- Will you adjust your *Why* by adding objectives that you once thought were out of reach?

The answers to these questions cause many owners to adjust or refine the answers to their Big 6 questions on their Transition Compasses. When "Bonnie" and "Jim" completed their Future Wealth Projection and their Wealth Development Worksheet, they learned they were in a great position to begin their Next Adventure.

Information = Confidence

onnie and her husband, Jim, were the owners of a family business. As the company's CFO, Bonnie provided the analytical balance to Jim's creative drive. During The Transition Roadmap Developer Process, Jim drew an amazing picture of the couple's Next Adventure. It was so amazing that Bonnie wondered whether they were wasting their time on a pipe dream. Those concerns disappeared when Bonnie dug into their Wealth Development Worksheet. For the first time, she felt she could embrace the Roadmap that we were developing.

But let's imagine that our analysis indicated they would not have the financial resources they needed—when they needed them—to finance their Next Adventure. And let's imagine that Bonnie and Jim engaged in The Transition Roadmap Developer Process years before their anticipated *When.* The Financial Wealth Projection and Wealth Development Worksheet would tell them exactly how much business value they needed to build and how much they needed to save from distributions along the way. This foresight would give them the time they needed to work toward building that additional enterprise profitability and value.

The Future Wealth Projection and The Wealth Development Worksheet work together to illustrate whether an owner's Next Adventure can become a reality, allowing them to make confident decisions today and in the future.

The Synergy of The Future Wealth Projection and The Wealth Development Worksheet

When we integrate projections about the performance of an owner's personal savings and investment assets (stocks, bonds, real estate, etc.) with a projection of 1) annual excess business cash flow and 2) growth or contraction in the value of the business between the present and their Next Adventure, the result is a plan that:

- Thoughtfully projects future business and asset performance using historical data as a basis for reasonable assumptions.

- Tells owners whether, based on the current facts and projected outcome of their personal and business lives, they will have the financial resources they and their businesses need to support their Next Adventures on the date they desire.

- Gives owners greater clarity and confidence to move to the next step of their journey: establishing *How* they will transition out of their businesses.

Note: To learn more about The Future Wealth Projection and The Wealth Development Worksheet, please visit: *www.TheSuccessionPlanningBook.com/Tools.*

Even if you don't plan to begin your Next Adventure for years, fixing your *How Much* as a compass point on your journey to your Next Adventure is critical. Solving for the variables and determining the gap (positive or negative) between where you are now and your Next Adventure minimizes guesses, questions and uncertainty. With documented objectives and realistic estimates, you can—with clarity and confidence—make smart decisions, anticipate your financial future, and envision the legacy you may wish to leave to future generations.

We know it can be intimidating to attach a price tag to a Next Adventure, but the confidence that comes from knowing your Next Adventure is actually achievable? That's *priceless.*

If you try to determine *How Much* before you complete The Future Wealth Projection and The Wealth Development Worksheet:

- You are making choices without any data related to how much cash/assets you personally need and how much your business can support.

- You cannot be *truly* confident that your Next Adventure will happen, because you are not *fully* confident you have the resources necessary to reach that stage of your journey.

- If you find out you miscalculated your *How Much*, you run the risk of either working longer than necessary in your business or living a scaled-back version of your Next Adventure.

If you answer the *How Much* question after you complete The Future Wealth Projection and The Wealth Development Worksheet:

- You gain clarity about whether your Next Adventure is possible in the time frame you desire.

- You have a powerful decision-making foundation that evolves in response to events or your changing desires.

- Financial forecasts, not anxious hopes, provide clarity regarding how much you will need from the transfer of your business ownership to achieve your objectives.

- You have a clear picture, so uncertainty becomes confidence, which quickly evolves into excitement about the journey ahead. You can relax and enjoy your life.

POINT OF INTEREST

As you explore your *How Much*, it is important to understand your current and future personal financial position relative to the funds you will need to live your Next Adventure with financial confidence. Take a look at the following three scenarios, and then circle the one that best reflects what you believe to be true for you today.

The Positive/Negative Gap

Negative Gap
(have<need)   ⟶   **Stay and Grow Until Ready Financially.**

Positive Gap
(have>need)   ⟶   **Leave As Soon As Desired.**

I Don't Know.   ⟶   **Find Out!**

CHAPTER TWENTY

THE *HOW:* HOW WILL YOU HARVEST THE VALUE OF YOUR COMPANY?

Every tree, every growing thing as it grows, says this truth,
"You harvest what you sow."

Rumi, 13th-century Persian poet

As you know, there are many ways to transfer a business to a successor: sales of equity or assets, gifts of equity or assets, or some combination of these. Each method, of course, has multiple pros and cons. The wide range of options can easily become a confusing maze for owners who attempt to figure out *How* they will transfer their companies (or which of these methods will work best for them) before they answer the first five questions: *Why, What, Who, When,* and *How Much.* Many owners become so overwhelmed in an attempt to weigh the pros and cons of all these methods that they simply abandon the succession planning project altogether.

Getting stuck—whether due to feelings of confusion, frustration, fear of what might happen or being overwhelmed—is not at all surprising, because owners who begin with the question of *How* have no compass to guide them.

You do.

You have set objectives for yourself, your spouse, family and business (your *Why*). You've identified your most important relationships and the paths you will not take as you honor your Deal Breakers. Based on these choices, you have a picture of where you are going: your Next Adventure.

You have also considered *What* you wish to transfer and how to choose a successor (your *Who*) in a way that is fair to you and to those you care about. You understand you can use your *When* to protect yourself, your family, successor and business. In the prior chapter, we discussed how to calculate *How Much* you will need and want from the business to live the great life you have planned during your Next Adventure.

By establishing your objectives and answering the first five of The Big 6, you have a measure to *assess which transaction method is best for you.* You have established the compass points you will need to guide you through your choice of options, but you will still encounter some difficult choices, or dilemmas. You will have to make choices that will yield some results you want and some you do not. Before we look at each option, please recall Principle 3: No transition is perfect.

Major Transaction Options

Owners face a myriad of transaction options when transferring business interests to a successor, so we created The Transaction Guide (Figure 20.1). This Guide provides owners with a visual and a high-level overview, and it introduces (and opens their mind to) options they may not have considered. But perhaps The Transaction Guide's greatest value is as a tool that you can use to coordinate input from all of your advisors as you ask them to present the pros and cons of the options you want to know more about or think might work for you.

Visit *www.TheSuccessionPlanningBook.com/Tools* for an expanded version of The Transaction Guide.

Our Guide is not designed for separate sit-downs with each one of your advisors (CPA, business advisor, attorney, financial advisor, etc.). That siloed approach will likely result in good advice from each of your advisors, but you will not receive the optimal result of this team's *coordinated* effort: the best advice for you.

Allow us to explain. Asking one advisor at a time which transaction option is best for you is similar to asking several people to describe the wind. All answers are correct—as far as they go. If, on the other hand, you share your objectives with your advisors and ask them to recommend—as a group—the options that best meet your objectives, you will receive the benefit of their joint thinking. We guarantee this approach will save you money, time, aggravation and confusion.

We expect that you work with highly competent advisors, and less-than-optimal advice is not a reflection on their competence. The fact is no advisor—working on

Figure 20.1

The Transaction Guide™

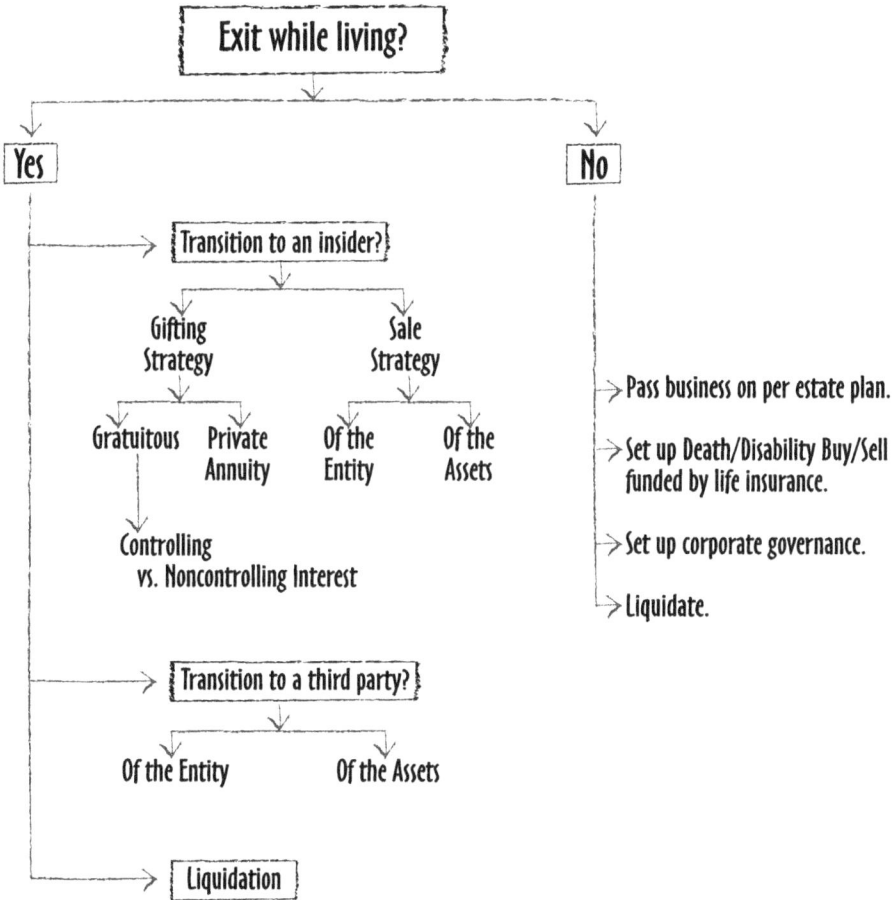

their own—can provide the assessment you seek unless you share with that advisor *all* of the objectives you want to achieve. The second reality is you have a business to run and build, relationships to nurture and enjoy, and activities and hobbies to pursue. Like our clients, you may not want to give up any of these activities to manage a team of advisors. In response, we organize and coordinate the activities of all of an owner's advisors. Our clients continue to make all the critical decisions but do so in the most timely, affordable and emotionally efficient way possible.

Now let's look at each of the major categories of transaction options. After a basic overview of each one, we'll look at how you can determine which options are best for you and your situation.

Transfers To Insiders

When transferring a business to insiders, you have three basic options that can occur at two possible times:

- A one-time sale of your stock, assets or membership interests—during your lifetime or at death.

- A sale over time of stock, assets or membership interests—during your lifetime and/or at death.

- Gifting (total or partial)—during your lifetime and/or at death—to individuals or in trust.

Sales To Third Parties

In third-party sales, parties outside your business and family purchase assets or stock (or membership interests of limited liability companies or partnerships) in arm's-length transactions. Third-party buyers typically prefer to purchase assets (rather than stock or membership interests) because assets do not typically come with prior liabilities.

Liquidation

A liquidation can be conducted via a public sale, private sale or auction.

Each of these three types of transactions involves many moving parts, so how can owners be expected to evaluate all of them and choose the best one? That's a task for you and your expert advisors. Your advisors can help you evaluate your options, but only if they know what your objectives are. Theoretically, all methods are possible, but practically, you will consider only those that achieve your specific objectives. That's the reason we ask owners to establish their objectives long before they consider their *How.*

There Is More At Stake Than Tax Savings

When owners reach the question of *How* and begin to consider their options, many are tempted to evaluate each through a tax lens. Consider "Peter" as a perfect example.

Peter's longtime dream was to turn his truck parts distributing company over to his two sons. Both in their mid-40s, they had worked in the business for years. Peter shared his dream with them before they even came into the company, so the sons were looking forward to becoming business owners.

As do so many owners, Peter first met with his CPA and attorney to ask them which transaction option was the most tax efficient. The CPA and attorney recommended that Peter hang on to ownership and use his estate to pass the business to his sons. They'd receive a step-up in basis—a great tax-saving advantage.

Peter went home after that meeting thrilled that he had a clear path forward. He told his wife, "Sue," what he'd decided to do, proud that he had found an answer to the question that had been nagging at him for months.

Sue looked him straight in the eye and said, "Kiss your grandchildren goodbye. While you are at it, kiss Christmas dinners goodbye and every other holiday we celebrate together." She turned and headed to her garden.

Peter knew all too well that when his wife was upset or angry, she gardened. What he didn't know was why she reacted the way she did to his great news. Peter followed her outside and offered to help her pull some weeds. His offer was met by silence. When he asked Sue what was bothering her, she put down the garden hoe and shook her head.

"You have promised our boys for years that they would own the company. You are now 72 years old and have made not one move in that direction." Peter tried to remind her that he was 73, but Sue continued. "How long do you expect them to wait? How long before they get to be the owners you keep telling them to be? How long do I have to wait to take some of the trips we've put off for years?" Before Peter could point out that he was giving the business to their boys, Sue headed straight for the house.

"Where are you going?" Peter asked.

"I'm going inside to pack. You may not be doing any traveling, but I am. I might as well take the trips you promised we would, since I don't think I'll be seeing the grandkids for a while." Peter was not following her argument, and Sue could tell.

"You have broken your promise to me," she continued. "You are breaking your promise to our sons. When you share your 'good news' with our boys, I don't expect they'll be bringing their kids around any time soon. I wouldn't be at all surprised if they decided to work somewhere else." With that, she slammed the back door and left Peter wondering how his good day had gone bad so quickly.

Luckily, the only person Peter had told about his plan was Sue. He hadn't talked to his sons and had signed no documents. Had he done either, he would have found it extremely difficult to put the genie back in the bottle.

As evening moved in, Peter sat on the patio, thinking about what his wife had said. He had to admit that he'd been so dazzled by the prospect of minimal taxes he had not given adequate attention to the important issues on the other side of the scale. Aside from breaking his promises, if he waited years (and he hoped it would be many!) to transfer his company, his sons would lose some of their prime wealth-building years. He also would lose the opportunity to see the places he had always told Sue they would visit one day.

As Peter turned to head inside, he realized how lucky he was to have two great sons who were ready, willing and able to take over the business. A longtime dream was coming true, and he wasn't about to throw that away for a lower tax bill.

While we have yet to meet one owner who relishes the prospect of paying more taxes than necessary, we have met many who decide a tax bill is less important than three issues that often don't appear on their initial list of objectives: minimize their risk, lower their stress level and enable their successors to "live like owners."

Risk Tolerance

As long as you own even part of your company, your assets are at risk. If a guy on one of your roofing crews slips and falls—even though he failed to follow safety protocols—you and/or your company could be held liable. If a customer slips in your parking lot or store, you could spend thousands on attorneys' fees and even more for a settlement or judgment. If a former employee discloses one of your critical product formulas to a competitor, you could lose millions of dollars in sales.

At the point in their lives when owners have a lot to lose, most simply aren't willing to put all they've worked for at risk. Risk tolerance is an important factor, for example, when owners weigh the benefits of a transfer at death (often a favorable option from the standpoint of tax minimization) against a transfer during their lifetimes.

Stress Level

Let's face it: there's a certain level of stress in owning a business. As owners, we have customer pipelines to fill, payrolls to meet and customers to satisfy. We wake up every day to an ever-changing competitive environment, evolving governmental regulations, and curveballs that we don't expect. As a result, many owners recognize the strain that stress puts on them and their families, so they include stress as a factor as they assess various transaction options.

Successor Lifestyle

When owners weigh various transfer options, they do well to take their successor's lifestyle into consideration—especially when their successor is one of their children. For example, the salary that owners anticipate paying their successors for the work they do in the business (while owners hold on to ownership) may not enable successors to live a lifestyle that is equivalent to the one the owners lived at the same point in their careers. Peter figured his plan to give his business to his sons at his death would be great for them (minimal taxes and no requirement to buy equity) and great for Sue and himself (no need to dip into their savings to support themselves during retirement). Well, Pete's sons, who both made a good salary every year, were not able to buy their own homes. Their mother paid her grandchildren's private school tuition and financed the minivans needed to transport them. Emotionally, their sons didn't feel like owners. That's not surprising, because they didn't live like business owners; in fact, they couldn't even afford to live in neighborhoods with business owners or socialize with them.

If you haven't included risk, stress and your successor's lifestyle in your calculations, it may be time to add these factors (and possibly others) to your Objectives Matrix. While no one has a crystal ball, you will have to choose a transaction option that balances the level of risk and stress you are willing to tolerate and how you want your successors to live, against other objectives such as tax minimization. Unlike owners who have not established their objectives, however, you have the means to find the balance that works best for you.

THE FOUR PAYMENT FACETS OF YOUR *How*

As you evaluate your transaction options, remember there are four issues related to payment that will likely affect your ultimate choice:

1. Time Frame: Over what time period do you want to receive payment for the value of your company?

2. Amount of Payment: How much do you want to be paid for your equity?

3. Form of Payment: In what form do you want payment?

4. Security: What level of assurance do you need that you will receive payment?

Time Frame

Transfers of ownership can occur all at once or in stages over a period of time. In both scenarios, owners must determine the point at which they will depart. Depending on their objectives, owners may choose to leave as soon as their successors are capable of leadership and have purchased more than 50 percent of the equity, or they may stay involved with their companies for some period of time.

Those owners who choose to stay involved for a period of time must work with their successors to determine the terms of that involvement and the length of that period. For example, will your continued involvement depend on how well the business is operating, or will you set an end date for your involvement regardless of how your business performs under your successor's leadership?

Amount Of Payment

It's natural for successors—particularly if they have been involved in the business for some time—to feel some degree of "ownership." If successors believe that they have contributed to the growth of the company for years, they may assume you will sell the company to them for a discount and/or with no cash up front. You, on the other hand, may want to be compensated for the efforts you've invested to grow a successful company and for the risks you have taken over the years.

Parents "Gloria" and "Philip" were no different: They wanted to be compensated fairly for their investment. Their daughter, "Angela," wanted to compensate her parents fairly and wanted to be recognized (compensated) for her contribution to the value of the company.

G*loria and Philip worked hard for 30 years to grow their manufacturing business into a healthy, vital company. Now in their late 50s, they wanted to work fewer hours and harvest some of the cash flow they'd been reinvesting into the company for years.*

For the past 10 years, their daughter, Angela, had learned the ropes, assumed greater responsibilities and had steepened the company's growth trajectory. Sensing that her parents were ready to move away from their 60-hour weeks and spend more time enjoying themselves, Angela decided to make them an offer. She lined up financing and prepared to start living her dream of owning her own company.

When Angela put together her offer, she took into account both the company's fair market value and her contribution to that value. When she proudly presented her offer to her parents, she was stunned by their reaction. Gloria and Philip were offended because they believed that their business was worth far more than Angela did. They were upset because they felt that she was trying to "steal" it from them.

Angela readily acknowledged that the company was worth more than she had offered, and she believed that her parents should just as readily acknowledge the contribution she had made to that value.

In addition, Gloria and Philip found fault with Angela's terms. First, Angela had "put them out to pasture" far sooner than they wanted. Second, because Angela secured the financing necessary to pay them in one lump sum rather than paying them for equity in stages, Gloria and Philip felt robbed. They had imagined that they would sell equity to Angela in segments so they could receive dividends over years. These dividends would provide them with the funds they would need to finance some of the "goodies" (vacations and toys) they wanted in their retirement.

Angela's offer failed to meet three of the four elements of her parents' How: timing, amount of payment and form of payment.

While Angela may have jumped the gun by making an offer before discussing her desires with her parents, Gloria and Phillip were too slow off the starting block. Had all three communicated their expectations and desires, they could have spared themselves unnecessary hard feelings and family stress.

As you may know (and as Gloria and Philip experienced), strong feelings and unfounded assumptions on either side can easily evolve into misunderstandings that irreparably damage relationships. You can minimize misunderstandings and the possibility of damaged relationships by communicating! If you are uncertain about how to begin, flip back to Chapter Five for some helpful hints about how to broach sensitive topics with successors.

Form Of Payment

Financing

Most successors are not able to pay for 100 percent of the equity/assets they are purchasing, so they secure outside financing from banks (as Angela did) or ask owners to carry promissory notes.

Before deciding whether to finance your successor's purchase of your equity, ask your advisors (CPA, financial planner, business advisor, tax attorney, etc.) as a group to help you assess the pros and cons of carrying a note. Assess the risk that your successor may not be able to pay the note, your willingness to use collateral to collect on an unpaid note, as well as whether entering a lender/borrower arrangement will affect the relationship you have with your successor. Depending on your analysis and the amount of time before your successor purchases your equity, you may be able to create a Roadmap that gives your successor time to secure outside financing. Owners who have long enough runways and the ability to shift a business's dependence from their shoulders to their successors' can transfer a minority interest to a successor so that lenders and advisors can develop confidence in the successor's ability to perform. Before you make a decision about financing, it is critical to take all of these factors into consideration and weigh them in light of your objectives.

Gifting

Gifting to successors is one strategy parents use to pass businesses to family members if that strategy is consistent with the parents' objectives. Again, you and your advisors will discuss your objectives, consider your time frame preferences and investigate whether you have the financial ability to give away the business *and* live the Next Adventure you anticipate. With all that information, you are able to assess whether the gifting option is the best one for you.

Security

An owner's choice of successor can be heavily influenced by how likely and/or how able that successor is—or will be—to pay the full purchase price. Is one successor more likely to default than another? If a successor defaults, are you willing to take the company back?

Security is typically an issue your attorney will spend a lot of time on in your purchase/sale agreement, so it needs to be planned out in light of your Objectives Matrix.

THE OPTIONS MATRIX™

As you can see from The Transaction Guide (Figure 20.1), you have numerous transaction options, but as you assess them in light of your objectives, several will rise to the top of your list. The tool we developed to help owners determine which of their top options satisfy the greatest number of objectives is The Options Matrix.

Figure 20.2 is a sample of an Options Matrix that one owner ("Joy") completed after reviewing her options with her advisors using The Transaction Guide. She decided that she wanted to exit while living and ruled out liquidation.

The Options Matrix should look a bit familiar to you since it takes The Objectives Matrix that you worked on in chapters Thirteen and Fourteen and expands it by several columns.

The first column to the right of the Deal Breaker column is the status quo which is always an option, even if it's not a good one. Taking no action is a road, but it is a road with a dead end.

The end of the road might be an owner's death, but it could also be the death of a business that an owner could reinvent but chooses not to. For example, think of the owner of the company that operated the ferries that crossed the Golden Gate Strait in the early 20th century. As he watched the construction of the Golden Gate Bridge, did he take steps to reinvent his business or did he maintain the status quo? We don't know, but the fact is, he had a choice.

In the far-right column is always the option to sell to a third party. Again, this may not be your first choice, but if The Options Matrix indicates that a third-party sale would accomplish most, or nearly all, of your objectives, you may choose to adjust course. For example, if an owner indicates that they prefer to transfer their company to their children, but a sale to a third party would accomplish all of their objectives except that one, they may choose to sell to that third party and give each child the funds necessary to start their own companies.

Between the columns titled "Status Quo" and "Sell to Third Party" are multiple variations of the transaction option (i.e., transition to an insider, a third party or liquidation) that an owner has chosen. In Figure 20.2 you can see that owner Joy has chosen to transition her business to insiders, in her case, to her sons "Ezra" and "Kaz."

Figure 20.2

The Options Matrix™

Owner/Entity	Objectives	Deal Breaker	Options Under Consideration				
Organize objectives by person or entity. Start with yourself because your objectives are critical. Add segments as needed.	List the objectives you want to achieve in the present or future.	Mark with an "x" the objectives that are non-negotiable.	Status Quo	Gift Kids 50/50	Gift Ezra 60/Kaz 40	Gift kids 40/40 with Ezra buying 20	Sell to Third Party
Joy	I am out of the day-to-day tasks but am still involved and engaged in the business.		red	green	green	green	yellow
	My net worth is $9 million, and the portfolio continues to grow.	X	green	yellow	yellow	green	green
My Spouse, Darrin	Darrin continues to enjoy his retirement – boating and working in his woodshop.		blue	blue	green	blue	blue
Us	We have gained free time to enjoy our mountain home for 3–4 months each year.		yellow	green	green	green	yellow
Our Family	I am fair to all of my children.	X	green	green	green	yellow	yellow
	Our family is happy together.	X	green	yellow	yellow	green	green
	The kids and their families continue to join us at the mountain house every summer.		green	green	green	green	green
	Darrin and I are a part of our grandchildren's lives by attending school and sports activities.		green	green	green	green	green
My Partners	I have made the kids partners in the business.		red	green	green	green	red
Employees/ Successors	The kids and I are having fun in the business.	X	red	green	green	green	red
	The employees are a part of the business's success and continue to give back to the community.		green	green	green	green	yellow
The Business	I have optimized taxes.		yellow	green	green	green	green
	The business continues to be a great asset to the community.	X	green	green	green	green	yellow

Options Matrix Key: Achieves Objective [green] | Objective Is at Risk [yellow] | Does Not Achieve Objective [red] | Objective Not Affected by Option [blue]

She uses her Options Matrix to compare several ways she might make that transition: 1) an equal gift to both children; 2) a gift of 60 percent to Ezra and 40 percent to Kaz; and 3) a combination of gift and sale.

Joy looked at each of her objectives and determined whether:

- Each transaction option achieved the objective.
- Each transaction option put the objective at risk,
- Each transaction option failed to achieve the objective.
- Meeting the objective was not affected by the transaction option.

Joy used green to indicate the objectives she believed were achievable, yellow for those objectives she believed were at risk, red for objectives that she believed could not be attained, and blue for those that could be achieved regardless of which path she chose.

Notice that we use the word "believed." We do so because what you believe to be true might—upon further probing and some creative thinking—not be true at all. It's our job to understand why owners assign the colors they do to each box and then question whether each is accurate.

In Figure 20.2 you can see that Joy believes that if she gives each of her children equal shares of the company, she will achieve as many of her objectives as she will by giving her children a smaller proportion of equal shares but having one child (Ezra) purchase ownership. A sale to a third party would put six of Joy's objectives at risk and fail to achieve two, while maintaining the status quo would put three objectives at risk and fail to achieve three. Perhaps most importantly, both the status quo and third-party options would fail to achieve one of Joy's Deal Breakers (having fun with her sons in the business).

Your Options Matrix enables you to zoom out to see a snapshot of how the scenarios you are considering compare to one another *and to your objectives.* A quick glance at the color blocks shows you which options are worth exploring further with your advisors. It shows your advisors how well various options match up with your objectives. Finally, your Options Matrix is visual evidence (for your successor and anyone else you show it to) that the option you will choose is not a whim or a default position; rather, it is the result of rigorous evaluation.

Earlier we asked you to answer the question *Why*, because your answers (the objectives now listed on your Options Matrix), as well as your spouse's and of anyone else, set the standard by which all options are measured.

With this assessment of your *How*, you have answered all of your Big 6 questions. The points on your Compass are set for the journey ahead, and it is now time to create your Transition Roadmap.

If you do not have a means to assess how various transaction options achieve your objectives:

- You can become so overwhelmed by the pros and cons of multiple methods that you abandon the transition planning project altogether. You waste time, money and energy on false starts and do-overs.

- You may choose a method that jeopardizes your most important relationships or your ability to meet your objectives.

- You can become so focused on one objective (for example, tax minimization) that you choose a transaction option that fails to honor your other objectives.

If you use a standard (your objectives) to evaluate your transaction options:

- You gain a clear picture of which transaction option is best for you, your spouse and those you will invite into your journey.

- You assign proper importance to your life's work and accomplishments, and you honor your financial future, your company's and your successor's.

- You may uncover objectives and Deal Breakers that you had not initially recognized and validate others.

POINT OF INTEREST

Create your own Transaction Guide by circling the possible pathways that you desire and/or that may make sense in light of your situation and objectives.

This is a first step in choosing a *How*. Once you have considered your best path, you can bring your Options Matrix into a discussion with your Cabinet of Advisors (see Chapter Twenty-Six) about the options that may work best for your particular *Why, What, Who, When* and *How Much*.

The Transaction Guide™

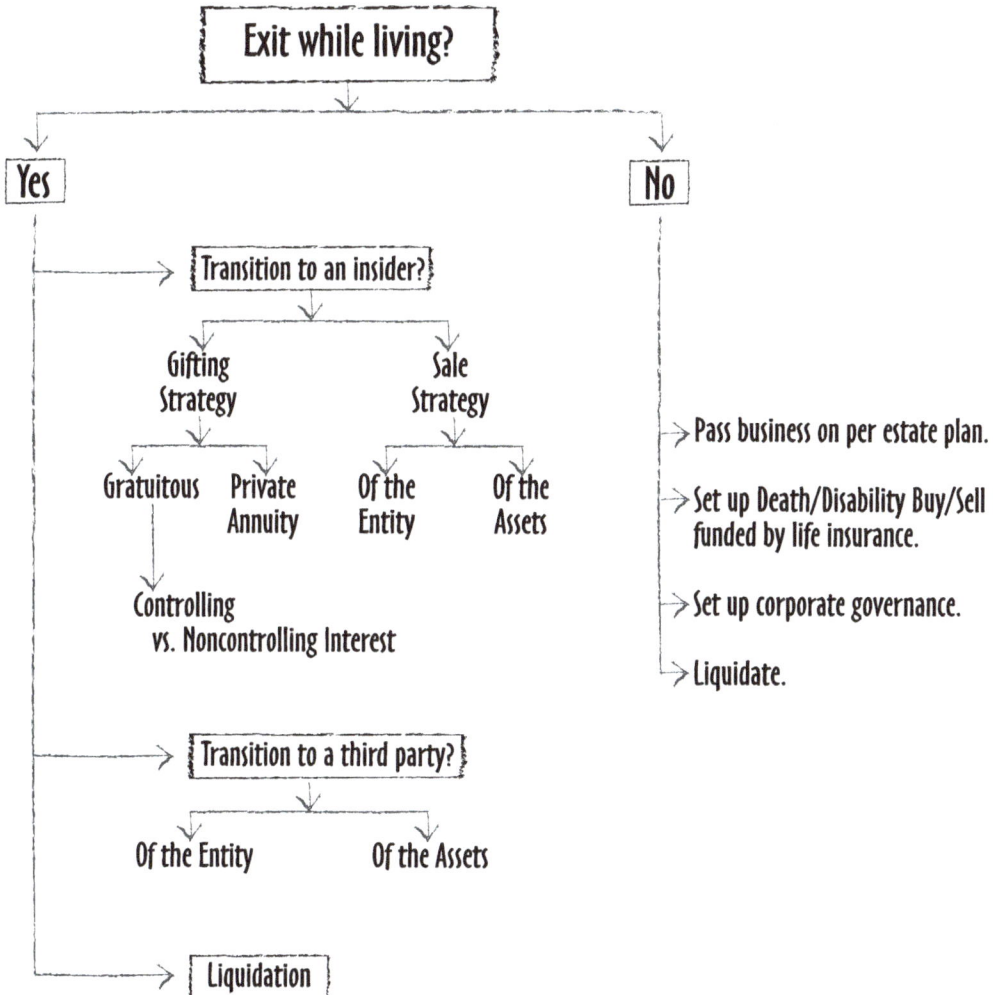

Exit while living?

Yes

→ **Transition to an insider?**

Gifting Strategy — Sale Strategy

Gratuitous — Private Annuity — Of the Entity — Of the Assets

Controlling vs. Noncontrolling Interest

→ **Transition to a third party?**

Of the Entity — Of the Assets

→ **Liquidation**

No

→ Pass business on per estate plan.

→ Set up Death/Disability Buy/Sell funded by life insurance.

→ Set up corporate governance.

→ Liquidate.

CHAPTER TWENTY-ONE

IT'S TIME TO TALK TURKEY

Show me the money!

Jerry Maguire, Fictional sports agent

Now that you have a framework for answering *How* and *How Much*, we turn for a moment to the nuts and bolts of getting paid for your business. The term "nuts and bolts" does not do the topic of getting paid justice. After all, part of the reason you put a lifetime of effort into your company is to reap a healthy return.

You are well aware that excess cash flow has funded your company's growth. Excess cash flow also plays a huge role in the success of your business transition journey. It supports your successor's salary and the continued growth of your company once you leave it. If your successor finances the purchase of your equity, excess cash flow must also support your successor's obligation to you or to the financing institution.

If you haven't already answered the following two questions about your company's cash flow, now is the ideal time to do so.

1. Are your personal financial assets and your company's cash flow strong enough to support the transition plan you have created?

2. Based on your company's cash flow, how and over what amount of time will the incoming owners buy, earn and/or work their way into full ownership?

The answer to the question of whether your financial position and the company's ability to generate cash flow are sufficient to support the transition plan you have described depends on:

- Whether your Next Adventure can be financed by the amount of personal assets you have and the proceeds from the sale of your equity.

- The financial resources your successor brings to the table.

- Your successor's financial expectations.

- Whether the company must grow to support your successor's salary and the purchase of your equity (either directly from you or via a bank loan).

The answers to the questions of how and how long your successors will pay you depend on:

- The amount of financial resources that your successors can bring to the table.

- The number of successors.

- Your company's level of excess cash flow.

We take all of these factors into consideration as we calculate whether you can achieve your *How Much* number. Perhaps you will have to adjust your plan by staying in your business longer than you had anticipated. Perhaps you will pivot to your Plan B.

Plan B

If you find that you cannot achieve all of your objectives—especially your financial objectives—you are not alone. Not all of the owners we work with get all the answers they want. Sometimes their successors cannot pay the price owners put on the business. In those cases, we pause and regroup. In doing so, some owners, like "Chuck and Debby Fuller," find that there's hidden gold in options they did not consider.

Chuck and Debby Fuller were in their mid-50s and enjoyed a very comfortable lifestyle thanks to the healthy and steady cash flow from their business. They didn't have very much in savings, so they were counting on the proceeds from the sale of their company and ongoing income from the business to continue living their lifestyle.

After helping them to prepare their Objective Matrices and evaluating their financial resources, we learned that unless they received a premium price for their business, they did not have the assets necessary to support their Next Adventure. We also learned that the success of their business depended on the knowledge in Chuck's head rather than on a management team and well-documented processes. This fact substantially lowered the value of their company.

The work the couple had put into answering their Big 6 questions did not deliver the outcome they desired, but it did yield clarity about their financial readiness to turn over ownership of their company. The Fullers made the decision to put a hard stop to their journey and consider their options.

Since they didn't have the assets they thought they had, the Fullers decided to dedicate themselves full-time to shoring up their personal finances and improving their business for a future transition. They grabbed the opportunity to build the skills of their management team and to put in place operational processes and procedures. They began to act based on reliable financial data. Through the execution of their Transition Roadmap, the Fullers became financially prepared and business ready.

If you overlook the importance of cash flow in whether and how much you will get paid:

- You may go too far in the wrong direction, investing time and money in a plan that takes you down the wrong road.

- You may have to take the company back if your successor is unable to pay you the full purchase price.

- Your team and customers could lose confidence in you as they watch you hit roadblocks.

If you assess how you will get paid and you must pivot to your Plan B:

- The outcome of the great work outlined in this book so far provides the foundation for this challenging and exciting part of your journey.

- You are closer to realizing four major objectives: keeping your relationships healthy, bringing others into your journey, harvesting your investment, and using proceeds to live your Next Adventure.

- You have established realistic goals and expectations related to cash flow.

Three quick questions for you to consider here:

1. Are your personal financial assets strong enough to support the transition strategy you have created?

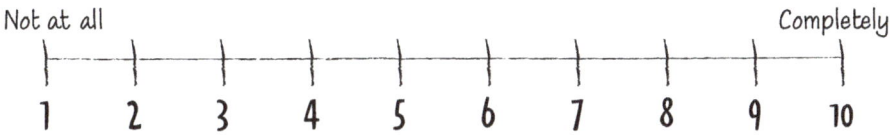

Not at all   Completely

| | | | | | | | | |
1   2   3   4   5   6   7   8   9   10

2. Is your company's cash flow strong enough to suppport the transition strategy you have created?

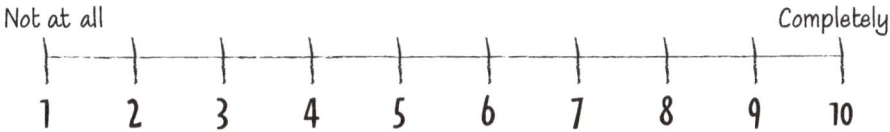

Not at all   Completely

| | | | | | | | | |
1   2   3   4   5   6   7   8   9   10

Your answers may be "I have no idea." (And that's okay.)

3. Regardless of whether your successor has to finance the purchase of your equity or you carry a portion of the note, how quickly do you want to be fully paid?

_____within 3 years?

_____between 3 and 5 years?

_____between 5 and 10 years?

_____within 10 years?

The Transition Roadmap Developer Process Overview™

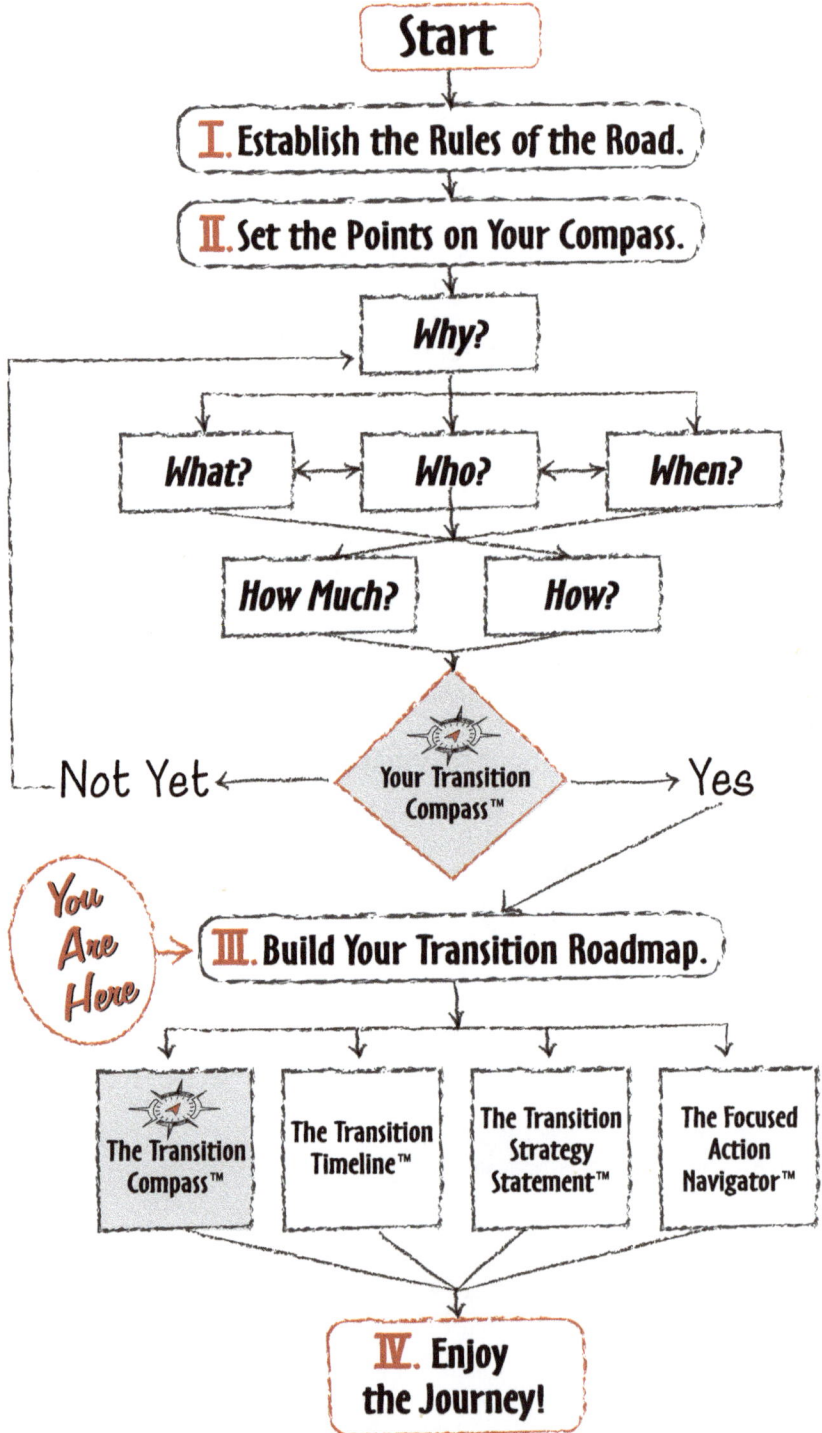

Start

I. Establish the Rules of the Road.

II. Set the Points on Your Compass.

Why?

What? — **Who?** — **When?**

How Much?   **How?**

Your Transition Compass™

Not Yet ←   → Yes

You Are Here →

III. Build Your Transition Roadmap.

| The Transition Compass™ | The Transition Timeline™ | The Transition Strategy Statement™ | The Focused Action Navigator™ |

IV. Enjoy the Journey!

SECTION III

Build Your Transition Roadmap

Congratulations! You have set the points on your Transition Compass: your *Why, What, Who, When, How Much* and *How*. You have untangled any issues you did not know how to organize. In addition, you have resolved any dilemmas that you suspected were impossible to handle. You have resolved dilemmas in a way that satisfies you and everyone you care about and that supports the business you have built.

Now the fun really begins. You will create your actionable Roadmap complete with:

1. An itinerary of milestones, including the dates by which you will reach them.

2. An inspiring summary of the goals you expect to achieve during and at the end of your journey.

3. A complete list of the actions necessary to move you from being an owner who has planned a transition to one who has successfully accomplished one.

We hope you can see how what once felt overwhelming has become a win-win-win-win-win situation:

Win 1: The succession plan you envision puts a premium on the relationships that matter most to you so that you will retain them as you move into your Next Adventure.

Win 2: Your plan will launch you into your Next Adventure.

Win 3: As your successor assumes greater responsibility, they will move toward their dream of owning and leading a successful business.

Win 4: Not only will your business be able to financially support your transition, but you have also positioned it to succeed after you leave and well into the future.

Win 5: Your customers will continue to receive the great experience/products/service they have come to expect from your company.

CHAPTER TWENTY-TWO

ELEMENT 1 OF THE TRANSITION ROADMAP: THE TRANSITION COMPASS™

Maps are living, breathing organisms that change on a daily basis...
Noam Bardin, CEO/Co-Founder of Waze, Inc.

A ll of the work you have done establishing your Compass points—*Why, What, Who, When, How* and *How Much*—is the foundation for your Transition Roadmap. With your destination set, or nearly so, your Transition Roadmap charts the route from where you are today to your Next Adventure.

Your Roadmap is made up of four documented components:

1. The Transition Compass

2. The Transition Timeline

3. The Transition Strategy Statement

4. The Focused Action Navigator

These four components enable you to communicate your transition plan to others and execute it with clarity and confidence. In a process with multiple moving pieces, your Roadmap keeps you (and the other people involved in your transition) focused on your priorities and your destination. It demonstrates your care for others, provides mile markers on the road to your destination and shows everyone the distance yet to be traveled.

All four elements of a Transition Roadmap adapt to change. If, for example, a successor needs more time to acquire a skill, we expand the Timeline. If there's a fundamental shift—like a significant change in business value—we adjust the *How Much*. If an owner marries or loses a spouse, parts of the owner's *Why* are likely to change.

Before You Get Started

We encourage you to be thoughtful and thorough as you think about how to integrate all the work you've done so far. We also encourage you to have some fun with this project! You are creating the Roadmap that takes you from successful business owner to successful Next Adventurer, while honoring all the people and things that are important to you. We hope you will bring the same excitement to creating your Transition Roadmap that you did to creating your first business. We know your Roadmap will give you confidence as you move forward, and freedom from the wondering and worrying you did before you had one.

> *We encourage you to enjoy creating your Roadmap. It's exciting planning your journey from successful business owner to flourishing Next Adventurer.*

The Transition Compass

The first element of a Transition Roadmap is your Transition Compass. As you'll recall from Chapter Twelve, a Transition Compass is made up of six points, or your answers to The Big 6 questions: *Why, What, Who, When, How Much* and *How*. (We addressed each of these questions in detail in Section II.) While it is important to set as best you can all six points as you initially create your Transition Compass, know that any points you were unsure of at first become clearer and some may change as you move through your Transition Roadmap Process. It is not at all unusual to adjust your answers as you explore your options in greater detail, gather new information, or encounter new obstacles and opportunities. What is important is that all of your answers work together.

In Figure 22.1 you'll see fictional owner Joy's answers only to the first question (*Why*) on her Transition Compass. These answers are her objectives for herself, others and her business, and she's indicated which objectives are Deal Breakers for her.

Joy's Transition Compass continues with her answers to the second question, *What* (Figure 22.2).

Once your Compass includes all of your answers to The Big 6 Questions (not just the Why and What that we've shown here) the first element of your Transition Roadmap is complete.

Figure 22.1

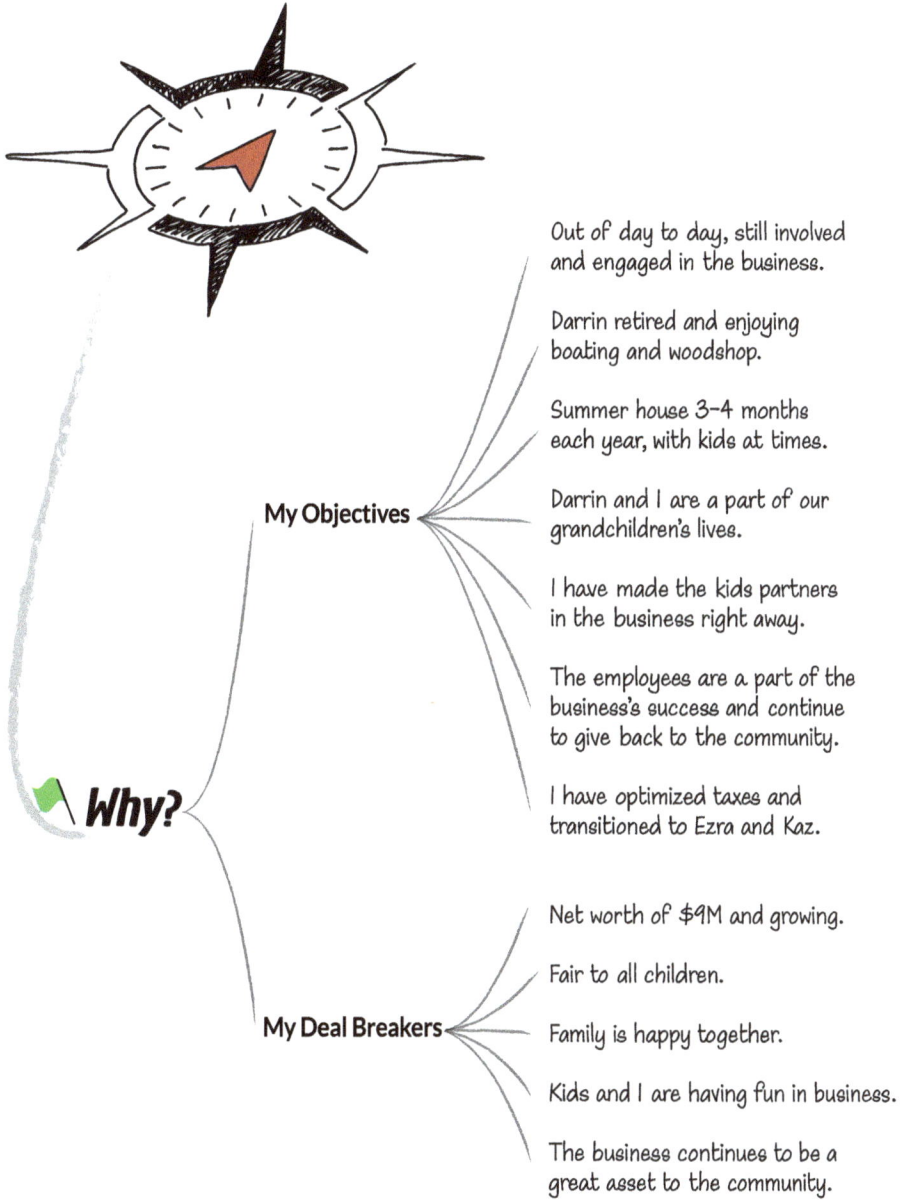

My Objectives

Out of day to day, still involved and engaged in the business.

Darrin retired and enjoying boating and woodshop.

Summer house 3–4 months each year, with kids at times.

Darrin and I are a part of our grandchildren's lives.

I have made the kids partners in the business right away.

The employees are a part of the business's success and continue to give back to the community.

I have optimized taxes and transitioned to Ezra and Kaz.

My Deal Breakers

Net worth of $9M and growing.

Fair to all children.

Family is happy together.

Kids and I are having fun in business.

The business continues to be a great asset to the community.

Why?

Figure 22.2

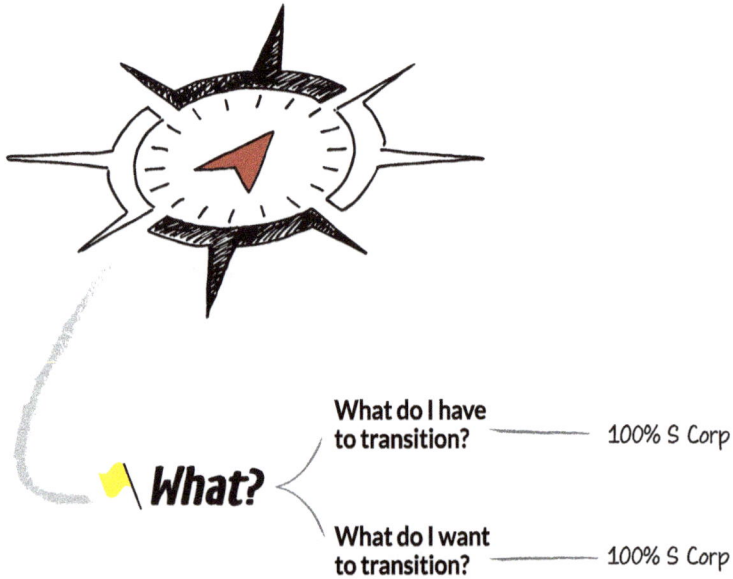

What?

What do I have to transition? —— 100% S Corp

What do I want to transition? —— 100% S Corp

Figure 22.3 is Joy's completed Transition Compass. As you can see, it shows her answers to The Big 6 Questions.

We create Transition Compasses that are unique to each owner. This format enables owners to view how they have populated each question and each sub-question. A Transition Compass is invaluable: When you lose your way in a host of decisions, opinions and options, your Compass provides an objective reference point to keep you headed in the direction you want to go.

Figure 22.3

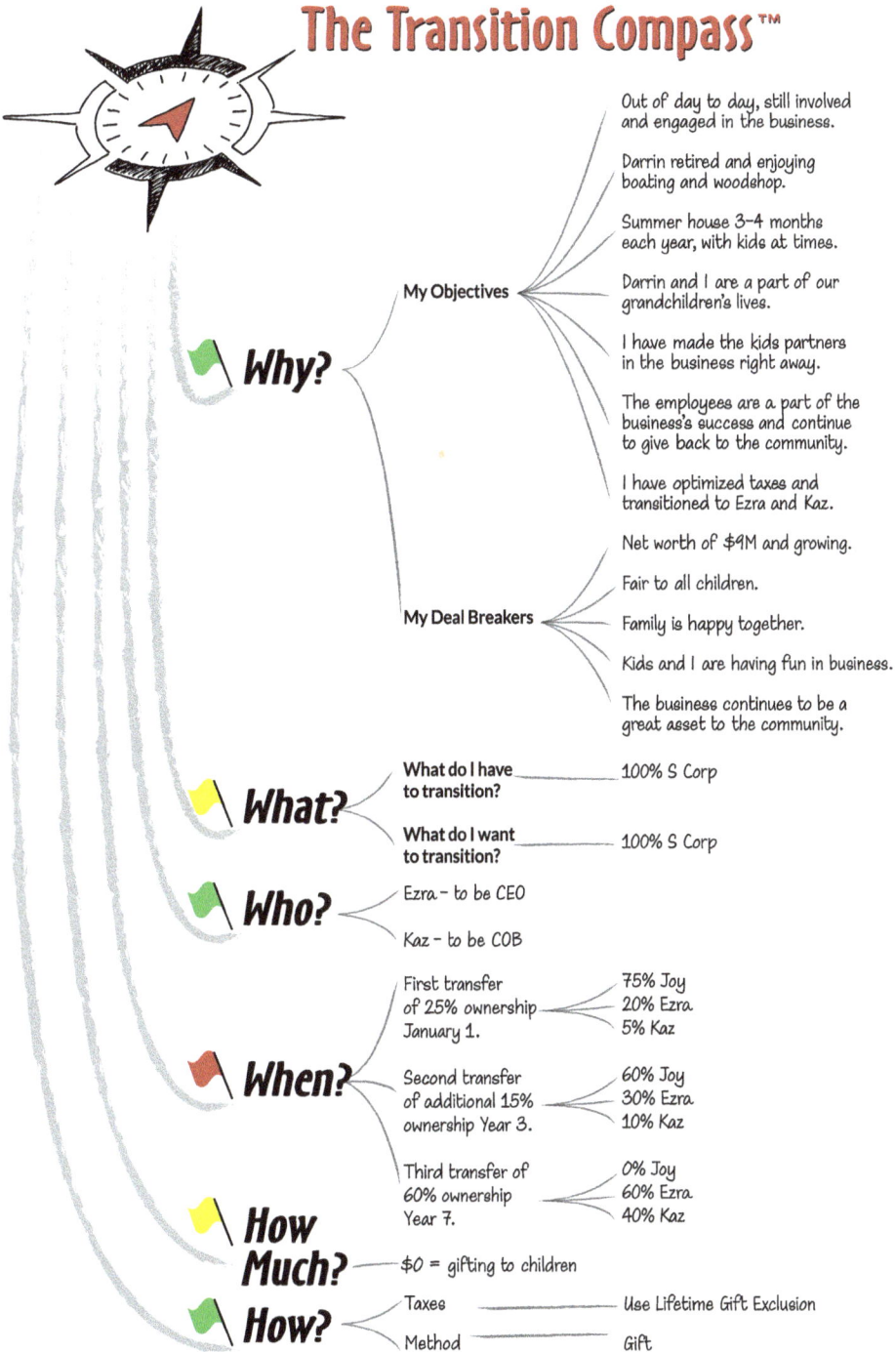

The Transition Compass™

Why?

My Objectives
- Out of day to day, still involved and engaged in the business.
- Darrin retired and enjoying boating and woodshop.
- Summer house 3-4 months each year, with kids at times.
- Darrin and I are a part of our grandchildren's lives.
- I have made the kids partners in the business right away.
- The employees are a part of the business's success and continue to give back to the community.
- I have optimized taxes and transitioned to Ezra and Kaz.

My Deal Breakers
- Net worth of $9M and growing.
- Fair to all children.
- Family is happy together.
- Kids and I are having fun in business.
- The business continues to be a great asset to the community.

What?
- What do I have to transition? — 100% S Corp
- What do I want to transition? — 100% S Corp

Who?
- Ezra – to be CEO
- Kaz – to be COB

When?
- First transfer of 25% ownership January 1.
  - 75% Joy
  - 20% Ezra
  - 5% Kaz
- Second transfer of additional 15% ownership Year 3.
  - 60% Joy
  - 30% Ezra
  - 10% Kaz
- Third transfer of 60% ownership Year 7.
  - 0% Joy
  - 60% Ezra
  - 40% Kaz

How Much?
- $0 = gifting to children

How?
- Taxes — Use Lifetime Gift Exclusion
- Method — Gift

POINT OF INTEREST

On "My Transition Compass," insert your thoughts about each of The Big 6 questions. (This form is available at *www.TheSucessionPlanningBook.com/Tools*.) You can summarize your *Why* per your Objectives Matrix. You'll see that we've left space for both the beginning and completion of your transfer of equity. If you want to transfer your equity in one lump sum, the dates in those spaces would be identical. Again, circle the flags that reflect your confidence level.

- A green flag means you already know the answer or are as confident as you can be at this point.

- A yellow flag indicates you are fairly certain about your answer.

- A red flag indicates you don't yet know the answer.

You might go back to look at The Transition Compass ratings you chose when responding to the Point of Interest exercise in Chapter Twelve. After thinking more deeply about your transition, have you changed the color of any flags?

It is very much the norm to not have all the answers to The Big 6 nailed down at this point. If that's the case for you, please write down your thoughts related to any unanswered questions at this stage of the process.

Your journey will include validating, verifying, exploring, and ultimately answering your Big 6.

My Transition Compass™

Why?
- My Objectives _____
- My Deal Breakers _____

What?
- What do I have to transition? _____
- What do I want to transition? _____

Who? _____

When?
- Begin transfer of equity _____
- Complete transfer of equity _____

How Much?
- How much do I need? _____
- How much do I want? _____

How?
- Taxes _____
- Payment _____
- Method _____

CHAPTER TWENTY-THREE

ELEMENT 2 OF THE TRANSITION ROADMAP: THE TRANSITION TIMELINE™

The best thing about the future is that it comes one day at a time.

Abraham Lincoln, 16th president of the United States

A Transition Timeline is a graphic representation of milestones that must be reached in order to transfer control of a business from owner to successor.

Note: We use the term "Transition Timeline" to refer to a collection of "sub-timelines" that relate to: 1) equity, 2) the individuals involved in the transition, and 3) the business itself.

By noting on The Transition Timeline the critical steps on the transition journey, owners clearly set and communicate their expectations, let successors know what they are committing to, and ensure everyone involved understands how much time they have to complete each project. Because your Transition Timeline organizes and keeps track of the critical steps on your journey, it shows you whether the deadlines you have set are achievable. Finally, creating a Transition Timeline makes all the work you have done so far very, very real.

The Transfer Of Control

A Transition Timeline illustrates how ownership and leadership of a business will transfer from owner to successor. Your Timeline might mark the date you will initially turn over responsibilities for day-to-day operations and the date your successor will have learned enough about operations to assume the role of CEO. While your successor is learning, you might take steps to create a board of directors (if you do not already have one in place). In that case, your individual sub-timeline would show the date you will become the chairman of the board. Once your successor demonstrates their ability to handle operations, you might turn over control of cash flow. At the same time you may plan to transfer portions of your equity but maintain majority control until your successor pays for that equity. If so, your equity sub-timeline will indicate when you will transfer various amounts of equity.

Set And Communicate Your Expectations

When you share your Transition Timeline with your successor and others who are with you on this journey, you show them what you want to happen, over what time period and how each task will be accomplished. With this information they can see what you expect of them and of yourself, and everyone can make informed commitments to the Timeline as a team.

Without a Transition Timeline that clearly communicates expectations in writing, owners can inadvertently initiate downward spirals of repeated disappointment. Let's say that owner Raquel expects successor Lola to manage human resources. Lola doesn't know that Raquel expects her to gain that knowledge within a certain time frame and fails to achieve Raquel's objective. Raquel interprets Lola's "failure" as a lack of engagement or skill when, in reality, Lola never knew exactly what Raquel expected of her. Raquel begins to doubt that Lola can "do the job," so Raquel takes over HR once again. When she does, Lola loses confidence in herself, and Raquel loses the opportunity to teach Lola a skill she needs to know to succeed. When this spiral continues, owners end up with successors who disappoint them, an outcome that is not the fault of the successors but of the owners who never communicated their expectations.

Of course, every person in your journey may not meet every one of your deadlines and expectations, because no transition is perfect! Despite that imperfection, the very existence of a Transition Timeline increases the odds of success for everyone involved.

Predictor Of Future Events

Transition Timelines take time and effort to create, but they are hugely valuable because they identify, in graphic detail, points where tasks and events are in sync and points at which they are not. For example, an individual's sub-timeline may make it obvious that it is *entirely possible* to teach a successor all the skills necessary to assume control of a business by the date on which the owner wants to leave. On the other hand, it may illustrate that *just the opposite is true.*

This predictive quality of a Transition Timeline is critical because it gives owners the opportunity to have conversations with others about possible solutions to problems the Timeline may reveal. These conversations are based on an understanding of the desired results. Keeping these conversations focused on those results helps to keep everyone aligned as you tackle any problems.

MARKERS ON THE TRANSITION TIMELINE

Two Endpoints

A Transition Timeline begins on the day an owner creates it and ends when they decide it should. The end of your Timeline might be the day you begin your Next Adventure. It might be the day you choose not to work in the business, or it may be your dying day. Your Transition Timeline is unique to you, but most that we design for owners extend from three to ten years.

The Timeline we created for our fictional owner "Joy" and her company "BizCo" covers a seven-year time frame (see Figure 23.1). As you may recall, she plans to transfer her equity to her two sons, Ezra and Kaz. Ezra is currently active in the business and will become the company's CEO when Joy steps down in Year 2 of her transition. Kaz is not active in the business but will join the company's board of directors when it is formed and become its chairman in Year 3.

Joy loves working with her sons, however, so she plans to remain in the business until she chooses to do something else, as indicated by the angel at the end of the business sub-timeline.

Milestones

In Figure 23.1, you see several items marked with red diamonds (e.g., Joy, Ezra and Kaz becoming members of the board of directors). Those items are milestones. Milestones mark a start date or end date for accomplishing critical steps involved in turning over a business to a successor. You will establish milestones for your business, the individuals involved (you and your successor, at a minimum) and the transfer of equity.

Figure 23.1

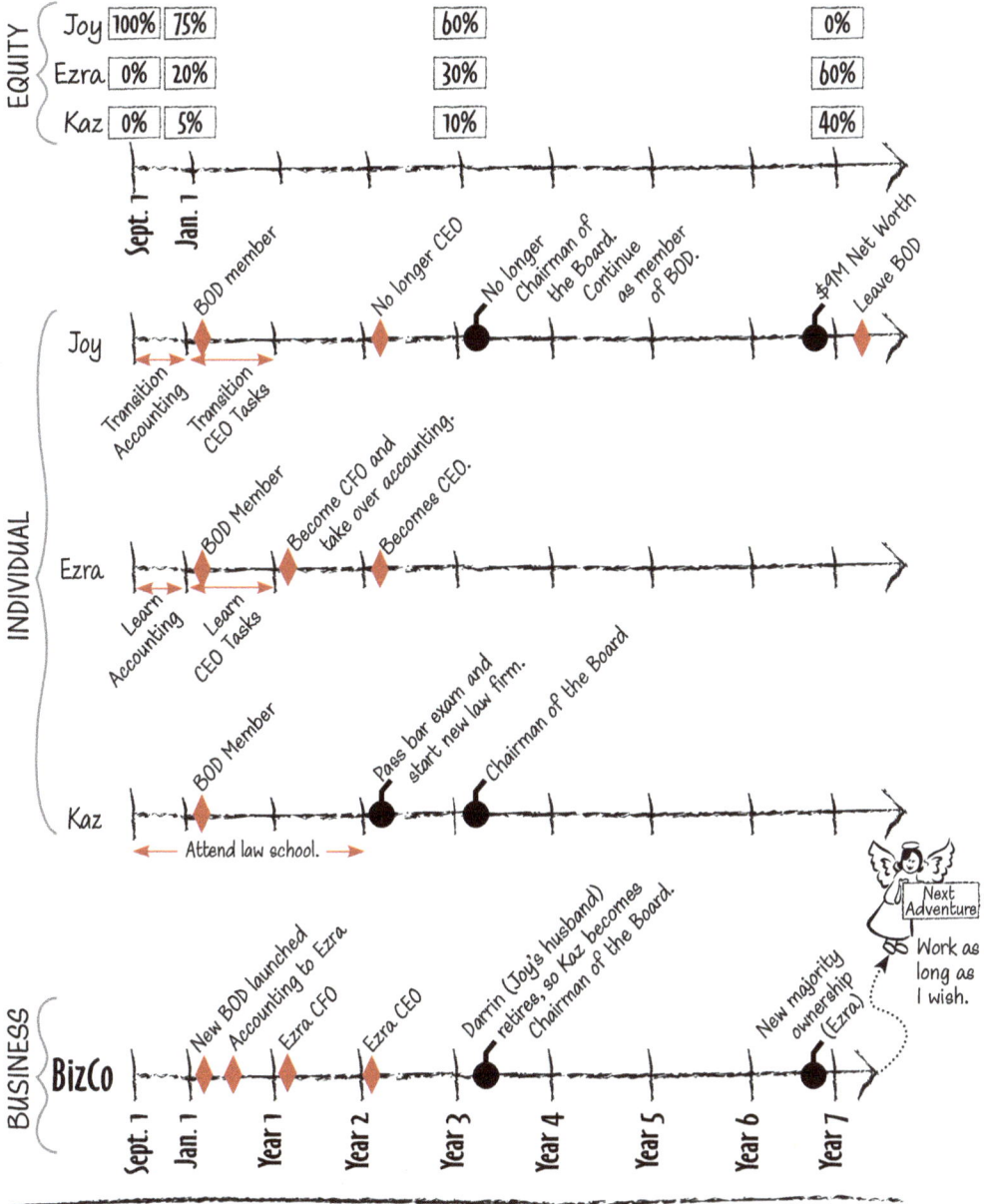

Joy's Seven-Year Transition Timeline

New BOD – Joy, Kaz, Ezra all elected by shareholders as of
Jan. 1 when they gain ownership interest.

Each owner has unique milestones. These might include the date on which an owner will be removed as a guarantor on all debt instruments and contracts, the date on which they finish paying college tuition, and the dates they will transfer management of both sales and cash flow. Joy's milestones include transferring responsibilities to her sons and setting up a board of directors. The number of milestones on your Timeline depends on the length of your time frame and whether you are a detailed, big picture, resistant or meticulous planner.

Triggers

Timeline triggers are if-then, or really, when-then events that must occur for your journey to continue. In Figure 23.1, one of the triggers on BizCo's timeline is *when* Darrin retires, *then* Kaz becomes chairman of the board. For another owner, a trigger might be "When the company grows to $100 million in revenue, then I will begin the transfer of my ownership equity." Joy doesn't know exactly when her husband will retire and her son will become chairman of the board as a result, just as the other owner would not know the date on which revenue will reach $100 million. Both owners, however, clearly communicate that when A occurs, then B will happen. Of course, there are milestones or steps that precede each of those triggers.

When compiled into a Transition Timeline, the individual, business and equity sub-timelines provide a visual representation of how each person involved and the business entity will accomplish:
1) putting the business and ownership in a successor's hands,
2) launching an owner on a Next Adventure, and 3) positioning a business for future success.

A trigger related to a successor might be "On the date my successor achieves the necessary certification, they purchase 50 percent of the company and assume the role of CEO."

Triggers come in all varieties, but yours are unique to you. Common to all is the fact that we can't set an exact date because meeting a specific date is not the goal. The goal is to achieve something (for example, a net worth of $9 million) before something else can happen (in Joy's case, transferring majority ownership).

Three Sub-Timelines: One Transition

As Figure 23.1 illustrates, a Transition Timeline is made up of at least three basic types of sub-timelines: one for your business, those for individuals involved (owner, successor and everyone else who will play roles in your journey), and one for the transfer of equity. You may decide to add sub-timelines for other businesses that you own and real estate to suit your situation. Let's review the function and features of each of the basic sub-timelines.

Sub-Timeline For The Business

The focus of our Transition Roadmap is the business, so we begin with the business sub-timeline. It maps out how the business will transfer from the owner's hands into the hands of a successor. As you can see in Figure 23.2, which shows *just the first year* of the business sub-timeline, we've marked milestones for events that relate to the business, such as establishing a board of directors. Other milestones on a business sub-timeline might include completion of a certification required to do business, such as a general contractor's license. If the CFO who has been with your company for years is retiring in 18 months, thus making the position available to your successor, that's also a milestone. Perhaps you give one of your children until the age of 25 to decide whether or not to join his older siblings as an owner of your business. That's a milestone.

Business triggers are those hard-to-pin-down events you can't put an exact date on. If you had a crystal ball, you could accurately estimate how changes in the economy or in demand for your product or service will affect your company. It's equally difficult to predict what effect the market will have on your ability to build wealth.

Figure 23.2

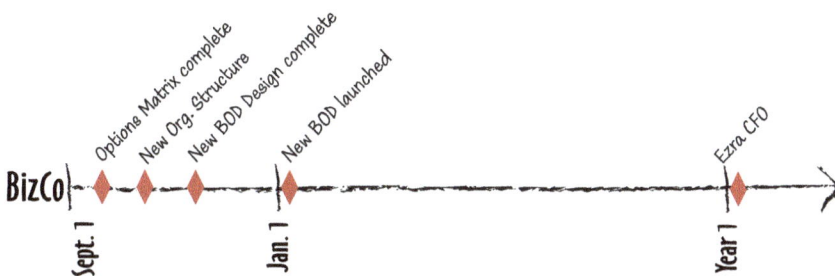

Joy's One-Year Business Sub-Timeline (BizCo)

Sub-Timeline For Individuals

Every business transfer involves—at a minimum—an owner and a successor. We create sub-timelines for each of them as well as any other individuals involved. On each individual's timeline we mark triggers and milestones that relate to the transfer of responsibility for—and control of—day-to-day operations from owner to successor. Typically, owners give up responsibility in stages, as they transfer their knowledge and successors gain skills.

Figure 23.3 illustrates the staged transition of responsibilities for Joy, Ezra and Kaz in just the first year of Joy's transition.

Figure 23.3

Joy's One-Year Individual Sub-Timelines

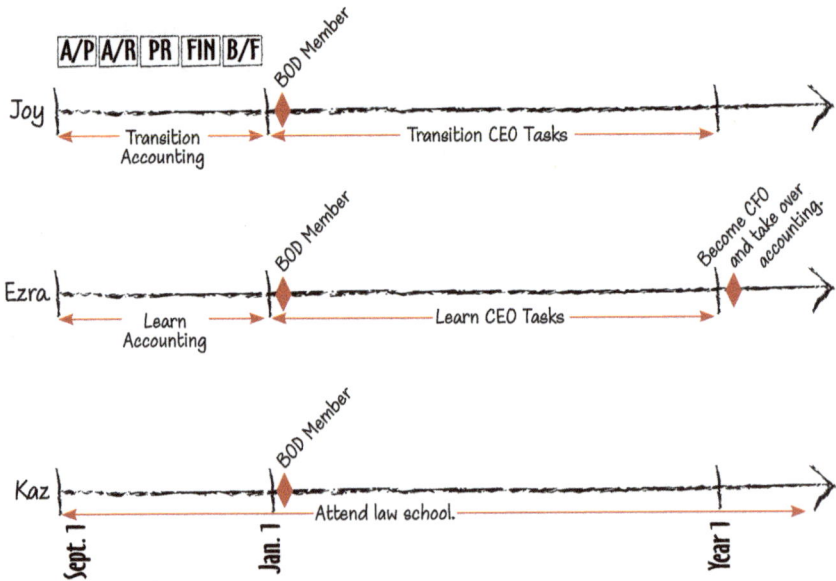

Note that in the first year Joy will transfer various accounting functions (accounts payable and receivable, payroll, financial statements and banking/finance) to her successor Ezra. On Ezra's sub-timeline we've marked the period during which Ezra is committed to learning these accounting functions and the day he will assume responsibility for all of them.

If there are others involved in preparing or assisting your successor, you may create individual sub-timelines to document the path forward for each of them. In some cases, it is appropriate to include sub-timelines for business partners, key employees, children and/or spouses who interact with the business either now or will interact with it during the span of the Transition Timeline. The purpose of multiple sub-timelines is to create harmony among all participants and the business.

Sub-Timeline For The Transfer Of Equity

The equity sub-timeline tracks the transfer of equity from owner to successors over the course of a business transition. We note the dates on which equity will be transferred (in a lump sum or in stages), name the individuals involved in the transfers and state the percentage of equity owned by each individual. In Figure 23.4, we see how Joy plans to transfer her equity to her sons over the seven years of her transition.

Figure 23.4

Joy's Seven-Year Equity Sub-Timeline

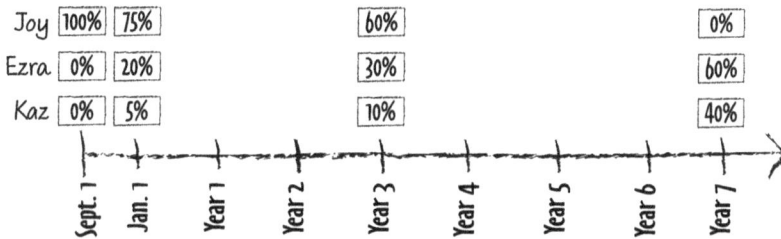

Joy	100%	75%		60%		0%
Ezra	0%	20%		30%		60%
Kaz	0%	5%		10%		40%

Sept. 1 — Jan. 1 — Year 1 — Year 2 — Year 3 — Year 4 — Year 5 — Year 6 — Year 7

Joy's seven-year Transition Timeline (combining her equity, individual and business sub-timelines) appeared at the beginning of this chapter (Figure 23.1). In Figure 23.5, we combine all three of Joy's one-year sub-timelines (equity, individual and business) to see what she and her sons will accomplish during the first year of her transition.

Joy's Transition Timeline provides everyone whom Joy invites into her journey a visual representation of how each person and the business entity will accomplish: 1) putting the business and ownership in her sons' hands, 2) launching her on a Next Adventure, and 3) positioning her business for future success.

Figure 23.5

Joy's One-Year Transition Timeline

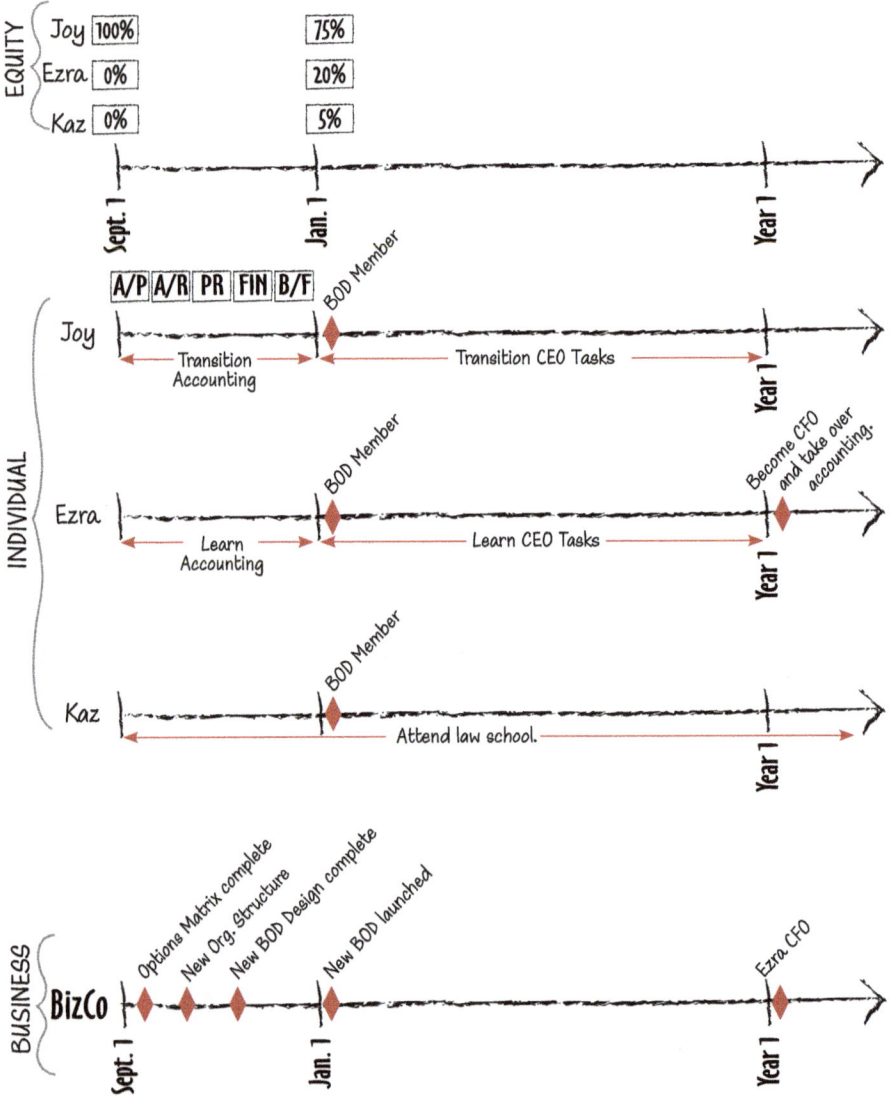

Planned Procrastination

From long experience, we know several things about owners and business transitions:

1. Owners must undertake numerous projects to reach the great outcome they seek (the successful transfer of their companies).

2. Owners, being the go-getter entrepreneurs that they are, feel urgency as they reach the Roadmap part of the Transition Roadmap Developer Process, so they want to attack multiple projects at once.

3. Owners, being human, will not achieve great outcomes if they attack all the component projects at once.

Our task as advisors is to persuade owners that doing too much at once is simply unsustainable. If we are unsuccessful, owners usually discover that fact on their own when they realize they can't continue to run their companies, work on all of their milestones at once, and sleep at night (much less maintain relationships with their loved ones).

When helping owners establish their Transition Timelines, we introduce them to the concept of *Planned Procrastination*. To illustrate that concept, let's look at a project that is far less complex than transferring a business: weight loss.

"Jim" wants to lose 50 pounds. To accomplish that goal, he must improve his sleep habits, learn about healthier food options and how to prepare them, and exercise more. If Jim tries to do all four at once, he's likely to make little progress or even fail, due to taking on too much at one time. Humans actually accelerate effectiveness and progress by making one or two life/behavioral changes at a time. Jim can utilize planned procrastination by first improving his sleep habits. Once he accomplishes that, he finds he has more energy to exercise. Once he's established a regular exercise schedule, he begins to study nutrition. With that knowledge, he starts preparing and eating healthier meals. By working at one task at a time, Jim eventually reaches his goal: a 50-pound weight loss.

Owners must take multiple critical steps (milestones). We help owners break down each milestone into its component steps, just as Jim did. One of Joy's milestones was to transfer accounting responsibilities to her son Ezra. To achieve that milestone, she first transferred accounts payable, then accounts receivable, payroll, financial statements and, finally, banking/finance. In the next chapter we'll introduce you to the organizational tool we use to help owners keep track of the progress everyone involved is making toward a milestone.

Focus+Planned Procrastination=Accelerated Progress

We use the same planned procrastination approach with successors. We give them time to focus on one area of the business, master it, assume responsibility for it, and then move on to the next area. This ongoing cycle accelerates learning. As you establish your milestones, you may want your successor to focus on more than one thing at a time, but remember the benefit of planned procrastination. It will help you prepare for your Next Adventure, and it will help your successor gain confidence in their ability to become the next leader of your company.

Planned Procrastination And Demographics

The cycle we've just described—focus on one area of the business, master it, assume responsibility for it, and move on to the next area—is more important than ever given today's demographics. Over the last two decades, we have seen the average age difference between owners and successors increase in both intergenerational and nonfamily transfers. The age gap is widening, in part due to the population numbers.

There are more Baby Boomers (those born between 1946 and 1964) looking to move on to their Next Adventures than there are Generation Xers (those born between 1965 and 1979, standing by to take the reins. According to the 2010 Census, there were 12 million more boomers in the United States than Gen Xers.*

This means more and more successors stepping up into ownership have, simply by virtue of their age, less business experience. To help successors climb the learning curve quickly, owners: 1) may have to flatten the learning curve a bit by increasing its length; 2) should adopt the planned procrastination approach to improve the efficacy of the transfer of knowledge from themselves to their successors, and 3) should commit to three rules of engagement that we discuss in Chapter Twenty-Eight (assuming the best of intent, being honest rather than accusatory, and being playful).

---

*"Gen X: America's neglected 'middle child,'" The Pew Research Center, by Paul Taylor and George Gao, June 5, 2014
https://www.pewresearch.org/fact-tank/2014/06/05/generation-x-americas-neglected-middle-child/

Timelines Adapt To Reality

Transition Timelines are extraordinarily flexible. They can extend or compress if a trigger occurs sooner or later than expected, or if a milestone is missed or it is achieved sooner than anticipated. If, for example, an owner reaches his goal of $9 million in net worth sooner than expected, their sub-timeline adjusts accordingly. If a successor fails to achieve the necessary certification on the expected date, their sub-timeline also adjusts accordingly.

Triggers can accelerate or decelerate the flow of events, but so too can an owner's or successor's sense of urgency, their progress through the assigned milestones or the appearance of unexpected obstacles.

If you would like to create your own Transition Timeline, check out Microsoft's Visio software.

If you travel without a Transition Timeline:

- It will be challenging to communicate the steps you (and others) must take to transition the business. Your successor and team may not engage at the level you desire, not due to lack of talent but to insufficient information regarding what you expect of them.

- When your desires and expectations are not met, you will lose confidence in the possibility of successful transition to your successor.

- You will likely feel as if you are carrying all of the full weight of this transition and must push your team forward every step of the way.

If you create a Transition Timeline:

- You break down the critical steps necessary to reach your desired destination. In doing so, you can communicate them in an organized way to others, identify potential delays, and understand the reasons those delays might occur.

- You set up your team and successor to succeed and engage in the journey. You set clear expectations with agreed-upon milestones for completion that people are able to commit to.

- You share responsibility and accountability with others, engage them, and pull them together for an outcome that benefits all.

POINT OF INTEREST

Using "My Transition Timeline," map out what you know about your equity, individual and business timelines. (This form is available at *www.TheSuccessionPlanningBook.com/Tools.*) Insert today's date as your starting point. In the equity boxes, record the current percentage of equity that you and your successor hold.

If you know your ultimate *When*, put that date at the end of the individual and business sub-timelines, and then add the appropriate number of tick marks to show the years between today and your *When*.

As you think about you and your business and complete your individual and business sub-timelines, write in the milestones and triggers you would like to meet. Doing so will spur your thinking about what your successor will need to do in order to align themselves to your individual and business sub-timelines. You can then follow the same procedure to complete the successor's individual sub-timeline.

Once you have sketched out sub-timelines for yourself, your business and your successor, go ahead and create additional equity transfer boxes that indicate when you would like to transfer some or all of your equity.

My Transition Timeline

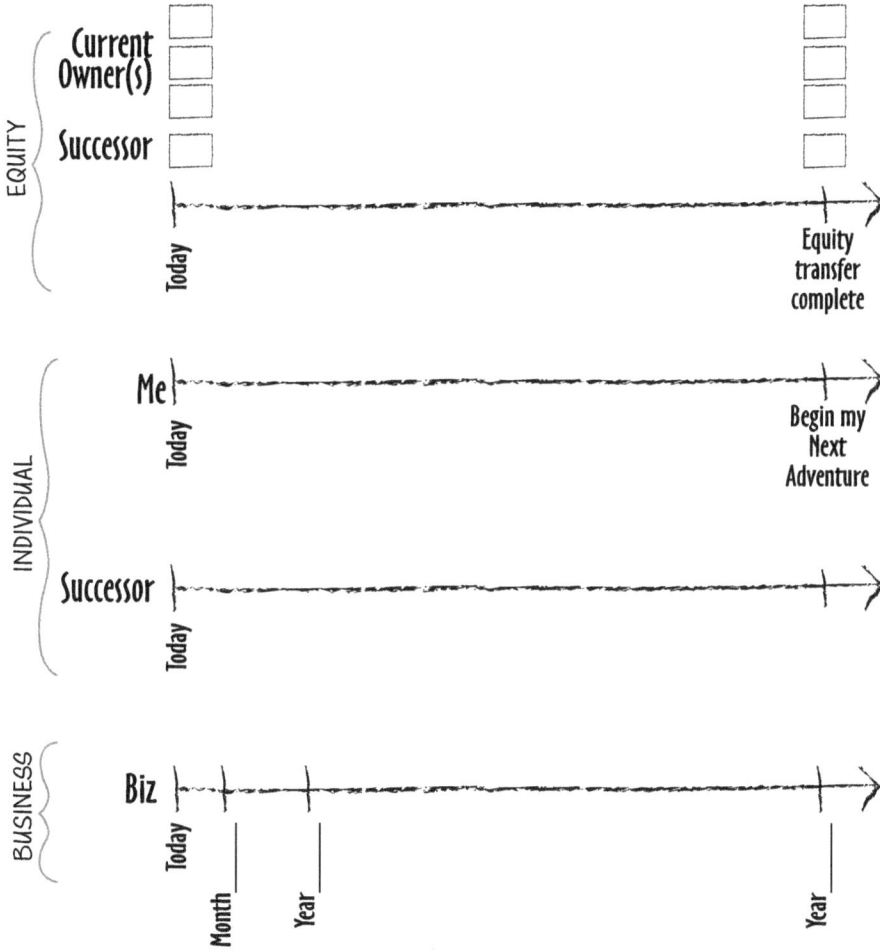

This is just the beginning of your Transition Timeline.

Issues will come to mind as you create these sub-timelines. The issues may be items you are unsure of or that you need or want to explore. Record them on the "List of Timeline Issues."

List of Timeline Issues

CHAPTER TWENTY-FOUR

ELEMENT 3 OF THE TRANSITION ROADMAP: THE TRANSITION STRATEGY STATEMENT™

Never limit yourself because of others' limited imagination;
never limit others because of your own limited imagination.

Mae Jemison, First African American woman to travel in space

The Transition Strategy Statement component of a Transition Roadmap provides a high-level, high-intention overview of the journey from business owner to Next Adventurer. It describes the future you envision for yourself, your family and your business. It is your opportunity to tell the story of your ideal journey. When choices become difficult, your Transition Strategy Statement grounds you in your vision.

Your Transition Strategy Statement may be as short as a couple of paragraphs or as long as several pages, depending on the complexity of the transition and level of detail you wish to include. No matter the length, write as if your vision of the future already exists. Figure 24.1 is owner Joy's Transition Strategy Statement.

Your Transition Strategy Statement is far more than a chronology of "We will do this, then this, then this." Establishing a chronology of events is the function of the Transition Timeline. Instead, The Transition Strategy Statement is a description of your reasons for moving out of business ownership

Without excitement about where we are headed, we all prefer the comfort of remaining where we are.

and on to a Next Adventure. When you begin to write your Transition Strategy Statement, we suggest that you:

- Refer to your original Objectives Matrix and summarize the objectives that have become the reasons you are making the effort to create a succession plan and move on to your Next Adventure.

- Write in the present tense when describing your Next Adventure.

- Include the answers to as many of your Big 6 questions as possible.

- Address how you will move forward to find definitive answers to any of The Big 6 questions that you have not yet confirmed.

An effective Transition Strategy Statement paints a vivid picture of your *Why*. It describes the positive energy that fuels the business transition. That positive energy will serve you well when all parties experience the losses (along with the gains, of course) that accompany change. The Transition Strategy Statement keeps everyone focused on a goal that they can connect with on an emotional level.

We encourage you to be brave as you write your Transition Strategy Statement. Be candid about how you expect your journey to progress, how you plan to address areas that might be problematic, and how you intend to approach the decisions that will need to be discussed and tackled. Be transparent about the information you still need to validate and verify before you can answer all of your Big 6 questions definitively. Write your Transition Strategy Statement in a way that if you were reading it for the first time, you would be motivated to engage in the transition and would feel that your role and input are valued. You want your team to have confidence in your ability to overcome any obstacles as you lead them to an outcome that will benefit everyone.

Figure 24.1

Over the past seven years, I have had a great time with my two sons! We have worked together to create a thriving business. Ezra is our CEO, and Kaz is an amazing chairman of the board and is a founding partner of his own law firm. The three of us make a great team as the board of directors.

We have navigated many ups and downs as I transitioned out of the day-to-day operations of the business. This great journey has not been without challenges, but our company and our relationships are stronger for having navigated them together.

Darrin, my husband, retired four years ago and is very happy boating and enjoying time in his woodshop. We are financially secure since achieving $9 million in net worth (and growing!).

We love being at our mountain home in the summers. Our children and grandchildren spend time with us, enjoying the cool weather and time on the lake. Our winter home in the South is lovely as well. We're so happy that we purchased a home that is close enough to our children to allow us to spend a great deal of time with our grandchildren. We enjoy attending their sports and school activities.

The business continues to be a great asset to our community, employing over 100 people. We support our local food bank and our church. I pop into the business when I want, and I enjoy the time that I have with my sons.

People ask me when I'm going to retire. I am having so much fun that I am pretty sure my answer will continue to be "I already am retired!" I'm living the way I want to live and have the freedom to spend my time as I wish. I am with my children and making a difference in people's lives. The business is transferred and is safely in the hands of the next generation. Life is great!

----Joy

If you don't take time to create a Transition Strategy Statement:

- You can become fixated on all of the possible pitfalls.

- The journey will not be as engaging as it can be, because you lack a positive, emotive statement of why you are intentionally crafting your transition out of your business.

If you create a thoughtful Transition Strategy Statement:

- Your story of what you will be doing and how your journey will end successfully becomes the positive focus that guides and inspires you.

- You enjoy sharing your amazing story as you navigate forward.

POINT OF INTEREST

Go ahead and write your Transition Strategy Statement. Remember this is a summary and not a book, so bullets are perfectly appropriate.

Whether you write bullet points or paragraphs, it is VERY IMPORTANT to express your feelings, how you want things to be and others to feel. You are taking a wonderful and rewarding journey! Your Transition Strategy Statement should reflect that.

Transition Strategy Statement

CHAPTER TWENTY-FIVE

ELEMENT 4 OF THE TRANSITION ROADMAP: THE FOCUSED ACTION NAVIGATOR™

Do not confuse motion and progress. A rocking horse keeps moving but does not make any progress.

Alfred A. Montapert, American engineer and philosopher

A Focused Action Navigator (FAN) is a detailed description of the specific actions (focus items) that you and your successor (at a minimum) must take to achieve the milestones that appear on your Transition Timeline.

We assign a due date (target completion date) for each focus item individuals must accomplish to reach a milestone. Target completion dates might be 30, 60 or 90 days out, depending on the complexity of the action to be accomplished or the number of components that an owner wishes to assign to an action. We prefer short time frames (30 days) because they commit people to almost immediate action and require all involved to communicate at least on a monthly basis. As each focus item is completed, we refresh the FAN.

A 30-day FAN is ideal for people who want to keep close tabs on what's being accomplished, are at the beginning of their learning curves, or need significant guidance or will benefit from frequent accountability checks. A 90-day FAN works for those who are well-trained in a particular task, are executing effectively, need a long period of time to complete a task, or don't require frequent check-ins to stay focused and on track.

If you enjoy checking off items on to-do lists, you will love the FAN.

Accountability

One primary benefit of a FAN is that it holds everyone accountable to the commitments they make, rather than to the expectations others have of them. To explain what we mean by that, we tell the story of the father who constantly reminded his son to pick up his own socks. The son agreed to do his best, yet day after day the father would find socks on the floor of his son's bedroom. The father finally asked his son, "Why can't you do this one simple thing: pick up your socks?"

The son replied, "Dad, I can't keep the socks picked up all the time, but I can pick them up each night before I go to bed."

Success rates improve when people are asked to commit to bite-size, realistic actions rather than to large, poorly defined ones.

Anticipates Obstacles

A FAN notes any obstacles we expect to encounter when working to accomplish a task. By identifying obstacles early in the process, owners and successors give themselves more time to work together to understand and resolve them.

Highlights What Is *Not* Happening

The greatest benefit of the FAN is that it illustrates whether a focus item is on track to being completed within the allotted period of time.

As Figure 25.1 illustrates, a FAN shows, at a glance, the status of a project:

- Green = We are on track.
- Yellow = We may not hit target.
- Red = We're off course or not doing well.

A FAN awash in a sea of red and yellow tells you that you are not moving at the pace necessary to accomplish a milestone in the time you allotted. A FAN that is mostly green indicates all is going according to your plan.

As you can see in Figure 25.1, Joy (the owner) is transferring to Ezra (her successor) all accounting functions (Focus Item) by January 31 (Target Completion Date). Ezra is taking a management accounting course (Progress), and within the next 30 days (30-day Focus) he will take action, i.e., complete the course. Also, within the same 30 days (the second 30-day Focus Action), Joy will begin the transfer of accounts payable so that Ezra can take over all A/P by September 30. The green in the Stoplight column

Figure 25.1

The Focused Action Navigator™

Focus Item	Progress	Leader	Notes/ Obstacles	Target Completion Date	Stoplight	30-Day Focus (Action)
Complete Options Matrix.	Put the Advisor Cabinet in place.	Joy	Attain objectives while optimizing taxes.	September 30	Timing with Scheduling	Set first meeting with Advisor Cabinet to explore legal aspects of our transition option.
Develop new org. structure to support Ezra as he takes over accounting and moves out of his current position.	Had a conversation with Joy to understand her thoughts. Need current, near-term and longer-term versions of org. structure to see how steps/stages will happen.	Ezra	Create a scalable structure that fully supports Ezra while Joy shifts. Manage employee perception and engagement in the shifting structure.	October 31	Need to complete Options Matrix.	Ezra take first stab at org. structure he would like to see then set meeting to review with Joy.
Develop board of directors' constitution.	Happy to be beginning the process.	Joy	Change behavior to take full advantage of more formal structure of governance.	November 30		Solicit proposals and hire consultant. Set first meeting with three of us and consultant to start the process.
Transfer accounting to Ezra fully by end of next year.	Ezra halfway through management accounting course.	Joy	Move enough off Ezra's plate to allow him to focus on and learn accounting.	January 31 Accounting Fully Transferred		Ezra complete management accounting course. Begin transfer of A/P Sept. 1, with intention of Ezra fully taking over by Sept. 30.

indicates that Ezra is taking the management accounting course as planned and Joy is on track with regard to transferring A/P.

You'll also note that Joy has written "Attain objectives while optimizing taxes" as a Note/Obstacle to completing her Options Matrix. That is her shorthand way of saying that it is important to consider the amount of taxes she and her company will incur as a result of each possible transaction option. In that, Joy, like most owners, wants to strike a balance between her interests and those of the various taxing entities.

Communication

The FAN functions as a communication tool in the same way as a Transition Timeline. FANs improve the quality and increase the quantity of communication between owners and successors.

The FAN And Your Transition Roadmap

Way back in Section I (Chapter Five), we talked about whom to invite into your journey and how and when to do it. Before you create your Transition Roadmap, your conversations with others are like fishing expeditions. You test your assumptions and the reactions of others to hypothetical situations.

With your Roadmap in hand, you can now dive into waters that, until this point, you were only fishing or sticking a toe in. Your Roadmap gives you a reference point for deeper and more specific conversations. You may share part or all of your Roadmap and invite others in to collaborate with you in planning and executing some of its elements. You can engage successors and explain why you chose your path, how you navigated dilemmas and what you expect your plan to accomplish. Your Roadmap paints an accurate picture of the path ahead, so other people can see how the process you have designed will work and how the process and the outcomes align with their own objectives. At this point, others can make much more informed choices about how and whether to join you.

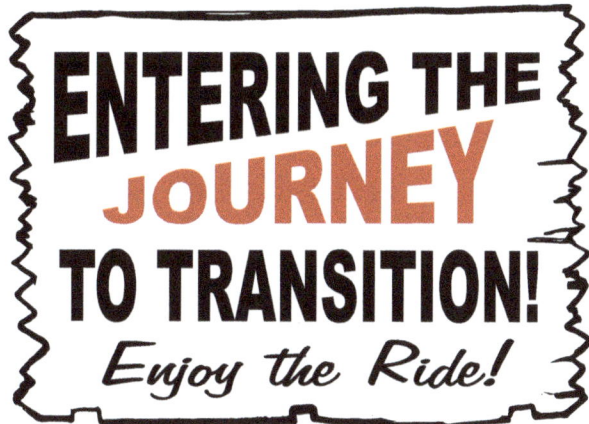

ENTERING THE JOURNEY TO TRANSITION! Enjoy the Ride!

Once you are prepared to discuss your Transition Roadmap with a successor, we suggest you follow three simple rules:

Rule 1: Prepare for these conversations. Know what your objective is. Decide what you will and will not share. Try to anticipate what your successor may think or feel, and determine how you might best respond.

Rule 2: Be honest and, as appropriate, practice vulnerability and transparency.

Rule 3: During these conversations, successors must absorb a huge amount of new information. They will have questions, so listen carefully to feedback and thoughtfully answer questions. After you present the outlines of your plan, ask about your successor's objectives. Listen carefully for any Deal Breakers, because successors usually have their own.

When you and your successor begin to "sing from the same hymnbook," together you will plan and script how to announce the transition plan to others. If the two of you do not tell the same positive story, opinions will multiply and rumors will begin to fly.

If you do not create a Focused Action Navigator:

- You have no way to determine whether you are progressing quickly enough to arrive at your Next Adventure on the date you wish, and you run a higher risk of being surprised by problems and delays as they occur.

- You will be challenged with expectations and commitments that are out of alignment.

- You will not know if a critical item is falling off the radar, thus putting your transition in jeopardy.

If you create a Focused Action Navigator:

- You, your successor and your team have a basis to talk about the focus items that you all have committed to complete.

- You have a means to assess whether everyone is progressing at the pace necessary to reach the dates on your Transition Timeline.

- You break large focus items into smaller pieces, thus improving the odds that you will complete them.

In the first column of your Focused Action Navigator, write the top four items that you need to focus on, in order to get started on your journey. The purpose is to identify the Focus Items that you must accomplish first.

In the Progress column, summarize what you have done (or are thinking about doing) related to each Focus Item. Next note the person who will lead the effort to accomplish each Item (the Leader), and record any related notes you want to remember or obstacles that may exist or arise. Write the date you hope to finish each item (the Target Completion Date), and then use a red, yellow, or green colored marker or pen to fill in each box in the Stoplight column (or just write in the word "red," "yellow" or "green").

Finally, for each Focus Item identify the specific tasks you will perform in the next 30 days in order to complete that action.

Review the 30-Day Focus column on your completed FAN. Ask yourself whether you have the time and commitment to accomplish everything in that column. If not, use our planned procrastination concept (described in Chapter Twenty-Three) to reevaluate. It is better to complete one task than to try to do five and not complete any of them.

Remember that this is a journey and every small milestone accomplished brings you closer to your ultimate transition. Every accomplishment makes it possible to enjoy the ride!

The Focused Action Navigator™

Focus Item	Progress	Leader	Notes/ Obstacles	Target Completion Date	Stoplight	30-Day Focus (Action)

SECTION IV

Enjoy the Journey!

We congratulate you for all the work you have done to reach this point: the final preparations for your journey to your Next Adventure. You now know where you are going and have set the compass points to keep you moving in the right direction. You recognize that no business transition is perfect and have seven principles that you can use to resolve any dilemmas that you encounter.

Now that you have outlined a transition plan that benefits you, your family, your successor, your company and your community, can you even remember losing sleep and feeling anything but confident?

Your confidence in your transition plan is invigorating, and your energy is contagious.

- Family members will appreciate the effort you put into helping them to achieve their Next Adventures.

- Your successor will see that you've created a plan to prepare them for ownership.

- Employees will see that, they will be taken care of after you leave the business, and the business will remain as successful as it was under your leadership.

- Financial institutions will be assured that you have put as much care into making your company successful after you leave as you did during the years you built it.

As rewarding as it is to see others share your excitement, you may be surprised to find yourself impatient. Impatience is completely normal because it inevitably takes time to teach your successor to do what you do and for your successor to fill your shoes.

The chapters in this section will show you how to smooth the road to your Next

Adventure. We will discuss the "owner and successor dance," during which you teach your successor what you know, and your successor grows into a successful leader. We will show you how a more formal form of business governance can improve your successor's and your company's odds of future success and make you more comfortable turning over the reins of ownership. Finally, we will introduce you to six attitudes that helped our 100 percenters succeed in reaching their Next Adventures and made their journeys both fulfilling and fun.

CHAPTER TWENTY-SIX

ADVISORS PUT THE ODDS OF A SUCCESSFUL BUSINESS TRANSFER IN YOUR FAVOR

The way of a fool is right in his own eyes, but a wise man listens to advice.

Proverbs 12:15 (ESV)

We've shown throughout this book that preparing yourself, your successor and your company to succeed once you move on to your Next Adventure is a journey: a journey that takes time and careful planning if you are to reach your Next Adventure with your relationships intact and your successor and business positioned to succeed. We've also illustrated how The Transition Roadmap Developer Process may increase the odds of a successful business transfer from dismal to 100 percent. Now we ask that you think of your journey, just for a moment, as a car race you very much want to win. You are sitting in the cockpit of one of the world's fastest grand prix racing cars. You know the course, and you are one of the best drivers on the circuit. Realistically, however, without the best pit crew you can afford, you don't have a chance at winning.

In the case of your business transition, winning means reaching your Next Adventure with the fewest possible hiccups or detours and with your important relationships healthy. It means leaving your company in the hands of a competent successor poised for ongoing success.

You and your advisors are similar to a race car driver and the members of a pit crew:

1. No one advisor can perform all the necessary tasks.

2. You choose your advisors.

3. Each advisor is highly-skilled in their area of expertise. They know how to reduce the risk of breakdowns and keep you performing at your peak.

4. Advisors make suggestions, but you are the ultimate decision maker.

5. Your advisors are highly-efficient and coordinate their efforts to put the odds of winning in your favor.

A Cabinet Of Advisors

It is impossible for anyone to be an expert in every facet of business succession. There is no way one person can fully understand, be current on, and have experience in contracts, tax law, business valuation, financial planning, human psychology, and deal structure (to name just a few elements). For that reason, you will assemble an Advisor Cabinet made up of multiple advisors who work together to help you reach your Next Adventure.

Choosing The Advisors To Serve In Your Cabinet

The beauty of an Advisor Cabinet is that you bring in the only ones you need at the times you require them to tackle tasks specific to your situation. For example, the makeup of a Cabinet for an owner whose successor is a family member is not the same as one for an owner who plans to sell to an outside third party.

Figure 26.1 illustrates the group of professionals that make up most Advisor Cabinets.

Figure 26.1

CABINET OF ADVISORS

Transition Strategist · Financial Advisor · Valuation Expert · Tax Accountant · Estate Attorney · Business Attorney

Your Cabinet may have some of these advisors, all of them and/or others.

Don't Hire Them (Quite) Yet!

The order in which you hire advisors, and when you hire them, is important. As you navigate your answers to The Big 6, you will gain clarity about which types of professionals you need and when you will need them. *This is your Cabinet.*

Every advisor you choose must understand that their purpose is to help you achieve your objectives. You will spend time assessing whether each:

- Is on board with your project as you envision it.

- Cares about your goals and the principles you are using to achieve them.

- Communicates as frequently and effectively with you and other members of your cabinet as you desire.

- Is available as you need them according to your timeline.

- Understands that they work for you—not your company or your successor.

Highly Skilled Advisors

A pit crew is made up of multiple people, each with very specific roles. Some pull off tires, and others put on new ones. Some stabilize the car while others use pneumatic wheel guns to unscrew and screw on wheels. Similarly, each of the members of your Cabinet of Advisors has a specific role to play.

Rather than change tires or wheels, your advisors will, as necessary, help you:

- Find your *Why*.

- Design your transition strategy.

- Keep relationships intact.

- Protect your financial well-being through financial and tax planning and proper insurance coverage.

- Create a tax-efficient structure for the transfer of ownership.

- Form new entities.

- Design or adjust your estate plan.

- Create successor development plans.

- Secure proper financing.

- Assign a value to your business by performing a business valuation.

- Sell or transfer real estate.

- Choose a business broker.

- Document and improve business processes, grow business value, streamline banking and capital/financial management procedures or create operational synergies.

- Build successor and team skills.

- Redesign the organizational chart or recruit high-performing managers to help the business succeed without you.

Do some or all of your current advisors have experience in performing these tasks? Can they anticipate pitfalls and suggest possible solutions in a transaction? Are they honest and candid with you? Do they tell you when you are headed in the right direction and caution you when you veer off course? If so, great. If not, or if your journey requires advisors that you do not work with on a regular basis (e.g., business valuation specialists), you will recruit new advisors to your Cabinet. Later in this chapter we discuss how to find skilled advisors.

You Are The Driver

Your advisors are accountable for meeting your deadlines. You should expect them to make suggestions and then carry out the decisions you make. For example, an estate planning attorney may suggest several possible strategies to gift a child part of your business while transferring different assets to your other children. You will choose the strategy that, in your opinion, protects your relationships and meets most of your objectives, while not violating any of your Deal Breakers. You are in the driver's seat.

Your advisors must understand the importance of confidentiality. They must keep news of the transition quiet until you decide to release the information. If a leak does occur, your advisors should be able to help repair any damage.

For your part, you must trust your advisors. That does not mean you take their advice without question, At the end of the day, however, you must trust that they are offering the best possible advice for your situation.

Choosing A New Cabinet Member

The professional advisors you trust and already do business with can be a great resource for referrals to experts with whom they have partnered on other projects. Other business owners and/or your own research can also lead you to quality referrals.

No matter the source of the referral, you will interview prospective Cabinet members much as you would when hiring a new employee. Your questions might include:

- Can you tell me about experiences you've had working on business transitions like mine?

- In what ways were those projects similar to and different from mine?

- How often did you interact with other advisors on those projects?

- How did you resolve any problems that arose during the projects?

- If I retained your services, how would you communicate with me?

- How does your fee structure work?

- Will you provide names of some owners you have worked with in the past? (Most professionals will supply a few references.)

As you would with a prospective employee, trust your instincts. If someone strikes you as a poor fit, you are probably right. Call an advisor's references and, at a minimum, ask two key questions: Would you would work with this advisor again? Why or why not?

Advisor Qualities

There is no room in your Cabinet for egos. The advisors you choose must collaborate well with you and with one another. No matter how you find professionals for your Cabinet of Advisors, we recommend that you look for the following key personal characteristics:

- Is open to possibilities.

- Is somewhat of a futurist. (Futurists are naturally focused on future results, conditions, consequences and scenarios.)

- Has experience participating as a member of a team organized to help business-owner clients transition their companies to successors in a way that meets the owner's objectives.

- Works well as a member of a team.

- Puts people, their relationships and their values first.

As you evaluate current and prospective advisors, trust your intuition. If someone doesn't feel like the right person, keep looking.

Compensating Members Of Your Cabinet

Your Transition Roadmap may include the dates on which you will hire certain professionals, as well as the periods of time when you will need their services. It might also include the fees that you expect to pay.

Highly skilled and experienced advisors may seem expensive; however, inexperienced, uncooperative, unavailable or unaccountable advisors cost money and your valuable time, and they may put your transition at risk.

One Race, One Next Adventure

Please consider the costs—emotional and financial—you would incur if you were unable to reach your Next Adventure. That's why the help of skilled advisors is crucial. Again, no one advisor is an expert at all the facets of a business transition. As consultants who are involved in business transitions every day, we know what we don't know. Our clients—all smart and successful people—recognize they don't know everything there is to know about business transitions. More importantly, they do know that they want to get it right the first time. As a result, they find and hire professional advisors who help them reach the outcomes they desire.

If you rely on too few advisors or on advisors who act alone:

- Their lack of expertise or experience in all of the areas you require it wastes your time and money and may derail your journey altogether. You will miss opportunities to optimize the transaction (e.g., tax-advantaged stock transfer techniques).

- When advisors work independently rather than as members of a team, they may provide conflicting information, overcomplicate matters and/or cause unnecessary detours and needless friction. Doing so can damage relationships with the people you care about.

If you assemble great advisors to work as members of your Cabinet:

- They can integrate your *Why, What, Who* and *When* with the *How Much* and *How* (i.e., tax, estate, legal, and financial investment strategies) to create your Transition Roadmap.

- You will receive creative and thoughtful advice rather than boilerplate documents.

- They smooth the road to your Next Adventure.

POINT OF INTEREST

In the first column of "My Cabinet of Advisors," write the names of the advisors that make up your Cabinet.

If you are still looking for any of these types of advisors, or your confidence level in the ones you have is low, don't worry. Finding the right advisors and creating a Cabinet to help you make your transition a reality is part of the journey. In fact, you may want to make putting your Cabinet in place a milestone on your Transition Timeline. You may also want to make interviewing a particular advisor a Focus Item on your FAN.

My Cabinet of Advisors

Advisor Type	Advisor's Name/Firm	My Level of Confidence in Their Ability to Take Me Through to My Next Adventure (High, Medium, Low)
Transition Strategist		
Financial Advisor		
Valuation Expert		
Tax Accountant		
Estate Attorney		
Business Attorney		
Others		

CHAPTER TWENTY-SEVEN

BUSINESS GOVERNANCE: THE BRAKES THAT POWER COMPANY GROWTH

Governance is possible only with assistance.
A single wheel does not move.

Chanakya, Hindu statesman and philosopher

As an owner, you are likely the CEO of your company, as well as the majority investor and shareholder, and the chairman of the board of directors. As CEO, you decide what needs to be done. If you are the only member of the board of directors, you unilaterally approve the CEO's proposed actions because they are in the best interest of the shareholder (you again!), and the return on investment appears to be reasonable, if not good. Informal governance has been very, very good to you.

If you are in business with a partner, together you likely discuss issues, make decisions and act on them. No committees or other obstacles prevent you from changing directions on the fly. What a great way to run a business!

If you are transitioning your business to a successor who will be a sole owner, informal governance may continue to work well for them. But will you be able to turn over the power to make decisions to a successor if you have no means of applying the brakes if one of your successor's decisions is a poor one? If you have multiple successors, how will they make decisions without good guidelines or processes in place? If some of the shareholders of your company are active and some are not, absent any formal governance who will make decisions? Without a structure for efficient decision-making, how will your company remain nimble in a dynamic business environment?

Business governance plays a huge role in the success of your business while you are transitioning it to a successor, because it gives your successor clear rules and marks boundaries. It provides a forum for you to share wisdom and experience with your successor and, with the right structure, gives you the means to put the brakes on any less-than-optimal decisions your successor may want to make. Essentially, business governance improves your odds of reaching your Next Adventure successfully, and your successor's and company's odds of future success.

Unless you install formal business governance, you put relationships—and even the future success of your business— at risk.

What Is Governance?

For our purposes, governance consists of: 1) the rules and processes that control both how decisions are made for and within the company and by whom, and 2) the types of decisions people in various positions are authorized to make.

Business governance puts in place a process for:

- Hearing and discussing all perspectives before making important decisions about major issues such as the direction of the business, debt, the acquisition of another business, or the purchase or sale of shares.

- Applying the brakes if new owners who lack experience take a wrong turn or move to implement their ideas without careful consideration.

- Including all owners in discussions in an organized and democratic way.

- Managing the input of owners who are not active in the business.

- Passing wisdom and insights from one generation to the next.

- Enabling members of an older generation (in family businesses) to learn from the next one, and allowing the younger generation to be heard regarding their vision and direction.

A formal form of governance (such as a board of directors) gives you the opportunity to:

- Observe how your successor thinks through and reacts to various situations.
- Create alignment through good communication.
- Offer your successors the benefit of your experience and guidance.

To successors, formal governance (through a board) gives them the opportunity to inject their energy into the company and begin to realize their vision for the future.

The most successful privately held companies rely on formal governance. Governance helps maintain relationships among management, minority shareholders and majority shareholders by providing a mechanism for all to present and hear multiple perspectives, and is a means for shareholders to ensure that the company is operated according to the wishes of more than one person. It gives CEOs access to expertise beyond their own. It makes senior management accountable for upholding the shareholders' high standards and for the performance of day-to-day operations. Given all of these benefits, why wouldn't you institute a formal form of governance?

Doing Things The Old-Fashioned Way

Some owners tell us they don't need "the hassle" of creating a board. They have run their companies just fine, thank you very much, by talking with their spouses and children over dinner and/or talking through issues with one or two trusted peers, and then considering their input and making decisions. We completely agree: That scenario works well when one person is the source of all decision-making. But your company and its ownership are about to change.

You are preparing to turn decision-making power over to a successor who may or may not be at your dinner table every night. Even if they are, do you want to use dinners, holidays and other family times to focus on the business? As you may suspect, those who are not actively involved in your business do not really enjoy being excluded from conversations. Even some of those who are active in your business prefer to use family time for fun and relaxation rather than as a forum for discussing or debating business issues.

Owners of family businesses—especially parents whose successors are their children—often tell us they do not need a formal board. They have a point. As long as the business is held in one family, the members of that family are all active in the business, and the entire family has dinner together every night, no one is left out of the conversation and everyone is present to express an opinion. We would point out to those owners, however, that adult children rarely live at home. These children have spouses and children who are generally not included in the owner's dinnertime conversations. But our stronger argument is that the best time to install a more formal vehicle for decision-making (a board) is before things get complicated! Between Generations 1 and 2, families may be able to sustain informal business governance. But as businesses move from Generation 2 to 3 and then (we hope) to 4, there are too many people and too wide a range of priorities to rely on informal governance—especially when there is a great alternative.

When you set up a board table to replace your dinner table, everyone invited to take a seat knows that the focus of discussion will be the business. They know when decisions will be made and that their voices will be heard. They know they will participate in lively debates about issues related to the business and then they will peacefully leave the room as friends, family or teammates.

We suggest you reserve your dinner table and family time for fun, relaxation and being together. Move discussions about your business to a designated platform to address concerns, issues, direction, opportunities and threats in an organized way. Just as they are at meals, those seated at a board table are free to disagree and express themselves, but unlike at the dinner table, everyone has a vote.

Governance Through A Board Of Directors

Although it may seem a bit formal in a private business, we suggest that you title the group that governs your company a "board of directors" or "board of governors." Whatever you decide to call that group, its official purpose is to represent and act in the interests of the members or shareholders. Board members have a fiduciary duty to the shareholders to keep a company running so it provides a healthy return on their investment. Board members create a vision for a company (what it wants to be) and determine how much cash it will take to achieve the vision. A board assesses risk, hires and manages the CEO, and helps the CEO reach the board's vision for the company, using a board-approved strategy and a budget.

A board of directors performs many functions, including assessing actions that could put the business at risk (e.g., the assumption of debt, purchase of another business, or purchase of the equity of one or more of the shareholders). The very existence of a multi-person board takes the pressure off one person to make all decisions, and it shifts the responsibility for decision-making to a group.

A board creates trust among its members by providing a place for open communication and thoughtful discussion. It provides a structure that allows individuals to make their best arguments, and others to judge the value of those arguments with their votes.

A Brief Guide To Governance

Here we've assembled and answered some of the most common questions owners ask when we suggest they install a structure for business governance.

Q: Who elects the board members?

A: Shareholders elect the members of the board during the annual shareholder meeting. This meeting can be held when all shareholders come together for a fun event or dinner. The agenda might include an overview of the business's performance for the past 12 months, the plan for the next 12, and the election (or reelection) of the members of the board whose terms are expiring.

Q: Who is typically elected to serve on a board?

A: Ideally a board is made up of individuals who understand how the business and its industry work and want to preserve and grow the business for the benefit of its investors. Membership on a board carries significant responsibilities (including fiduciary) to act in good faith and loyalty to all of the investors they serve. We recommend that owners carefully consider whom they want to serve on their boards (and whose boards they serve on!), because board membership carries potential liability. We also recommend that owners seriously consider directors and officers insurance.

The most successful boards are diverse in terms of experience and perspective. Owners of private and family businesses should attempt to achieve similar diversity in their boards.

In a family business, a board may be made up of some combination of family members who are active or not active in the business, and possibly even nonfamily members or nonvoting advisors. Directors or nonvoting advisors who are not members of the family tend to add an important "outside" perspective. A position on a board is not a reward. It is recognition that an individual has an understanding of how the business runs, and the knowledge or experience necessary to help the company overcome challenges.

As the following story illustrates, all board members must be able to leave their personal agendas at the door of the boardroom and put the health of the business first. If they cannot, they are not capable of fulfilling their fiduciary duty to the shareholders.

> *When the founder and owner of a small chain of dry-cleaning businesses died, his family began to navigate the transfer of ownership and management to the next generation. Upon the recommendation of the company's attorney, the family set up a governing board. Board members included the son and daughter who were essentially running the business, as well as three of their siblings who were, for the most part, inactive in the business. All was well until the CEO (the daughter active in the business) informed the board that there was no money to fund the annual shareholder distribution.*
>
> *Due to some extraordinary operational expenses and lower-than-expected revenue (thanks to road construction in front of the company's flagship store), cash flow was a fraction of what she expected. The CEO wanted to devote available cash flow to expenses rather than to shareholder distributions.*
>
> *The CEO's siblings who were not active in the business did not take the news well. Their father's generous distributions had funded a good portion of the lifestyles they had become accustomed to enjoying. Rather than face the hard facts, they used their votes to oppose their sister's recommendation and issued hefty distributions to all shareholders. That one vote by the board left the company mired in debt and was a primary reason the company did not have the cash to survive the economic slowdown that occurred just a few months after that meeting.*

Unable to put the business ahead of their own interests, the board members made a decision that destroyed this business. Everyone lost a major source of income, and company employees lost their jobs. Had all members of the board understood how the business operated and the funding requirements to remain healthy (including through a downturn), they might have voted differently and this company likely would have had a very different outcome.

Q: How much paperwork is involved in setting up a board?

A: Your company's articles of incorporation and/or bylaws may provide a foundation for how your board will be set up, but, in our experience, many of these documents are either too basic or outdated to provide much guidance. You may need to meet with your business attorney to amend your existing documents and possibly create a new document (or constitution) to govern your board.

Typically a business constitution contains more than simply the nuts and bolts of the board makeup and function. A constitution should be an asset for the business, and we believe it is very important to include the history of the business as well as a list of its values. For example, values can include:

- We believe in approaching decisions from a perspective of abundance. There is enough for everyone.

- We are committed to devoting time and effort to planning, because we believe it leads to better outcomes for all.

- We believe in serving our employees and greater community as we grow in our success together.

- We believe in the value of reaching agreement. To that end, we will keep open minds and listen without judgement.

A business constitution then outlines the workings of the board. At a minimum, your company's constitution should designate:

- The purpose and values of the board members.

- The number of people on the board (usually an odd number to prevent ties in voting).

- The responsibilities of board members beyond working to further the interest of shareholders (e.g., required or optional service on a committee).

- The action shareholders, board members, the CEO and management team are authorized to take.

- The officer positions, a definition of each officer's role and explanation of how officers are selected.

- Remuneration (if any) for serving on the board or any committees.

- The length of the term that directors will serve and whether the terms are staggered or not.

- The process/rules for resolving disputes.

- The process for removing or substituting a board member if required.

- The type, number and responsibilities of any committees.

- The frequency of meetings throughout the year and the plan for what will be done at particular meetings. Many owners will assign specific agenda items to specific meetings. For example, in January the board will approve the budget for the new year; during the March meeting the board will review the prior year's financials; in April the board will review the company's tax returns; in September the board will conduct strategic planning for the following year; and in October the board will discuss tax planning for the following year.

Your company's constitution is unique to your business. We suggest you hold a few meetings using your constitution to see which guidelines work for your company and which do not. You can establish strict rules on decision authority as you set up your board, and you can loosen them as your confidence in your CEO and board members grows and they gain experience. Many owners incorporate their best board practices into their formal corporate documents.

Q: How often does a board meet?

A: Regularly. That might mean once each month, quarter or six months. Boards meet in person, remotely or in some combination of the two. The frequency depends on what the business is doing and how much interaction is required by the board to guide the business. For instance, if the business is making acquisitions, the board may need to meet more often than if the business is simply working within its current structure and improving efficiency for the year, which can be handled by the CEO and the management team.

Q: Does the board operate by one member, one vote?

A: One vote per member is a typical voting structure for a board of directors. That's a contrast to the voting structure for shareholders, where percentage of ownership determines the weight of one's vote. In this way, majority shareholders have more influence on the election of board members, but elected board members are equal in their influence at the board level. This structure provides greater diversity in ownership and promotes balanced governance at the board level.

Q: What's the difference between a shareholder and a member of the board of directors?

A: A shareholder is a person who has an equity position in the business. Shareholders are financially invested in the business. Individuals invest in private businesses in the same way individuals buy stock in large public corporations. Shareholders typically meet at an annual meeting. At that meeting they elect board members to replace those whose terms are expiring.

Directors meet frequently. It is their responsibility—and fiduciary duty—to oversee the business and provide a return on the shareholders' investment through profitable business operations. There are actions a board cannot take without the approval (by vote) of the investors/shareholders, such as selling the business, entering into debt greater than a specified amount, making an acquisition, adding new shareholders, or changing the shareholder agreement. These are actions that are likely to impact the shareholders' return on their investment and/or require additional investment from them (i.e., a capital call).

Q: How does a board "manage" the CEO?

A: A board hires, sets compensation for, reviews and fires (if necessary) the CEO. It also supports the CEO, acts as their mentor and sounding board, and helps them to be successful. A board clearly defines the limits of the CEO's authority and determines the types of actions a CEO can take unilaterally and which actions require board approval.

Q: Which actions are typical of a board of directors?

A: Boards typically approve a company's strategic plan and annual financial budget. The board may develop strategy on its own, work with the CEO, or leave it up to the CEO and the executive management team depending, of course, on the company's practices, and competence and authority of the CEO and executive team. A board determines if and how well a business is executing its strategic plan. In general, a board helps to guide a business in good times and navigate through challenging times.

Q: How are meetings run?

A: Meetings follow an agenda that includes old business and new business. During the meeting the board secretary creates meeting minutes that summarize discussions, any votes, decisions and all issues that arise during the meeting.

Many boards use some form of parliamentary procedure (such as Robert's Rules of Order) to give meetings a structure and preserve the rights of all members. When we recommend the use of parliamentary procedure, many owners think we've gone a bit overboard. Over time, however, these same owners find this proven methodology to be the simplest and most effective path to efficient governance.

Q: When is the best time to create a governing board?

A: The ideal time to create a board is before you begin your business transition journey; the rules of governance you create on your own can give you more autonomy than might rules both you and a successor create together. Note: In family businesses it is easier to institute formal business governance when Generation 1 hands over the reins to Generation 2 than it is when Generation 2 passes the reins to Generation 3. Typically there are fewer people involved in Generation 1 to Generation 2 transfers than there are in transfers from Generation 2 to Generation 3.

Creating a governance structure before you really need it develops the framework for new behaviors at a time when there are fewer people involved and those people are closely connected. Once you reach G2 to G3 transitions, there are typically more family groups involved, more communication is required, and more people are only tangentially attached to the business. Dinnertime conversations are not possible when there is more than one dinner table!

Q: Until owners sell all of their equity and move on to their Next Adventures, what is their role as an owner and as a shareholder on the board?

A: As owners transfer ownership according to the timelines they set for the transfer of equity, and as successors assume greater levels of responsibility, owners migrate out of the day-to-day operations. Some choose not only to leave their "jobs," but also to leave the company's board. Typically owners move from CEO to chairman of the board as their successors mature. In doing so, they make room for their successors to take the lead. Only owners who have instituted proper governance are comfortable throttling back their involvement from CEO to shareholder and/or director.

Q: What is the biggest challenge in setting up a board?

A: Creating a formal form of business governance is easy. What's difficult is changing behavior to align with the new structure of governance. Behavior doesn't change overnight simply because there's a new form of governance in town. It may take a year or two before a board really gels. Owners who are accustomed to making decisions often continue to do so without realizing that "things don't work that way anymore."

When owners behaviorally avoid (even unintentionally) new terms of governance, successors tend to become frustrated. Those successors justifiably object to owners making decisions when successors on the board should have been consulted. Like anything else, practice makes perfect. As an owner you have to practice a new form of oversight and decision-making.

The shift from the governance by one to the governance by many benefits the business in the long run and requires those working in the business to change. It also benefits owners who report enjoying the better sleep and lighter step that come with sharing the burden of decision-making with others.

The Evolution From Speedboat To Cruise Ship

When one person makes all business decisions, a business can move quickly, like a speedboat. Governance by a board makes a business more like a cruise ship, in that it takes a crew to move the ship from place to place. The advantage of a business cruise ship is that its crew adheres to rules and procedures that govern decision-making. That's very appealing to owners who are justifiably concerned they may find out about poor decisions when it is too late to rectify adverse consequences. Proper governance slows things down, requires communication and distributes decision-making power. By defining the limits of authority, governance enables a company to remain nimble in a dynamic business environment. In essence, proper governance provides the best of both worlds: the agility of a speedboat with the discipline of a well-run ship.

Family Councils

A family council is an entity that complements a board of directors. It is similar to a board of directors in that it is governed by a constitution that directs who is eligible to serve on the council, how they are voted in, how long they serve, etc. Its purpose, however, is to deal with family—not business—issues. For example, a family council decides whether relatives, while they are students, can work part-time in the business. It determines whether the family will pay a stipend to members who attend college or complete a certain degree program.

In many ways a family council acts like grandparents. It shows equal care for all family members and takes actions that communicate how much it values each member. By giving all family members the same opportunities, it can create equality among various branches of the family. We often recommend family councils to owners who wish to keep their growing family working as one unit for the benefit of all.

Each family council is as unique as the family that creates it, and the number and variety of family-related issues that a council might handle are almost endless. For those reasons, it can be a challenge to structure the council that functions best for you and your family. Still, family councils are highly valuable when you are preparing for the business to be multigenerational, so please don't hesitate to contact us if you'd like to explore the topic of what a family council might accomplish for your family.

Embrace Change!

When there is a change to how business decisions are made, people react. Owners who must teach their successors to make decisions worry about what will happen when successors make mistakes. Successors wonder how they are supposed to learn to make decisions when owners are constantly looking over the successor's shoulders or continue to make all decisions.

As we've discussed, business transitions occur in stages that are marked by the transfer of knowledge and wisdom from owner to successor. Change—even if made in stages—can be disconcerting to owners. We assume owners who are considering transferring a business want change, and they worry that by sharing decision-making with others they are putting the success of their businesses at risk. Our response to these owners is that proper governance and the preparation of successors minimizes the risk to their businesses.

While change can concern owners, it can exhilarate successors. If, in their enthusiasm, successors try to take the reins prematurely or fail to listen well to the owner's voice of experience, proper governance and the preparation minimizes the damage successors can do to a business.

There is always tension between those who want to move quickly and those who want to move more deliberately. The goal for both parties is to find the middle ground that keeps the business successful and makes everyone happy to be where they end up.

We suggest to owners that they trust that they have chosen and trained their successors well. Enjoy your successor's excitement! Successors *should be* energized and eager to adjust the direction or vision of a company or initiate a new growth strategy. With longer runways ahead of them, successors *should be* excited about a bigger future for the business. Appreciate your successor's enthusiasm and be generous in sharing your experience. Proper governance is the rich soil where new energy and seasoned experience combine to produce great outcomes for your business and its investors.

If you expect governance by several to work as well as governance by one, and you do not put a formal structure in place:

- You will experience justifiable discomfort as you give up your decision authority, because there are no rules or processes that put the brakes on poor decisions or help to guide better decisions.

- Your successors may ultimately become frustrated when they are not included in decision-making and may give up hope that you will ever be able to let go.

- Your successor may interpret your justifiable reluctance to transfer decision-making authority as a lack of trust.

If you create a formal means of business governance:

- You share decision-making with others in stages. Distributing decision-making power to others removes some of the weight you've carried as the sole and ultimate decision maker.

- Your successor has a forum to share their energy and vision of the future, while you have a forum to share the wisdom of your experience. The company benefits both from your successor's energy and your guidance.

- Your company remains agile enough to respond quickly to changes in its environment as you successfully let go of day-to-day responsibilities, replacing unspoken rules and unmarked boundaries with clearly defined roles and limits of authority.

What is your current governance structure? Which person or group (shareholders, board of directors, executive management team) is making the decisions and has the authority to do so?

Take a moment to fill in the Business Governance table. Note that in the second column you identify the types of decisions that currently are made within each level. Completing this table is usually very enlightening.

Business Governance

Level	What types of decisions are made at each level? Make a short list. (See examples that follow this table.)	Who currently leads each of these groups?	Number of Members In The Group (Please list their names—even if it is a member of one—you!)
Shareholders			
Board of Directors			
CEO/ Executive Management Team			

Sample decisions: debt, capital purchases, approval of strategic plan and budget, addition of a new owner/shareholder, sale of part or all of the business, etc.

Now write what you learned as you completed the table: any observations, feelings or thoughts that came to mind.

CHAPTER TWENTY-EIGHT

THE DANCE OF SUCCESSOR DEVELOPMENT

If you want to go fast, go alone. If you want to go far, go together.
African proverb

*I*n this chapter we look at the three phases of a business transition as a dance:

Phase 1: You are the leader who teaches your successor the steps.
Phase 2: You and your successor alternate the lead.
Phase 3: Your successor leads and you follow.

We also share three guidelines designed to minimize the number of times you and your successor step on each other's toes, and increase your odds of joining that elite group of owners (the 100 percenters) who have successfully transitioned their businesses to others.

Phase 1: You As The Leader/Teacher

Most owners are doers; they decide, act and lead decisively. They know their businesses so intimately that they rarely give thought to how they do what they do. They simply enjoy it. In the first phase of your dance, you are a master dancer and the natural leader. Your successor has never led, so you lead, while teaching your successor the steps—even if teaching does not come naturally to you.

An important part of teaching is the ability to break what appear to be (and often are) complicated tasks into their component parts and explain each part in sequence. Elizabeth often tells the story of her years as a student in the petroleum engineering program at the Colorado School of Mines. She was not eligible to take a third level course called Calculus for Scientists and Engineers until she had successfully completed the first and second level courses. Had she attempted this Calc III course right out of the gate, she has no doubt she would have failed it. Instead, Mines organized the material sequentially and at increasing levels of difficulty to maximize student success. Elizabeth tackled the courses in order and aced the highest-level course.

We apply two lessons from this story to our work with owners. First, success in growing a business does not equate to success as a teacher. Owners know their "subject" so well that they typically and unwittingly skip steps as they teach it. To no one's surprise, except possibly the owner's, successors struggle to master the subject and often fail. The second lesson is less obvious, but no less important. Calculus courses offered at an engineering school that consistently ranks in the top five in the world are not easy. Success requires great teaching, but it also requires student ability and a healthy dose of student desire.

We can't wave a wand and make you a great teacher. Breaking down how you do what you do into bite-size pieces and creating an organized curriculum designed to enable your successor to take on increasingly difficult tasks may not be two of your strengths. Luckily, you can hire coaches who know how to do exactly that. Part of our job is to help owners organize an efficient transfer of knowledge.

But before you decide that teaching is or is not for you, let's look at what's involved. Here are some of the pieces of "what you do" that you must teach your successor in order for them to wear your CEO and ownership hat comfortably.

Finance. An understanding of financial operations; reporting and interpretation; how capital investment, debt structure, operating capital and taxes affect cash flow; and how to make decisions that keep the business financially healthy.

Operations. An understanding of how to deliver on the company's promise to customers and also maintain and increase the margins that support the business.

Sales and Marketing. An understanding of customers' current and future needs and wants; how to keep the pipeline full; the value of brand; and how to assess new opportunities.

Leadership. An understanding of how the structure of the company influences business success; how to engage a team; how to listen, respond and delegate effectively; and how important it is to develop the strengths of empathy and emotional intelligence.

People. An understanding of how people are wired and operate; how to recruit, hire, retain, compensate, motivate and inspire them; and how to create a healthy culture.

Investment in the Business. An understanding of how to analyze which business segments to invest in or not (as well as how and when) in order to keep the business competitive and thriving.

Trends. An understanding of how to identify trends in the business environment that create opportunities and threats, and how to respond effectively to opportunities and threats. Teaching your successor how you intuit what's ahead is a challenge, but it is one of the most important things that you will teach them.

Effective Decision-Making. An understanding of how to make decisions thoughtfully and on a timely basis; how decision-making is an often-complex exercise that requires attention, motivation and self-control; how time limits and stress affect decisions; and how sometimes you must go with your entrepreneurial intuition.

Effective Negotiation. An understanding of how to negotiate effectively in both complicated and simple situations, and how to communicate clearly with all parties at the negotiating table.

Systems and Processes. An understanding of all the business's systems: how they work, why they exist, whether they are effective and how they could be improved.

Key Performance and Results Indicators. An understanding of which numbers you watch and why.

The "Umbrella." An understanding of how a change in one business segment impacts all other segments; of what is working and what is not; and of the fact that decisions don't always result in the consequences one expects—and how to respond when that happens whether the consequence is an unexpected boom or bust.

In your Transition Timeline you established time-stamped milestones to indicate what you must teach and your successor must learn. These milestones illustrate the order in which successors assume responsibility and authority within the business.

Please remember that successors do not become champion dancers overnight. As we mentioned in Chapter Twenty-Three, if you set milestones and work through them step by step, you give your successor the opportunity to gain a greater understanding of how to do what you do, and you gain confidence in their ability to lead.

Phase 2: Owner And Successor Alternate The Lead

Perhaps you have watched two people try to lead while dancing together. There's a struggle for control, many missteps and at least a few bruised toes. In this second phase of the dance, successors begin to assume greater levels of responsibility and owners must let them. During this phase successors make mistakes. When owners begin to give up the lead and successors begin to take it up, conflict, miscommunication and misunderstandings are almost inevitable. It feels a bit awkward.

For example, you may pause to let your successor assume a responsibility or make a decision, and your successor either doesn't know what you expect or steps up in a way you do not anticipate. Conversely, your successor may follow your steps, while waiting and wondering why you won't stop leading. Both successors and owners will, at various times, feel as if they are waiting for the other. It often happens that as successors gain confidence, they believe they can accomplish a task for which owners know the successors are unprepared.

Executing a business transition takes time because it involves a change in behavior. Successors must learn to lead, and owners must learn how to step aside and sometimes follow. Be patient with yourself and your successor.

All of these scenarios are totally natural, so expect them. But natural does not mean they are painless. We've developed three rules of engagement designed to reduce the number of misunderstandings and keep open the lines of communication.

1. Always assume the other party has the best of intentions. To keep lines of communication open, you ask questions when you don't understand why someone does something. To shut down communication, you assume you know the other person's motives.

2. Be honest and never accusatory. Dishonesty and accusations are the fastest way to torpedo any type of business transfer.

3. Be playful. Don't leave your sense of humor at home. Humor, positivity and lightheartedness can help smooth even the roughest waters.

Consider the situation father "Ned" and son "Adam" encountered as they entered Phase 2 of their dance.

Every day Ned was in the office an hour before other employees arrived and was often the one to shut off the coffee maker at the end of the day. Once his son Adam took responsibility for supervising the company's work crews (both local and those working in other cities), Ned expected to see Adam there early as well, but that wasn't the case. Adam arrived at the office around 9:00 a.m. each morning. Ned let it go for a week or so, but then began to question his decision to make Adam his successor. "Now that he's had a taste of being in charge," Ned thought, "he doesn't think he has to work as hard. Maybe he feels entitled or he's getting lazy."

After two weeks of imagining what Adam was doing for the first two hours of every day, Ned confronted him. "If you aren't dedicated enough to this company to get to work on time, you aren't the one to take over for me."

Adam justifiably felt attacked. "Work on time?" he shot back. "What do you think I'm doing from 7:00 until 9:00 every morning?"

"I don't know. Are you wasting time at an expensive gym?" Ned asked. "Or do you think just because this place will be yours one day that you don't have to earn it?"

Before storming out of the room, Adam turned to his father and only refrained from shouting because the door was open. "Before you step foot in this office," he said, "I've already called every project manager. I know what they are doing that day and what they need from us. I'm sorry if you think that's 'wasting time.' "

Mother "Libby" and son "Jack" also encountered problems in Phase 2 of their dance.

Jack was nearing the end of the Transition Timeline we had created. As one of the last milestones, his mother (Libby) had turned over responsibility for the financial aspects of the company to him. As was his standard practice, Jack checked the company's account balances before making a significant purchase. He was shocked to see that the cumulative balance was at least $300,000 greater than it had been when he'd checked two days earlier.

Libby was flying back that day from a 10-day vacation, so Jack waited until the next morning to confront her. Without so much as a "How was your trip, Mom?" Jack pounced.

"If you don't trust me, why don't you just come right out and say so?" he began. "You said we were going to be honest with each other, but it looks like only one of us is keeping up our end of the bargain."

Libby looked clueless and hurt, as she struggled for words. "What are you talking about? I knew something bad would happen if I took so much time off. What was it?"

"You're wondering what happened?" Jack asked. "That's rich coming from the woman who waited months to turn over the finances, and when she finally does, without letting me know, she dumps $300,000 into the bank!"

As soon as Libby recovered her composure, she said, "Jack, that $300,000 is cash I've been meaning to put back into the company for the past six months. It's been on my mind, so I took care of it before I got on the plane."

Now let's imagine how these conversations might have gone if the participants had assumed that each other had the best of intentions, had been honest without accusing, and they had brought some humor to the situation.

Ned might have said, "Adam, I'm a morning person, and I know you are too. That's why I know you are doing something productive before you get into the office. If it has to do with house-training your new puppy, spare me the details. If not, I'm curious. Can you tell me what you are doing every morning?"

Similarly, Adam could have paused before responding to his father's question about dedication and asked himself, "I wonder why he thinks I'm not working?" He might have remembered his father prided himself on being the first one to the office each morning, and Adam could have explained that his phone put his kitchen table "in the office."

Jack might have asked his mother, "Mom, can you walk me through your thinking on that $300,000 deposit? I love what it does for cash flow, but I can't find the account for 'windfall' on the general ledger."

Phase 2 requires patience on your part and on the part of your successor. Remember that successors do not learn by osmosis, and crash courses almost always lead to, well, crashes. You are handing off a business that at the beginning of your journey is too much for your successor to handle. At the same time, with little or no experience as a follower in this dance, you may find following more difficult than leading.

> *Sure he (Fred Astaire) was great, but don't forget that Ginger Rogers did everything he did...backwards and in high heels.*
>
> Bob Thaves, Creator of Frank and Ernest

Be patient with yourself and with your successor. Your goal is to help your successor gain the skills required to master running and building your business. That means you must teach your successor to solve problems—a skill they cannot acquire if you constantly step in to save them from making mistakes. When you resist the impulse to lead the dance, you put the odds of a successful transfer in your favor.

Phase 3: Your Successor As The Leader

Once you have taught and mentored your successor well and they have mastered the tasks you set out, your successor will assume the lead in this dance. At this point, your role is to follow the lead of your successor before you leave the dance floor. When you do, you may find your successor is not leading in the same way you did. They may do the steps a bit differently (as Adam did), or they may not be as graceful as you were. In fact, you may not be a very graceful partner when put into the role of follower. Again, all of this is totally normal. Your successor will never know absolutely everything you do or do everything exactly as you did, because they don't have your experience and talents. They bring their own to the dance floor. They will lead in their own way from their own experiences.

The Payoff

Running a successful business gives most owners a sense of purpose. While executing their Transition Roadmaps, they find satisfaction in teaching something that they have loved to do and have done well. Deep satisfaction is what we want for you. We want you to be able to look back at the trajectory of your business life and see the pinnacle not as the day you receive the final payment for your equity (although that is a high point!). Instead, the pinnacle is the day that, because of your hard

The most successful owners don't just star in their succession plans; they generously turn the spotlight over to their successors.

work and patience, your successor confidently leads your company. It is the day you embark on your Next Adventure.

If you fail to understand the give-and-take of teaching a successor to lead:

- You and your successor will have many unnecessary communication failures, which not only diminish the chances of successfully executing the business transfer, but also damage relationships with others you care about.

- Your successor may grow frustrated with themselves or with you and decide not to travel the path you created to your Next Adventure.

- Any confidence you do have in your successor will be misplaced. Without proper training, your successor will be unprepared to assume leadership successfully.

If you effectively teach your successor how you do what you do:

- You *and* your successor gain confidence in their ability to lead, and you minimize the number of times that you and your successor step on each other's toes.

- You cap a successful career with perhaps a leader's greatest accomplishment: teaching another person to lead.

- You position your company to succeed and remain a contributor to its community.

POINT OF INTEREST

When you think about where you are with your successor, are you leading, following or somewhere in between? Circle a number on the "Leading/Following Scale" to rate where you are with regard to leading/following.

Leading/Following Scale

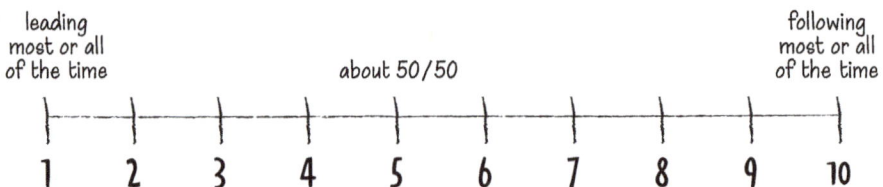

leading
most or all
of the time   about 50/50   following
most or all
of the time

| | | | | | | | | | |
|1|2|3|4|5|6|7|8|9|10|

On the "Leading/Following Accelerators" chart, write down what needs to happen in order for you to move toward a 10 on the Leading/Following Scale—if you are not already there. Remember to consider conversations, initiatives, commitments, or any other methods you could use to help you accelerate the transition of duties and roles.

Leading/Following Accelerators

CHAPTER TWENTY-NINE

NOW IT'S YOUR TURN

One idea, well executed, can change your life forever.
Dr. Tom Hill, Co-author of *Chicken Soup for the Entrepreneur's Soul*

At the beginning of this book, we recommended you use seven principles to increase the odds that you would transfer your business successfully and join our elite group of 100 percenters. At this point we hope you can see how each principle applies to your journey to your Next Adventure.

Principle 1: Put relationships first.

A business transfer is only successful if it protects or enhances your relationships with the people who are important to you, and good communication is the key to healthy relationships. Knowing when, how, what and with whom to communicate not only avoids and solves problems, but it also brings people closer together.

Principle 2: You are in charge of your journey.

It is up to you—not your successor—to lead the journey until your successor is ready to lead and you are confident you can step away. It is a privilege to create a plan for the ongoing success of your company.

Principle 3: No transition is perfect.

You will make difficult choices whose outcomes (intended and unintended) you cannot always accurately predict. You may not know until long after you make a decision whether an outcome is wonderful or detrimental. What you do know is how to move forward with the grace, confidence and compassion that have served you so well.

Principle 4: It's your Next Adventure: Go for it!

What comes after your business transition could be the most meaningful phase of your life. Let your vision of your Next Adventure inspire and motivate you.

Principle 5: Choose your destination with intention.

Avoiding the fact that all owners leave their businesses at some point or ignoring the dilemmas that can arise during a transfer of ownership does not make these dilemmas disappear. Instead, doing so robs you of the opportunity to take charge of what you want the transfer of your businesses to accomplish for you, your family, your successor and your company.

Procrastination only reduces the amount of time you have available to deal with whatever challenges come your way.

Principle 6: Step away from mutual dependency.

Ultimately the growth and well-being of your business will be in your successor's hands. If your business depends on you for its success, or you depend on your business for your identity, your Next Adventure is at risk. Teaching your successor to lead your company successfully and envisioning your Next Adventure end this mutual dependence and increases the odds that both your successor and your business will be successful.

Principle 7: Your Transition Roadmap is indispensable.

One hundred percent of the owners who have completed The Transition Roadmap Developer Process have successfully transferred their companies to their successors. Your Roadmap keeps you moving forward, shows you alternate routes when you run into roadblocks, and keeps all parties accountable when circumstances change.

We are confident these principles and The Transition Roadmap Developer Process will put the odds in your favor that you will execute the transition out of your business successfully and that these odds will improve exponentially when you approach your journey with the following six attitudes.

Attitude 1: Flexibility

With a Transition Roadmap in hand, you have the tools in place to:

• Know what you want the transfer of your business to accomplish (your Objectives Matrix).

- Know how (and in what order) to set new points on your Transition Compass.

- Assess various transaction options (your Options Matrix).

- Identify and assign time frames for all the tasks that you must now accomplish (your Transition Roadmap).

If necessary, you are prepared to initiate your Plan B. Even if you do not have to change paths, the business environment is always changing, so are tax laws, estate vehicles, investment performance, etc. We recommend you meet with your successor, key people (including your spouse and others) and your Cabinet of Advisors at least annually to review the progress you have made in creating and updating your Transition Roadmap and to make plans for the following year.

Attitude 2: A commitment to—rather than expectation of—action

One of the benefits of a Transition Roadmap is that it puts into writing the commitments you are making to your successor, and those your successor is making to you. In executing your Roadmap, the commitment you and your successor have made to each other and to this journey becomes crystal clear.

You and your successor are teammates in this process. Great teammates act with honesty, transparency, vulnerability and integrity. They give each other permission to call each other out when something isn't going well, and they support and help one other do what it takes to get it right.

Attitude 3: Humility

It's okay to ask questions and not have all the answers. Only by asking questions will you discover new options and opportunities. Only by asking and listening will you learn new information about what others need or desire.

Attitude 4: Positivity

When something unexpected happens along your journey, you have a choice: You can consider alternatives and new opportunities or view the unanticipated event as one more obstacle blocking your path. You can become frustrated, or you can acknowledge that things have not gone as you planned and come up with a new strategy to proceed. Frustrated owners often become stuck (and aren't very fun to be around). Positive owners ask, "What can we do to move forward?" and find the way.

Attitude 5: Abundance

Your business has provided you and your family financial security and a sense of identity. It has given your employees the ability to provide for themselves and their families, and it has made positive contributions to your customers and community.

When you live from a position of abundance rather than scarcity, gratitude—for who you are, for who others are and for what you have—is second nature.

Attitude 6: Gratitude

You own a successful business. You have (or will soon have) a successor who wants to step into your shoes. You have designed a great Next Adventure. Sometimes blessings are easy to overlook. Counting them is a great way to stay centered.

Bon Voyage

If you started reading this book while concerned that transitioning out of business ownership would require you to make big sacrifices, we hope you now realize that a shift in your life is inevitable; giving up what you most desire is not. If you picked up this book while frozen in place because you worried there could be consequences to your decisions that you do not intend, we hope we have put your mind at ease. Unintended consequences are always a possibility, but when we put relationships first, we minimize the chances that one of those consequences will be a damaged relationship.

As you conclude this book, we hope we have given you a new perspective on transferring your business to a successor. We hope you understand that you can leave your business in the hands of a successor in a way that is a win for you and all involved.

Our greatest hope is that this book is just a first step on your journey and you are now excited to move ahead. Reach out to your advisors, reach out to us, download tools from our website (*www.TheSuccessionPlanningBook.com/Tools*) and continue your journey! Use all the resources available to you, including blog posts, podcasts and programs available at *www.TheSuccessionPlanningBook.com* to keep learning how to craft your Transition Roadmap and take control of your destiny. We would be privileged to help you join our group of clients who have beaten the odds and transferred their businesses successfully. Give us a call at 303-790-0754 or email Elizabeth at *Elizabeth@TransitionStrategists.com* or Laura at *Laura@FirstWaveFinancial. com* so we can help you to maintain your momentum!

POINT OF INTEREST

As you move forward, we wish you a sense of gratitude and feelings of abundance, joy and excitement. You have already built a great business. Now you are prepared, confident and empowered to begin your journey to your Next Adventure.

For this last Point of Interest, we ask you to write down your commitment to yourself. Remember, *it is up to you to make your Transition Journey happen.* What will you commit to doing in order to create the transition journey that will get you to your Next Adventure and leave your business in the capable hands of your amazing successor while your relationships remain healthy?

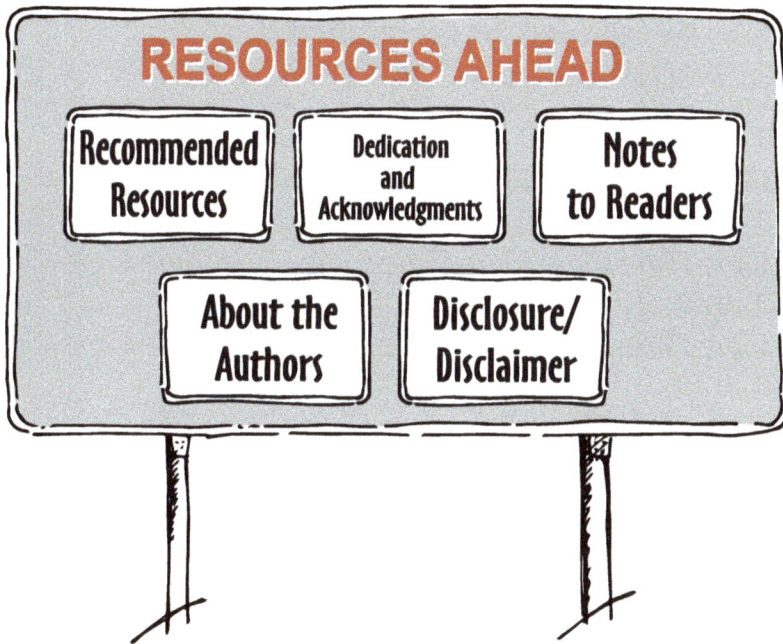

Recommended Resources

No one person is an expert in every facet of a business transfer. We've been working with owners for years, and we are constantly learning from other expert advisors. In the hope that this book is the launchpad for your planning process, we've created a list of some of our favorite resources.

Tools On Our Website and Points of Interest
(www.TheSuccessionPlanningBook.com/tools)

Points of Interest
The Business Owner Transition Confidence Survey™
The Transition Compass™
The Transition Timeline™
The Objectives Matrix™
The Transaction Guide™

Books

Accelerate Your Entrepreneurial Flight: How to Energize Business Value and Entrepreneurial Growth by Elizabeth Lake Ledoux and Melvin J. Wernimont, Ph.D., vNacelle, LLC, 2013

Are You Worried About Your Money? How to Gain Confidence About Your Money in a Rapidly Changing World by Thomas L. Kirk, FirstWave, 2013

Bridging Generations: Transitioning Family Wealth and Values for a Sustainable Legacy by Roy O. Williams and Amy A. Castoro, HigherLife Development Services, Inc., 2017

Built to Sell: Creating a Business That Can Thrive Without You by John Warrillow, Portfolio, 2012

Every Family's Business: 12 Common Sense Questions to Protect Your Wealth by Thomas William Deans, Ph.D., Detente Financial Corp., 2009

Family Business Governance: Maximizing Family and Business Potential by Craig E. Aronoff and John L. Ward, Palgrave Macmillan, 2010

The One Thing: The Surprisingly Simple Truth Behind Extraordinary Results by Gary Keller and Jay Papasan, Bard Press, 2013

Preparing Successors for Leadership: Another Kind of Hero (A Family Business Consulting Group Publication) by Craig E. Aronoff and John L. Ward, Palgrave Macmillan, 2011

The Decision Book: 50 Models for Strategic Thinking by Mikael Krogerus and Roman Tschäppeler, W.W. Norton & Company, Inc., fully revised 2018

Tongue Fu!®: How to Deflect, Disarm, and Defuse Any Verbal Conflict by Sam Horn, St. Martin's Griffin, 1993

Understanding the Growth of the Entrepreneur: How to Accelerate Your Growth as an Entrepreneur by Melvin J. Wernimont, Ph.D., and Elizabeth Lake Ledoux, 2014

Who Not How: The Formula to Achieve Bigger Goals Through Accelerating Teamwork by Dan Sullivan with Benjamin Hardy, Hay House, Inc., 2020

Organizations

Strategic Coach®, Business Coaching for Growth-Minded Entrepreneurs *https://www.strategiccoach.com/*

TIGER 21, The premier peer membership organization that helps high-net-worth wealth creators and preservers navigate the challenges and opportunities that success creates. *https://tiger21.com*

Women's Business Enterprise National Council (WBENC), The largest certifier of women-owned businesses in the U.S. and a leading advocate for women entrepreneurs. *https://www.wbenc.org*

American Business Women's Association® (ABWA), Leadership, education and networking support and opportunities for business women of diverse occupations. *https://www.abwa.org*

Women Presidents' Organization® (WPO), Worldwide affiliation of women presidents, CEOs and managing directors of privately held, multimillion-dollar companies. *https://womenpresidentsorg.com*

Software

Microsoft Visio

This downloadable software is a powerful and very flexible tool that allows users to put a wide variety of documents into one document separated by tabs and pages.

Using it, you can create timelines, organizational diagrams, flowcharts, tables, text and more. We have used Visio for years to design and organize plans in one central, easily accessible file.

MindManager

This downloadable software creates maps for projects, processes and connecting ideas. We use it to create Transition Compasses.

Dedication And Acknowledgments

We dedicate this book to you and to the hundreds of business owners who have trusted us to help them navigate one of the most challenging and exciting phases of a business owner's career. We are inspired by the legacies you are creating for a new generation of owners (and their families) as you mentor your successors and move on to your next great adventure.

We acknowledge our amazing writer, Kathryn Bolinske; our rock-star graphic designer, Sandy Cochran; our incredible marketing strategist, Olivia Omega; our fabulous longtime supporter, Tom Kirk; and all those who helped us to bring this book to life, including Dawn Dorsch, Trina Gorsuch and Kevin Ward.

We are forever grateful to our husbands and families, who inspire us to put relationships first in our lives and our practices.

Elizabeth Ledoux
Laura Chiesman

Notes To Readers

Case Studies

For nearly 30 years, we have had the privilege of working with owners of companies in a wide variety of industries. We draw on those experiences to illustrate concepts in this book, but we have changed all identifying information. Unless otherwise noted, any resemblance to actual owners is purely coincidental.

Word Choices

Throughout this book we refer to an owner's spouse. Note that we use the term "spouse" as a generic term to indicate a wife, husband, significant other or life partner.

Trademarked Terms and Tools

The following terms and tools are trademarked by Laura Chiesman and Elizabeth Ledoux:

The Business Owner Transition Confidence Survey™
The Business Owner Transition Confidence Spider Graph™

The following terms and tools are trademarked by vNacelle, LLC dba The Transition Strategists:

Next Adventure™
The Focused Action Navigator™
The Objectives Matrix™
The Options Matrix™
The Transaction Guide™
The Transition Compass™
The Transition Roadmap Developer™
The Transition Roadmap Developer Process™
The Transition Strategy Statement™
The Transition Timeline™
The Wealth Development Worksheet™

The following terms and tools are trademarked by First*Wave* Financial:

The Future Wealth Projection™
Wealth*Coach*™
Wealth*Confidence*™
Wealth*Plan*™

About The Authors

Elizabeth Ledoux

CLAYTON JENKINS PHOTOGRAPHY

Elizabeth Ledoux is the founder of The Transition Strategists, an international boutique consultancy offering transition and succession planning strategies to family and private businesses as well as individuals. She is also a thought leader and sought-after speaker, addressing the topics of business succession planning, navigating transitions for companies and leaders, strategic growth, and the business journey.

With a career spanning over 30 years, Elizabeth has compassionately and effectively helped hundreds of business owners navigate the complex family dynamics that come with family business shifts. She believes that whatever you want to achieve in life and in business is possible when the relationships that surround and support you are whole and intact. One hundred percent of the family businesses that Elizabeth has helped are thriving, a track record that crushes the dismal statistics related to the transition of family businesses.

Elizabeth is an entrepreneur at heart and has founded several businesses, including BizMultiplier LLC, SofTeach, and ROCG. In 2003 she was named as an owner of a Top 100 Women-Owned Business in Colorado. The Harvard Business School has recognized Elizabeth's work linking the growth and development of the entrepreneur to company success.

As a fifth-generation Coloradoan, Elizabeth loves the outdoors. When not on the slopes, she is golfing, fly fishing, or enjoying nature.

Elizabeth serves as a Denver Chair for TIGER 21, the premier peer membership organization for high-net-worth wealth creators and preservers. She served as the Denver Chair and Calgary Chair of the Women Presidents' Organization.

In addition to *It's A Journey*, Elizabeth is a coauthor of *Accelerate Your Entrepreneurial Flight: How to Energize Value and Entrepreneurial Growth* (2013) and *Understanding the Growth of the Entrepreneur: How to Accelerate Your Growth as an Entrepreneur* (2014).

Learn more about Elizabeth's work in developing and implementing successful transition strategies at *www.TransitionStrategists.com*.

Laura Chiesman

For over 25 years, **Laura Chiesman** has developed financial planning and wealth management strategies for individuals and families to enable them to achieve their immediate and lifetime financial goals. As a business owner, CERTIFIED FINANCIAL PLANNER™ (CFP®) professional and Certified Divorce Financial Analyst® (CDFA®), Laura brings a unique perspective to comprehensive plans that deliver peace of mind in uncertain times.

As a Wealth*Coach*™ Laura tailors each person's financial plan and wealth management strategy to their resources, needs and goals. When working with business owners, she partners with The Transition Strategists (a consulting firm that works with owners in the U.S. and across the globe) to create business transition and succession strategies that support an owner's desire to maintain important relationships and that create a clear path to a bright future for owners, their businesses and their successors.

As president of First*Wave* Financial, Laura leads her team of financial professionals as they deliver independent, objective and trusted planning and investment strategies designed to help their clients transform financial complexity and confusion into simplicity and confidence. As a volunteer, she brings the same energy to her community. She is a governing board member of Genesis House, a shelter for women and children, and serves on the Community Foundation for Brevard board, an organization that matches nonprofit organizations to philanthropists. As the 2019 Campaign Chair for the United Way of Brevard, Laura was privileged to help raise millions of dollars to improve the health, education and financial stability of thousands of Brevard County, Florida, residents.

Laura is an active member of the Oceanside Charter Chapter of the American Business Women's Association and the Women Presidents' Organization. Laura's commitment to these organizations reflects her willingness to share what she has learned in her career and to learn from other entrepreneurs.

Laura is a speaker and author on the topics of wealth management and financial issues, investment and retirement planning, life events and transitions, and business succession.

For resources and information about Laura's work in wealth management and financial planning, visit *www.FirstWaveFinancial.com*.

Disclosure/Disclaimer

While this publication is designed to provide accurate information related to the subject matter covered, no portion of the book's content is or should be construed as a substitute for individual investment, financial planning, transaction, and/or transition planning advice from any consulting professional(s), including Elizabeth Ledoux, financial professional(s), including Laura Chiesman, or other members of The Transition Strategists or First*Wave* Financial. Each individual's circumstances are different. All forms of business transactions or succession planning pose some inherent risks. Individuals should seek business consulting, financial, legal, tax or other professional or expert advice or assistance from independent professionals, based upon the individuals' particular circumstances.

Laura provides advisory services solely in her capacity as a Wealth*Coach*™ of First*Wave* Financial, a registered investment advisor located in Satellite Beach, Florida. First*Wave* Financial and its affiliates, and their respective officers, directors and employees specifically disclaim any liability for any damages (whether direct or indirect, special, general or consequential), loss (including loss of business and profits), or risk (personal or otherwise) that is incurred as a consequence, directly or indirectly, of the use or application of any of the contents of this publication, which contents are provided "as is."

Elizabeth provides advisory services solely in her capacity as a Transition Strategist of The Transition Strategists. The Transition Strategists and its affiliates, and their respective officers, directors and employees specifically disclaim any liability for any damages (whether direct or indirect, special, general or consequential), loss (including loss of business and profits), or risk (personal or otherwise) which is incurred as a consequence, directly or indirectly, of the use or application of any of the contents of this publication, which contents are provided "as is."

The authors make liberal use of case studies and examples. All identifying information has been changed, so ANY resemblance to actual individuals, living or dead, or companies is purely coincidental. No reader should construe any discussion in the book of actual client experiences as an indication or assurance that an existing or prospective client will experience a certain level of results if First*Wave* Financial or vNacelle, LLC dba The Transition Strategists are engaged, or continue to be engaged, to provide investment advisory or transition consulting services. Mention of specific companies, organizations, or authorities in this book does not imply endorsement by the authors or the publisher.

Neither the information in this book, nor any opinion expressed in it, constitutes a solicitation for the purchase or sale of a security or other investment. A copy of FirstWave Financial's current written disclosure statement discussing its advisory or transition consulting services and fees is available upon request.

If you have ANY QUESTIONS regarding the disclaimers and limitations related to the information contained in this book, FirstWave Financial's Chief Compliance Officer, Laura Chiesman, CFP®, is available to address them.

IT'S A JOURNEY
THE MUST-HAVE ROADMAP TO SUCCESSFUL SUCCESSION PLANNING

Elizabeth Ledoux and Laura Chiesman

ABOUT SKY TO SEA PUBLISHING, LLC

Sky to Sea Publishing, LLC produces inspirational books for people experiencing life and business transitions. Such change always requires navigating uncharted territories, and it often involves shifting/creating wealth, exploring next adventures and understanding personal fulfillment. We believe great relationships in and out of business enhance life. Sky to Sea is committed to publishing content that supports and engages people in developing their best lives.

It's A Journey
© 2021 Elizabeth Ledoux and Laura Chiesman
All rights reserved.
Sky to Sea Publishing, LLC
1300 Highway AIA, Suite 103
Satellite Beach, FL 32937

ISBN 978-1-7363623-0-3

www.ingramcontent.com/pod-product-compliance
Lightning Source LLC
Chambersburg PA
CBHW052337210326
41597CB00031B/5283